On the Frontier
of Science

- *Eisenhower's War of Words: Rhetoric and Leadership*, Martin J. Medhurst, editor
- *The Nuclear Freeze Campaign: Rhetoric and Foreign Policy in the Telepolitical Age*, J. Michael Hogan
- *Mansfield and Vietnam: A Study in Rhetorical Adaptation*, Gregory A. Olson
- *Truman and the Hiroshima Cult*, Robert P. Newman
- *Post-Realism: The Rhetorical Turn in International Relations*, Francis A. Beer and Robert Hariman, editors
- *Rhetoric and Political Culture in Nineteenth-Century America*, Thomas W. Benson, editor
- *Frederick Douglass: Freedom's Voice, 1818–1845*, Gregory P. Lampe
- *Angelina Grimké: Rhetoric, Identity, and the Radical Imagination*, Stephen Howard Browne
- *Strategic Deception: Rhetoric, Science, and Politics in Missile Defense Advocacy*, Gordon R. Mitchell
- *Rostow, Kennedy, and the Rhetoric of Foreign Aid*, Kimber Charles Pearce
- *Visions of Poverty: Welfare Policy and Political Imagination*, Robert Asen
- *General Eisenhower: Ideology and Discourse*, Ira Chernus
- *The Reconstruction Desegregation Debate: The Politics of Equality and the Rhetoric of Place, 1870–1875*, Kirt H. Wilson
- *Shared Land/Conflicting Identity: Trajectories of Israeli and Palestinian Symbol Use*, Robert C. Rowland and David A. Frank
- *Darwinism, Design, and Public Education*, John Angus Campbell and Stephen C. Meyer, editors
- *Religious Expression and the American Constitution*, Franklyn S. Haiman
- *Christianity and the Mass Media in America: Toward a Democratic Accommodation*, Quentin J. Schultze
- *Bending Spines: The Propagandas of Nazi Germany and the German Democratic Republic*, Randall L. Bytwerk
- *Malcolm X: Inventing Radical Judgment*, Robert E. Terrill
- *Metaphorical World Politics*, Francis A. Beer and Christ'l De Landtsheer, editors
- *The Lyceum and Public Culture in the Nineteenth-Century United States*, Angela G. Ray
- *The Political Style of Conspiracy: Chase, Sumner, and Lincoln*, Michael William Pfau
- *The Character of Justice: Rhetoric, Law, and Politics in the Supreme Court Confirmation Process*, Trevor Parry-Giles
- *Rhetorical Vectors of Memory in National and International Holocaust Trials*, Marouf A. Hasian Jr.
- *Judging the Supreme Court: Constructions of Motives in Bush v. Gore*, Clarke Rountree
- *Everyday Subversion: From Joking to Revolting in the German Democratic Republic*, Kerry Kathleen Riley
- *In the Wake of Violence: Image and Social Reform*, Cheryl R. Jorgensen-Earp
- *Rhetoric and Democracy: Pedagogical and Political Practices*, Todd F. McDorman and David M. Timmerman, editors
- *Invoking the Invisible Hand: Social Security and the Privatization Debates*, Robert Asen
- *With Faith in the Works of Words: The Beginnings of Reconciliation in South Africa, 1985–1995*, Erik Doxtader
- *Public Address and Moral Judgment: Critical Studies in Ethical Tensions*, Shawn J. Parry-Giles and Trevor Parry-Giles, editors
- *Executing Democracy: Capital Punishment and the Making of America, 1683–1807*, Stephen John Hartnett
- *Enemyship: Democracy and Counter-Revolution in the Early Republic*, Jeremy Engels
- *Spirits of the Cold War: Contesting Worldviews in the Classical Age of American Security Strategy* Ned O'Gorman
- *Making the Case: Advocacy and Judgment in Public Argument*, Kathryn M. Olson, Michael William Pfau, Benjamin Ponder, and Kirt H. Wilson, editors
- *Executing Democracy: Capital Punishment and the Making of America, 1835–1843*, Stephen John Hartnett
- *William James and the Art of Popular Statement*, Paul Stob
- *On the Frontier of Science: An American Rhetoric of Exploration and Exploitation*, Leah Ceccarelli
- *The Good Neighbor: Franklin D. Roosevelt and the Rhetoric of American Power*, Mary E. Stuckey

ON THE FRONTIER OF SCIENCE

AN AMERICAN RHETORIC OF EXPLORATION AND EXPLOITATION

Leah Ceccarelli

MICHIGAN STATE UNIVERSITY PRESS • *East Lansing*

Michigan State University Press
East Lansing, Michigan 48823-5245

Printed and bound in the United States of America.

19 18 17 16 15 14 13   1 2 3 4 5 6 7 8 9 10

LIBRARY OF CONGRESS CATALOGING-IN-PUBLICATION DATA

Ceccarelli, Leah.
On the frontier of science : an American rhetoric of exploration and exploitation / Leah Ceccarelli.
  pages cm.—(Rhetoric and public affairs series)
  Includes bibliographical references and index.
  ISBN 978-1-61186-100-6 (pbk. : alk. paper)—ISBN 978-1-60917-391-3 (ebook)
  1. Research—United States. 2. Research—Social aspects—United States. 3. Scientists—United States.
4. Rhetoric. 5. Communication in science. I. Title.
  Q180.U5C43 2013
  507.2'073—dc23   2012049442

Book design by Charlie Sharp, Sharp Des!gns, Lansing, Michigan
Cover design by TG Design
Cover art © Shutterstock.com/Pan Xunbin. All rights reserved.

Contents

⌘

Acknowledgments

⌘

This book has benefitted, as all my scholarship has, from the encouragement and thoughtful commentary of many colleagues in the fields of communication, rhetoric, and science studies. To reduce the feeling of déjà vu for my readers, I chose not to seek journal publication for any of the work that would go into this book. But my arguments will be familiar to some of you nonetheless, since I have presented portions of it in invited lectures at University of Memphis, University of Texas at Austin, University of Utah, University of Puget Sound, Carnegie Mellon University, and University of British Columbia, as well as at a number of scholarly conferences and in public lectures at my own institution, University of Washington. The comments and suggestions of the many people who listened to me talk about this subject in those venues have been much appreciated. I also am thankful to the Rhetoric Society of America for its Career Retreat for Associate Professors, to Barbara Schneider and Jen Bacon who joined me in a writing group that came out of that workshop, and to our career mentor, Krista Ratcliffe, who encouraged us to set and meet our writing goals. Two of my departmental colleagues, LeiLani Nishime and Christine Harold, joined me in a writing group when the term of that other one ended, seeing me through the end of this project and beyond. I am grateful to them as well as to the many graduate students I have introduced to fragments of this work, knowing that they would offer me the honest feedback I needed to improve it. I would especially like to recognize the research assistance of ML Veden and Patricia Narvaes.

In addition to recognizing the intellectual support I have been fortunate enough to receive, I would like to acknowledge some of the financial support without which this project could not have been completed. I am thankful for funding received as a Faculty Fellow in the 2011 Summer Research Consortium, an initiative of Biological Futures in a Globalized World, hosted by the Simpson Center for the Humanities (University of Washington) and sponsored by the Center for Biological Futures (Fred Hutchinson Cancer Research Center) through Prime Contract No. HHM402-11-D-0017. The Simpson Center also granted me a Crossdisciplinary Research Conversation Award in 2008–2009 that allowed me to have some concentrated research time as well the opportunity to work with Celia Lowe. My own Department of Communication at University of Washington provided me with some funding for the acquisition and translation of texts, and I benefitted from my College's approval of intensive research quarters and a sabbatical to focus my time on writing.

I am especially grateful to Marty Medhurst and to his manuscript reviewers for their timely and extremely helpful editorial direction. Your work is recognized and appreciated. I dedicate this book to my parents, Richard and Madeline Ceccarelli, and to my spouse Tim Smith and our children, Kyler and Serafina.

Introduction

⌘

In 1984, President Ronald Reagan campaigned for reelection by appealing to a mythic vision of America as "a shining city on a hill."[1] Democratic National Convention keynote speaker Mario Cuomo responded by evoking another powerful American myth.

The Republicans believe that the wagon train will not make it to the frontier unless some of the old, some of the young, some of the weak are left behind by the side of the trail. "The strong"—"The strong," they tell us, "will inherit the land." We Democrats believe in something else. We Democrats believe that we can make it all the way with the whole family intact, and we have more than once. Ever since Franklin Roosevelt lifted himself from his wheelchair to lift this nation from its knees—wagon train after wagon train—to new frontiers of education, housing, peace; the whole family aboard, constantly reaching out to extend and enlarge that family; lifting them up into the wagon on the way; blacks and Hispanics, and people of every ethnic group, and native Americans—all those struggling to build their families and claim some small share of America.[2]

1

The mental picture developed by Cuomo here is incongruous: pioneers in a wagon train, typically envisioned as circling in defense against hostile Indians, are imagined to be lifting up those very same "native Americans" to protect them with the rest of the family huddled inside. The mixing of images from different historical eras is strange too, with Roosevelt imagined to be lifting the nation from the Great Depression while wagon trains are traveling across the frontier. Likewise, the phrase "to new frontiers of education, housing, peace" is, on its face, oxymoronic. When schools and homes have been built and a social structure of peaceful security has been achieved, it is only after an old frontier has been conquered; these institutional signs of settled comfort do not align with our understanding of what awaits us on *new* frontiers. Yet despite the illogic of these images to a critical reader, the message Cuomo conveyed to his immediate audience through this use of the frontier myth was powerful and unambiguous, securing a symbol of American greatness for his party while temporarily denying it to the opposition.[3]

Cuomo's speech was not unusual in its use of frontier imagery. The symbol of the frontier is pervasive in American culture. Within a five-mile radius of my home, there are eight businesses that lay claim to a frontier ethos: two restaurants (Frontier Room and Frontier Café), a bank (Frontier Bank), a gift shop (Frontier Gallery), a laboratory that specializes in trace metals analysis (Frontier Global Sciences), the regional office of a construction company (Frontier-Kemper Constructors), a surety bond agency (Frontier Bonding Services, Inc.), and a claims adjusters office (Frontier Adjusters of Seattle). Lest you conclude that this surfeit of businesses associating themselves with the frontier is due to my location in the western part of the United States, you should know that a Google Maps search of New York and Chicago produces a similar density and variety of businesses carrying the "frontier" moniker.

The term also appears frequently in the setting of the research university. A search through my university's web pages turns up several scientists describing their work with a frontier metaphor. For example, there is an article identifying a specific experimental area as a "frontier" of particle physics; an essay titled "Endless Frontier Postponed" claiming that reduced federal funding for basic research in computer science will result in the United States ceding leadership over the "opening" of new areas of scientific discovery; and the promotional material for a lecture in the Global Health Department about why lesbian, gay, bisexual, and transgender (LGBT) rights should be seen as "the Final Frontier" that "will liberate us all."[4] The fact that frontier justice has rarely been liberatory for those in the LGBT community, or that frontier themes like rugged individualism and international competitiveness often operate counter to the goals of scientific knowledge production in disciplines like computer science and particle physics, did little to deter these researchers from selecting frontier language to convey the excitement and opportunity they associate with their favored subjects.

The historian Patricia Nelson Limerick encapsulated the ubiquity of "frontier" language in modern American culture when she pointed to a popular science article titled "Velcro: The Final Frontier." The sense in which a fabric fastener can be metaphorically compared to a frontier, much less to the "final" frontier, is self-evidently absurd. Yet the meaning of such rhetoric is immediately understood by readers: that "makers, marketers, and users of Velcro stand on the edge of exciting possibilities." Such diverse and often bizarre uses of the term "frontier" are signs that it acts as "virtually the flypaper of our mental world; it attaches itself to everything" in American public discourse despite the fact that the frontier myth is "jammed with nationalistic self-congratulation and toxic ethnocentrism."[5]

In this book I examine the unconsidered entailments of this mythic appeal in the metaphoric construction the "frontier of science," particularly as this metaphor is used in the contemporary public address of American scientists. As the rhetorical theorist Kenneth Burke put it, the terms we choose when we communicate "necessarily constitute a corresponding kind of screen" or filter on our perceptions, with each such "terministic screen" having its own way of directing our attention and shaping our thinking.[6] By examining the historical development of this terministic screen, as well as some recent uses of it, I set out to answer three questions: What is selected and what is deflected by this metaphor? What effects might these selections and deflections have on the scientific research projects of those who use the metaphor? What moves do rhetors make when they try to escape the flypaper trap of this metaphor?

With respect to the first question, my research into the history of the metaphor as well as some recent uses of it by American scientists suggests that when the terministic screen of the frontier shapes our understanding of science in America, it narrows our perception of who is qualified to undertake scientific research (ruggedly individualistic men), the motives that guide scientists (progressive), the means and proper actions they take to achieve their goals (competitive and exploitative), and the setting in which they work (unclaimed territory). These findings align with the work of the historian Richard Slotkin, whose study of the frontier myth demonstrates that this "venerable tradition in American political rhetoric" also serves as a "vein of latent ideological power," in which separation and conflict are envisioned as necessary precursors to progress.[7] Scientists interpellated through this metaphoric filter are asked to see themselves as risk-taking, adventurous loners, separated from a public that both envies and distrusts them, but that nonetheless comes to rely on the profitable discoveries they bring back from the frontier of research. This frontier metaphor constitutes American scientists as stereotypically male, with a manifest destiny to penetrate the unknown, and a competitive desire to claim the riches of new territory before others can do the same. The negative consequences of this image of the scientist are particularly striking in an era when there are more women than men in the recruiting pool for scientific careers, and when the most pressing research questions facing scientists require the ability to work cooperatively with others on problems of global significance.

The second question I take up in this book follows from this recognition of a rift between the metaphor and the needs of contemporary science. As the rhetorical critic Tarla Rai Peterson once put it, the goals legitimized by the frontier metaphor "are not always congruent with the goals of those ensnared in its web."[8] This is especially true when rhetoric designed for one audience is overheard by another, or when some audience members begin to develop a more ambivalent relationship to a myth that they had previously embraced. Limerick affirms that while "clear and predictable on most occasions, the idea of the frontier is still capable of sudden twists and shifts of meaning, meanings considerably more interesting than the conventional" connotations it engenders.[9] In this book I expose some of those twists and shifts of meaning, particularly as the term is used by American scientists and received by publics with different sensitivities to those meanings. A close look at the public rhetoric of two biologists, Edward O. Wilson and Francis Collins, demonstrates that under the influence of this terministic screen, the frontiersman's erasure of land ownership rights for the native inhabitants of "wilderness" territory is carried over to the scientist's erasure of indigenous rights to biological products. By looking at audience reception to this public rhetoric, we come to see that resistance to the research projects being promoted by these scientists was amplified by the decision to frame those projects through a frontier metaphor. When a commonplace so familiar that it is used without reflection encounters unintended audiences, or purposes that conflict with its connotations, or ambiguities of public memory, the resulting rhetorical product can be strange, illogical, and counterproductive. Identifying these incongruities can help us to better understand individual texts and their influence, and perhaps help scientists begin to loosen the grip of this ubiquitous metaphor over their rhetorical imagination.

The third question raised in this book follows from the implication that it is desirable for rhetors to escape the pull of the frontier of science metaphor by removing it from their rhetorical toolkits, or at least using it more mindfully. One of the public arguments by Collins attempts to do just that, acknowledging some of the troubling implications of the metaphor when viewed from the perspective of those who were pushed aside by the Euro-American conquest of frontier territory. But a critical examination of that text in its context shows that it is a superficial move that misses the point of its own denunciation. Another, different sort of escape from the pull of the frontier of science metaphor is attempted in President George W. Bush's first speech on stem cell research. Bucking a long tradition of American presidential rhetoric that praises scientists for their pioneering spirit of opening new frontiers of knowledge, Bush reframed the boundary that separates civilization from the unknown, reconstituting it as a line that should not be crossed. In the short term, his rhetorical reconstruction of territory across the frontier as a deadly and dystopian space was successful at subverting the appeal of an American pioneering spirit that always presses forward toward new biological futures. But in the long term, this reframing failed, as his opponents successfully invoked the frontier myth to identify his attitude toward science as incompatible with the American way. The ultimate failure of both progressive and conservative attempts to counter the influence of the frontier of science metaphor tells us much about the ongoing power and reach of this cultural trope. Coming to recognize how hard it is to escape its appeal is a first step toward developing a more sophisticated relationship to it.

In answering these three questions about the frontier of science metaphor, this book demonstrates the pathological entailments, effects, and attempted evasions of a powerful American commonplace. Research that is characterized as being on the frontier of science imagines science in a way that neglects some of the qualities that are most important to the production of successful scientific research today, like collaboration across national borders, respect for nonscientific publics, and a professional culture capable of recruiting the best minds regardless of gender. American scientists are using the frontier myth unreflectively, developing appeals that seem perfectly reasonable to them and to some of their audiences, but that undermine their goals with other audiences who interpret and evaluate those appeals in transnational contexts. The solution to these problems is not a simple affair; explicit denouncements of the metaphor have little impact on the worldview it endorses, and attempts at reframing can be short-lived. To demonstrate these points, this book narrates a rhetorical history of the frontier of science metaphor and scrutinizes the appearance of this trope in the contemporary public address of American scientists and politicians talking about science. Such criticism will help readers develop a better understanding of how the frontier metaphor dogs American science, and how such rhetoric might be better managed in the future.

The Need for Rhetorical Criticism of Scientists' Use of the Frontier Metaphor

Multiple intellectual communities, from scholars of rhetoric, to researchers in the interdiscipline known as "science studies," to scientists themselves, will find something of value in this close look at the frontier of science metaphor. The approach to inquiry that I take is developed primarily from the first of these communities, or rather from two overlapping branches of rhetorical scholarship that have been too infrequently combined—namely, "public address" and "rhetoric of science." This book engages in public address scholarship by enlisting the conventional techniques of that research community and by examining, for the most part, its prototypical artifact—namely, orations. It engages in rhetoric of science scholarship insofar as it uses rhetorical concepts and sensibilities to examine the discourse of scientists, showing how the symbolic inducements that scientists choose help to shape the scientific research that gets done. The metaphor of the frontier in the public address of scientists is an important subject that has been largely overlooked in the literature of both the public address and rhetoric of science research communities. This book examines that metaphor, and in doing so, makes contributions to each of these two branches of rhetorical scholarship.

THE FRONTIER AS METAPHOR:
A CONTRIBUTION TO PUBLIC ADDRESS SCHOLARSHIP

Despite the significance and ubiquity of the frontier of science metaphor, there has been, to date, little sustained rhetorical analysis of it. This paucity of research is not due to a lack of interest in frontier rhetoric, since rhetorical critics have long written about the power of the frontier myth in American public address. A sign of just how substantial this research has been is the fact that two recent articles on the use of frontier rhetoric begin with an acknowledgment that rhetorical studies of the frontier myth have been "numerous" and "robust."[10] This abundance of scholarship has established that the frontier myth is broad in scope and flexible in application, always telling a story of national identity rooted in a history of heroic adventure and ever-expanding vistas.

In one of her many studies of the frontier myth, Janice Hocker Rushing expertly summarized the temporal, spatial, and characterological contours of this rhetorical appeal for Euro-American audiences: "From birth to maturity, America has drawn upon the frontier for its mythic identity. Whether fixed upon Columbus sailing the ocean blue or Buffalo Bill conquering the Wild, Wild West, the American imagination remains fascinated by new and unknown *places*. Lured by the sea, then the plains, we are a people of the promised land, the New World, the untamed frontier. Since the beginning, the pioneer spirit has shaped the American Dream and infused its rhetoric."[11] Rushing's statement that the frontier myth is tied to an American national identity is undisputed; all who study the myth make similar statements. Her delineation of the myth as extending from Columbus to the cowboy is also standard among scholars who examine this commonplace of American public address. A mythic vision of the American frontier spirit is not limited to a narrow historical period in which new states were added to the nation along a western border; instead, the frontier myth is a central component of the American story writ large, from the prehistory of the nation in which a people discovered and entered a "New World," to the development of that nation and the expansion of that people across a continent, taming an extensive wilderness and profiting from the riches to be hunted, mined, or cultivated there.

We see the same wide scope for the myth being established by Slotkin, who began his three-volume study of the American frontier myth with reports of the first European conquests in the New World and ended his study with the film genre of the modern western. The theme that unifies this long history of the "myth of the frontier" in America is "the conception of America as a wide-open land of unlimited opportunity for the strong, ambitious, self-reliant individual to thrust his way to the top."[12] The protagonists who populate this frontier narrative are the men who "tore violently a nation from the implacable and opulent wilderness"—that is, the adventurers, land-boomers, Indian fighters, traders, missionaries, explorers, hunters, and settlers who made their fortunes from their bold actions in a untamed land.[13] Other historical figures who might have been found on the frontier, like the Indians whose land was "discovered" and conquered by European immigrants, are most often elided in the myth or made out to be part of the hostile scene, elements of the wilderness to be tamed rather than heroic characters to be emulated.

My own analysis of the frontier myth in the public address of American scientists follows the lead of Rushing and Slotkin, turning up metaphoric links to a broad range of Euro-American protagonists, from prospectors to pioneers, all of whom are represented as rugged heroes with an adventurous spirit that impels them to separate from the safety and familiarity of civilization to seek the unlimited opportunities that exist beyond the horizon of the known and established.

Since a relationship to new territory is what defines the frontier hero, those invoking the myth in recent times have had a rhetorical difficulty to overcome. Once the United States was settled, there was no geographic American frontier to conquer. New spaces of adventure had to be invented for the men who continued to carry the nation's pioneering spirit within them. Rhetorical scholars have provided a great deal of insight into how this shift toward new frontier lands has been accomplished by American rhetors.

For example, one line of research shows how a mythic American frontier identity was used in the twentieth century and beyond to justify adventures into new non-American terrestrial domains. In one of his many excellent studies of the frontier in American public address, Leroy Dorsey emphasized the myth's heroic and progressive contours as applied by John F. Kennedy to motivate people to join the Peace Corps, so they could exercise their pioneering spirit in underdeveloped countries.[14] In another study that carefully details the use of the American frontier myth, Ronald H. Carpenter revealed how this cultural commonplace was tragically applied throughout the twentieth century to justify imperialist military actions overseas, as rhetors imagined "contemporary American combatants as frontiersmen" who engage in violent ventures in foreign lands.[15] More recently, Mark West and Chris Carey described how George W. Bush tactically deployed the American myth of frontier justice to frame American combat operations in Afghanistan and Iraq in a way that could be judged by American audiences to be a meaningful and appropriate action.[16]

In addition to examining how a frontier appeal can be used to inspire and justify American adventures abroad, rhetorical critics have studied the extension of the frontier myth into extraterrestrial space. According to Rushing, "America has constantly sought new frontiers as the old are tamed" in order to preserve "the backdrop of its identity" against a constant change of scene, so it is worthwhile to see how this has been accomplished in film and speech that imagine a new frontier in outer space; in looking at such texts, Rushing demonstrated some of "the dangers of applying old mythic values to a new mythic scene."[17] Other scholars who have examined the extension of frontier rhetoric into outer space concur that this use of the myth is compelling and problematic, conjuring "a positive, romantic, masculine image of life in the West" as "a way of ignoring or pushing aside the possible negative aspects of the exploitation of space."[18]

Yet another extension of the frontier myth has been into cyberspace, as computer-generated environments accessed over the Internet are conceived to be territory in need of exploration and colonization. As the rhetorical critic James McDaniel put it, the current "new frontier rhetoric" of cyberspace "articulates itself frequently in terms of nineteenth-century fantasies and tropes of Manifest Destiny, in which God's will was invoked to justify and motivate the stretch westward," with leaders in the computer industry promoting this view by making reference to a new Oklahoma land rush of digital territory, complete with surveyors of the digital landscape and cyber-colonists.[19] Other scholars concur that virtual worlds are frequently conceptualized as being like "the New World of the Americas and the western frontier of the United States," spaces in which heroic individuals can escape the restrictions of the Old World and extend "the ideology and rhetoric of the European 'age of discovery' and American expansionism."[20]

Each of these rhetorical studies tells us something important about how the frontier myth has been applied to new spatial domains, carrying with it the image of a hardy, risk-taking, self-reliant American identity and erasing anything that might run counter to such a vision. But what rhetorical critics of American public address have not yet studied in sufficient detail is how the frontier has been used as a metaphor for nonspatial subjects. The anthropologist Beverly Stoeltje made an important distinction that helped me recognize this point. She argued that to speak of "the Frontier of Space" is to apply "myth in contrast to metaphor." In discourse that proclaims outer space to be the final frontier, "the term 'Frontier' . . . serves as the abbreviation, the synecdoche that sums up the myth or the entitlement which tells the story of the sociopolitical process known as Exploration and Conquest of the Unknown," a process that is then "extended from the earth to the skies."[21] This is also the case when the American frontier is extended from the western territorial frontier to new Third World places when rhetors use the myth to justify modern imperialist adventures in foreign lands. Such spheres of influence are not *like* a new frontier; they *are* a new spatial frontier for Americans to enter. Likewise, as new media scholars David J. Gunkel and Ann Hetzel Gunkel point out, "the virtual environments created in the nonspace of cyberspace are not to be understood as something like a frontier; they are, quite literally, a new world—a very real space (albeit one which is entirely virtual) that is open to exploration and colonization . . . not analogous or comparable to the frontier; they are quite literally a new territory."[22] This computer-generated terra nova does not occupy real estate, but in a very real sense it is perceived to be a type of terrain, to be moved through, purchased, and developed. In each of these cases, where the frontier myth is extended by American rhetors to justify adventures in foreign lands, outer space, or cyberspace, a new location is found to replace the American wilderness territory that did so much to mold the character of the mythic frontier hero.

The subject of this book is something different: the frontier of science *metaphor* extends the frontier myth not into another spatial location but into an endeavor, a profession that occupies only the figurative space of an *intellectual* (rather than a literal or even virtual) territory. The appeal to explore a frontier of science does not actually call Americans to cross a border into a new domain. Instead, the frontier works here as both myth and metaphor, evoking a compelling story about American character traits in heroic situations to describe a type of knowledge work and to set apart a class of people who are engaged in that work. In the early twentieth century, this metaphorical frontier of science was introduced as a compelling rhetorical substitute for the vanished American terrestrial frontier, and it has been serving that function ever since in the public discourse of American scientists and politicians.

Since it is the terrain that shapes the character of the frontier hero, whether adventuring in the American West, foreign lands, outer space, or virtual reality, it is reasonable to ask what happens when the myth of the frontier is applied to something that lacks this essential spatial dimension. The metaphor of the frontier of science does not include a harsh scene that molds a heroic agent; regarding this metaphorical frontier, there is no literal or even virtual territory for the scientist to enter and master. With a bountiful and unforgiving setting being so important to our understanding of the frontier, the metaphor must somehow carry over this essential feature of the myth. My research on the rhetoric of Wilson and Collins in particular suggests that when the frontier of science *metaphor* is deployed by biologists, the spatial component of the myth finds a way to reassert itself in an analog between wilderness territory and the bodies of organisms, whether they be the bodies of new species that are to be mined for their biological wealth or the microscopic interiors of people whose genomes are to be mapped by scientists staking a claim to promising new genetic sequences. In short, frontier as *metaphor* carries entailments that force us to think of the subject being discussed as if it were a spatial territory, ripe for exploration and exploitation. By examining the extension of the frontier myth into a metaphor for new knowledge in the biological sciences, and taking a close look at the particular spatializations that are implied by that metaphor, we can learn something new about the way this powerful cultural appeal works to influence the thinking of the rhetors who use it and the audiences who respond to it.

So how can we think about new knowledge as something other than frontier territory? A popular metaphor used by rhetorical critics is Burke's depiction of scholarship as a parlor in which an unending conversation is being hosted, with individual scholars entering and then exiting a vigorous discussion.[23] Under the terms of this metaphor, new knowledge does not claim space, but instead, is the consensus acknowledgment of an insightful point in an ongoing dialogue.

Burke's metaphor is fitting to characterize the contribution to new knowledge that I offer with this book. One of the main conversational turns that I present is a claim that the frontier myth, a rhetorical appeal so frequently discussed by public address scholars who have entered the parlor before me, works also as a *metaphor* for new scientific knowledge, with a particular spatialization of scientific "territory" as the outcome.

This turn in the conversation is not the only scholarly contribution that I make in this book. Several other groupings of scholars in the public address parlor will find that portions of this book speak to issues relevant to their ongoing conversations. For example, those interested in public memory studies should find value in my analysis of modern attempts by some rhetors to escape the pull of a powerful cultural myth, as a nation's collective understanding of that myth shifts over time.[24] They should also find a point of interest in my contention that some resistive audiences are able to invert the appeal of this myth by emphasizing its less admirable features.

Those scholars of presidential public address who discuss the rhetorical construction of national identity should appreciate my documentation of presidential speeches that identify U.S. scientists as quintessential Americans, fearlessly pressing forward to make discoveries that lead to a better future for the nation.[25] Such identification of scientists with an exceptional American ethos works to diminish citizens who are not scientists, or who question the onward rush of scientific research.

Those public address scholars interested in metacriticism, or the study of how critical practice develops in the field of rhetorical inquiry, will attend to the approach to criticism that I take, as I deliberately move between scholarly traditions that have, at times, been seen as existing in tension with each other. In this book, I embrace both instrumentalist and constitutive approaches to rhetorical criticism, I undertake the close reading of carefully structured speech texts while also piecing together fragments to illuminate the ideograph *frontier*, and I adopt both an intentional focus on rhetorical design and an extensional focus on audience reception.[26] The degree to which I am able to successfully unite approaches that have been presented, in the past, as conflicting "methods" of rhetorical criticism aligns this work with the work of contemporary conversationalists in the parlor who proclaim the end of method as a guiding force for public address research, and who champion the rise of a multidimensional critical practice that is driven more by the desire to answer specific questions about rhetoric than by any desire to brand or warrant new critical methodologies.[27]

Meanwhile, in an adjoining parlor, rhetoric of science scholars take part in another set of conversations that I also engage with this book, conversations that should also be of interest to other science studies scholars and to scientists themselves.

The Public Address of Scientists:
A Contribution to Rhetoric of Science Scholarship

Rhetoric of science is a thriving subdiscipline, but to date there has been very little scholarly examination of the frontier of science metaphor in the public address of scientists. There are a couple of reasons this pervasive trope in the public communication of scientists has not yet been widely discussed. First, although the rhetoric of science has been analyzed by a number of accomplished scholars over the last couple of decades, the public address of scientists is a genre that has not yet been closely scrutinized. Until recently, studies of the rhetoric of science have focused mostly on scientists communicating with other scientists, or on popularizations written by science journalists. As Jeanne Fahnestock recently pointed out, the public discourse of scientists themselves is "an area that deserves far more attention."[28]

Second, those few studies that *have* examined the public rhetoric of scientists have mostly focused on other themes. For example, Thomas Lessl produced an early study of how scientists present themselves to the public at those "rhetorical junctures, in proemial and perorational moments, as well as in editorials, biographies, advertisements—whenever rhetorical demands cause the public scientist to step out momentarily" from his or her other duties as researcher or educator. What Lessl found in such public discourse was "the voice of a priest." This priestly metaphor that Lessl introduced was useful for characterizing the relationship that scientists pursue with public audiences. However, while Lessl did not note it, almost every block quote that he included in this article contained the voice of the frontiersman as well. Reading these fragments, we see: a call to membership for a Planetary Society that describes a "series of voyages of exploration and discovery" designed to entice people to support the scientific study of the solar system; a paragraph from a National Aeronautics and Space Administration

(NASA) booklet that ends by depicting the scientific ethos in terms of the heroic explorer ("they have always gone into the unknown; they have always pushed the frontiers of human knowledge outward"); and passages from Carl Sagan's eulogy for a famous planetary scientist who complained that younger scientists had "come gunning for him" since his status led to him "being treated as 'the fastest gun in the West.'"[29] In each textual fragment representing the scientist's public voice, the figure of the frontiersman beckoned; yet Lessl concentrated instead on the figure of the priest.[30] My book corrects this absence of interpretative attention by listening to the voice of the frontiersman in the public address of scientists.

Although Lessl failed to attend to the frontier rhetoric that appeared in the texts he examined, he did well to focus on the public appeals of scientists themselves in developing his portrait of a scientific ethos, because such a focus is more likely to be meaningful to scientists. Many rhetoric of science scholars aim to influence scientists, encouraging them to be more thoughtful about their rhetorical choices. A recent review of rhetorical scholarship about science-public interactions concluded that a number of critical scholars adopt "a melioristic set of goals—identifying errant or problematic features of specific public representations of science" while holding out "the possibility of reconciliation or revision," and other scholars are even more direct in offering "the resources of rhetorical analysis for making more productive public rhetorics of science rather than solely for oppositional critique."[31] My own work aligns with this type of scholarship, analyzing public texts to help scientists understand how to improve their communication. But unlike much of the rhetoric of science literature, I focus almost entirely on the public rhetoric of scientists themselves, under the assumption that scientists are not likely to recognize the relevance of rhetorical criticism if that critique focuses mostly on popularizations written by nonscientists. Scientists already suspect that media sources mischaracterize science to the public, and they are liable to take little responsibility for such distortions.[32] This book highlights the frontier rhetoric used by scientists themselves when they speak in public in order to help scientists recognize that they are complicit in promoting the public image of science that is developed from that language use.

Of course, while they are complicit, scientists are not the only ones using frontier language to describe scientific activity. Rhetorical critics who examine scientific popularizations that are authored by nonscientists have already begun a conversation about the presence and significance of the frontier of science metaphor in mass media texts. Such analysis has the potential to alter the thinking of the journalists, entertainers, movie producers, and cartoonists responsible for such texts. For example, Joanna Ploeger's analysis of the rhetoric of an IMAX documentary explained how the last third of the film "links the western explorer to the modern scientist." This "depiction of science as an extension of the western frontier mythologizes rather than illuminates the actual practice of science," according to Ploeger.[33] More recently, Maureen Burns and Joan Leach examined an internationally syndicated newspaper comic strip that portrayed scientists as frontier explorers, creating a "highly problematic" ideology that obscures the ways in which science really works.[34]

There also are a number of scholars who have included a critique of the frontier metaphor as a small part of their larger examination of images and language in popular treatments of science.[35] But most of these studies include little analysis of the public pronouncements of scientists themselves, focusing primarily on mediated texts authored by journalistic science writers.[36] I believe that a demonstration that scientists are using frontier language in their *direct* communication with public audiences offers a critical finding that is less easy for scientists to dismiss as being about someone else's discursive choices.

I should note that a handful of scholars have focused on the appearance of the frontier myth in the direct public communication of scientists. The use of the frontier metaphor by scientists to promote high-energy physics research has been studied in some detail. For example, the historians Adrienne Kolb and Lillian Hoddeson recognized that "the frontier myth has been of central importance in the self-image of American scientists," and yet scholars "have not devoted much attention to that issue." To correct this, they documented the "frontier imagery [that] passed into the writings and speeches of the four founders of Fermilab" as well as the use of frontier rhetoric by physicists making arguments for the construction of the Superconducting Super Collider.[37] The science studies scholar Alice Domurat Dreger also documented scientists using the frontier metaphor when she examined the arguments of scientists to Congress and the public about the worthiness of the Human Genome Project.[38] She concluded that geneticists "found genome-as-unexplored-territory metaphors compelling because the language matched well their sense of the project."[39]

In this book, I extend this scholarship on frontier language in the self-presentation of American scientists by interrogating the history of the frontier of science metaphor, locating some of the initial uses of this trope in American public discourse. To demonstrate the current popularity of the metaphor and develop a more full investigation of the implications of its contemporary use, I examine its presence in some recent public speeches by American scientists from various disciplines. I then trace the appearance of this trope in three case studies from the rhetoric of biology that have been selected because they demonstrate some of the specific difficulties faced by those who wrestle with frontier rhetoric in our contemporary world. In almost all instances, I examine the public address of scientists—that is, their relatively unmediated appeals to prospective supporters, patrons, voters, and new recruits to a scientific career.[40] In doing so, I turn the conversation in rhetoric of science scholarship toward the public rhetoric of scientists, with the intent of making the critical insights of rhetorical inquiry more meaningful to the scientists and scientists-in-training whom many rhetoric of science scholars like myself seek to influence with our teaching and research.

Theories of Myth and Metaphor

Another set of conversations that I enter in the rhetorical parlor centers around theories of myth and metaphor. Scholars have produced a small industry of research on the two main rhetorical concepts that I use in this study. It is beyond the scope of this book to thoroughly review that research or to develop new argument threads in ongoing debates over how myth and metaphor work. However, it is worthwhile at this early point in the book to set out some basic definitions and introduce some vocabulary for talking about texts in which myth and metaphor align to create a specific rhetorical appeal. It also is worthwhile to consider what others who have critically analyzed this literature have to say about the limitations of this kind of research. In entering the scholarly conversation about theories of myth and metaphor, I pay particular attention to critical exchanges about the proper use of these concepts, as such conversations have helped to shape the specific approach to rhetorical inquiry that I take in this book.

Myth: A Cultural Ethos Exposed
through Rhetorical Criticism

One of the most prolific writers on myth in the field of rhetorical criticism was Rushing, who defined myth as "a society's collectivity of persistent values, handed down from generation to generation, that help to make the world understandable, support the social order, and educate the society's young."[41] Rushing acknowledged that myths share deep archetypal structures, but what is most significant about her definition of myth for this project is her claim that a myth is fundamentally cultural—that is, it upholds the values of a particular society.[42] As the rhetorical critic Michael Osborn put it in his eulogistic reflection on Rushing's corpus of research, she truly understood "the essence of myth," that it is "a vital cultural resource" that "serves rhetorically to premise, to justify, and to warrant codes of behavior that in turn mold specific programs of action."[43] Even Robert Rowland, who critiqued Rushing's broad definition in favor of his own narrow definition of myth, agreed that "at a minimum, a myth is a story about heroic characters who serve as personal or societal models."[44] Critics who might disagree about other matters regarding the concept of myth agree that when a myth is used in a rhetorical text, it calls up a cultural ethos that audience members from that culture are encouraged to emulate.

A myth establishes that exemplary ethos by anchoring the values of a particular culture in a narrative of that culture's past. As Dorsey said, a myth "is a persistent story of extraordinary historical experiences and protagonists, real or fictive, which explain and empower a community's origin and sense of self."[45] As a story, it emphasizes some aspects of its subject and neglects others. Dorsey, drawing on literary theorist Roland Barthes, noted the "chimerical tendency of myth—to promote a sort of memory loss about history and yet create sacred knowledge from that same history."[46] Offering up a selective history, myth re-creates its target audience in its romantic, idealized image. By exposing that image and its implications as only one way of thinking about that community's foundation and identity, a rhetorical critic can help to weaken the myth's power in a particular case and expand the rhetorical possibilities for self-identification available to that community in the future.

This might sound easy, but Rowland has warned critics who seek to expose a mythic appeal in a rhetorical text that their efforts are susceptible to two interpretive errors. They might incorrectly identify a narrative as mythic when it does not actually rise to the level of myth, or they might argue that a text is drawing on a particular myth without sufficient evidence that the myth is being evoked.[47]

It is with this conversation in mind that I have selected the texts to be examined and the critical practice to be employed in this book. Regarding the first potential pitfall, Rowland himself has acknowledged that stories about the frontier fit the most "narrow definition of myth," and that "frontier mythology" is an important cultural resource for American rhetors. Since I focus on the application of such a "well-known societal myth," there is no danger that I am misapplying the concept of "myth" in using that term to talk about frontier rhetorics.[48]

Rowland's second admonition, that critics should avoid the temptation to identify the existence of a particular myth in texts that show little sign of its presence, is the more significant one for this project. In setting out this caution to critics, Rowland asked a rhetorical question that is especially pertinent to this book: "Are all works about cancer or science or education or ocean research or any number of other subjects mythic, since some have referred to those subjects as a 'new frontier'?"[49] With this question, Rowland suggested that the barest mention of the word "frontier" by a scientist is insufficient to warrant a claim that an appeal is being made to the frontier myth.

Some critics respond to this warning by disputing its assumption, disagreeing with Rowland's dismissive attitude toward such minimal signs of a mythic appeal. Replying to Rowland's rhetorical question, Osborn defiantly answered in the affirmative, arguing that such oblique references to research frontiers are mythic "if the embedded mythic pattern is dominant and sensitive enough to be evoked by the metaphorical allusion."[50] Rushing offered a similar response, drawing on one of the earliest studies of myth in rhetorical criticism to argue that because myths are so well known, mere insinuation through passing reference or gesture is enough to evoke a myth in a text.[51]

In making their argument for a more liberal attitude toward the identification of myth, Osborn and Rushing advocate a critical practice that would pay close attention to the most subtle of signs that a mythic appeal exists in a text. Although I agree with their arguments against Rowland's cautionary restriction, I understand his concern as well, and so I have selected the texts to be examined in this book carefully, ensuring that they meet Rowland's more stringent standard of providing sufficient evidence of the presence of mythic appeals. In almost all of the cases I examine, the texts activate the frontier myth by extended, explicit reference to heroic characters from the cultural story (for example, Lewis and Clark) and to the symbols of their mythic exploits (for example, survey maps).[52] Because these texts make elaborate and overt comparisons between old and new frontiers, my claim that they draw upon a mythic appeal is supported with more than sufficient textual evidence. An examination of the reception of some of these texts shows that there is also intertextual evidence that audiences were influenced by the frontier imagery in them, providing further proof of the presence and significance of these mythic appeals.[53] By tracing the abundant explicit references to the frontier myth in public arguments about American scientific research, as well as some of the more subtle signs of frontier language appearing in those texts and in the responses of audiences, I expose the mythic appeal of the frontier of science and its likely influence on the attitudes of both speakers and audiences.

Metaphor: A Selection and Deflection Exposed through Rhetorical Criticism

Metaphor is defined by Kenneth Burke as "a device for seeing something *in terms of* something else. It brings out the thisness of a that, or the thatness of a this," allowing us "to consider A from the point of view of B [which] is, of course, to use B as a *perspective* upon A."[54] Like myth, metaphor selects some aspects of a subject to emphasize, while deflecting our attention from other aspects of that subject. Rhetorical criticism of metaphor is often undertaken to expose the way our attention is being directed in one way rather than another by the cognitive and affective framing mechanism of particular word combinations.

Ironically, the best way to talk about the concept of metaphor seems to be through metaphorical language, with theories of metaphor frequently using the terminology of conveyance, spatial overlap, cooperation, and filtering. So, for example, a metaphor can be described as the interaction of two ideas, a tenor (or principal subject) and a vehicle (or figure).[55] In the case of the frontier of science metaphor, "science" is the tenor, and "frontier" is the vehicle. The interaction of these ideas creates a "system of associated commonplaces," which is defined as a set of inferences and connotations available to a speech community when the two ideas are brought together. Some details that might be associated with the tenor are made more prominent by its connection with the vehicle, while others are suppressed, and vice versa. Like a screen, the metaphor filters and transforms our perception.[56] As Osborn put it in a recent summary of his career-spanning work on rhetoric and metaphor, this ability to "control perceptions: how we see and encounter the world in which we live" is "the first, most basic function of rhetorical language—including metaphor."[57] This might be why metaphor has been a subject of such interest to rhetorical critics over the years.[58] In shaping our perceptions, metaphor can have a tremendous influence on what public policies we adopt and on our conceptions of ourselves and others, restricting our options to those that are conceivable within the imaginative constraints of the worldview being proffered by that specific language choice.[59]

In addition to establishing and explaining the power of metaphor, one of the contributions that rhetorical critics have made to theories of metaphor is classificatory. Osborn has written much about archetypal metaphors, such as metaphors that include vehicles of light or dark-ness; these are popular and persuasive in public discourse because of their timeless and universal appeal.[60] Although he has not written about it in as much detail, he also introduced terminology to identify another type of metaphor that appeals specifically to the values and interests of a particular culture. The "culturetypal" metaphor uses the sacred words of a society, expressing their key values and thus resonating with spe-cial force for that audience.[61] Archetypal metaphors are more likely to work cross-culturally, while culturetypal metaphors appeal to a particu-lar discourse community. The frontier of science, as it is presented in the cases examined in this book, is an example of this latter type of metaphor, carrying a special meaning to a Euro-American audience that might not be shared by other audiences.[62]

As with the study of mythic appeals, a review of the literature on metaphor indicates that there are at least two interpretive errors that rhetorical critics are vulnerable to when examining metaphors in a text. Rhetoricians might incorrectly identify something as a metaphor when it is not one, or they might claim that a particular entailment follows a metaphor without providing sufficient evidence that it does.

Ever since George Lakoff and Mark Johnson popularized the study of conceptual metaphors that underlie our everyday speech, like the cluster of expressions that perceive argument as a war (I *defended* my claims; he *shot down* my argument; I will *attack* each of his points), there has been an explosion of rhetorical criticism that collects the conventional, typically unnoticed metaphorical vehicles that make up a text, vehicles that, upon being recognized, reveal a text's overall orientation.[63] The critic's exposure of these patterns of literalized metaphors can ground a compelling argument about the limitations of a text's essential worldview, and in so doing open us to alternative perspectives that are suppressed by the routine language choices made in that text. However, by focusing our attention on conventionalized, or "dead," metaphors, this approach to metaphoric analysis can encourage rhetoricians to mark as metaphorical some word combinations that may no longer really function as metaphors at all. For example, Osborn has confessed that he "wince[s] over some of the liberties taken with 'metaphor' by Lakoff and Johnson," Fahnestock would prefer a "narrower" definition of metaphor than they use, and Randy Allen Harris has remarked that the metaphors they identify are "dormant-unto-literality" and that the general framing phenomenon they describe is more accurately named analogy.[64] Rhetorical critics who follow the lead of Lakoff and Johnson by tracing the use of conventionalized metaphors in public address are vulnerable to the same critiques of their work.

Scholars reviewing the literature on metaphoric criticism have also pointed out that the analysis of metaphors can result in critics spinning out chains of connotations for isolated metaphors while failing to respect the emotional or cognitive weight of the rest of the text or without seeking evidence of audience reception to support their claims about the troubling influence of those chains of connotations. For example, David Douglass identified this error when he argued that the tendency in the field has been "to isolate vehicles and conduct an interpretive deconstruction of their implications for tenors," a "seduction" for critics who enjoy the "vivisection of language" but an approach to criticism that contributes little to understanding because these critics fail to seek evidence of their interpretations in "any real-world auditor's interpretation."[65] Sharing this concern about metaphoric criticism, Celeste Condit has undertaken a research program to counter untested critical presumptions about the impact of specific isolated metaphors.[66]

Sensitive to these interpretive dangers, yet impressed by the potential of metaphoric criticism to reveal ideologies and prejudices that might otherwise remain unnoticed and unexamined in a text, I adopt an approach to metaphoric criticism that is responsive to the critical concerns that my colleagues have identified in our ongoing conversation about this subject. To avoid the mislabeling of metaphor, I have selected texts where terms such as "scientific frontier" are activated by multiple references to symbols from the frontier myth, making it more than a literalized, dormant, or dead metaphor in those texts. I also am careful to support my claims about the entailments of such metaphors, offering evidence of reception whenever it is available to demonstrate how different audiences orient toward these language choices, and attending to other contextual material that influences the interpretation of the frontier metaphors present in these texts.

In adopting this critical approach, I have been influenced by applied linguistics scholar Cornelia Müller's "dynamic view" of metaphor, which distinguishes truly dead metaphors from entrenched metaphors that are conventionalized but that may be either asleep or awake, depending on the degree to which they are activated in a given text by various contextual cues like repetition, clustering of source domain expressions, and elaboration.[67] So, for example, the word "frontier" is a dead metaphor insofar as we consider its primary meaning drawn from Old French into Middle English, ultimately from the Latin *frons*, meaning forehead or front part. The metaphoric nature of this primary meaning of a frontier as territorial border is opaque to ordinary readers; only etymologists would recognize that the standard definition of this term is drawn from a metaphoric comparison between an anatomical feature, the forehead, and the front part of a political state. However, when the word "frontier" is used to refer to the development of new knowledge, as in the frontier of science, the metaphoric nature of this more recently developed meaning for the term is fairly transparent to contemporary audiences; we are likely to recognize the term as metaphorical, a comparison between the move into promising new geographic territory and intellectual achievement. As it is used today, the frontier of science is not a novel metaphor, but it is still recognized by auditors as metaphorical, and it may be activated to lesser or greater degrees depending on how much the surrounding text emphasizes its metaphoric nature by highlighting the analogic connection.

The texts that I have selected for analysis in this book all awaken the metaphor of the frontier of science with extended references to the myth of the frontier that foreground the relationship between tenor and vehicle. Some of those references unambiguously point to symbols of westward expansion across the American continent, as when the frontier of science metaphor is accompanied by an elaborated comparison of the Superconducting Super Collider to a wagon train. Other references that awaken the frontier of science metaphor in these texts are terms from the broader myth of the frontier in America, the scope of which has been established by scholars such as Rushing and Slotkin to extend from "discovery" of the New World during the Age of Exploration to contemporary cowboy culture; in these cases, the frontier of science metaphor is accompanied by language that compares scientists to Columbus, or to prospectors, or to hunters or trappers in a vast wilderness, always drawn by the lure of the unknown and the promise of great riches. Yet other references that awaken the frontier of science metaphor are more oblique, archetypal metaphors of directional movement that, in close proximity to the metaphor of the frontier of science, play into a mythic frontier appeal, as when scientists are imagined to be blazing ever forward, or crossing boundaries, or climbing ever upward. Each of these references underscores the frontier of science metaphor as it appears in the texts examined in this book, activating the metaphor for audiences that encounter these texts. That the metaphor is activated is confirmed when those audiences respond to these texts with identical or similar language, carrying forth the metaphor and its associated commonplaces, either in a way that affirms the intent of the author or counters it.

How Frontier Rhetoric Shapes Science

This book is organized into five chapters that move from historical to contemporary times, from a broad overview of scientists' use of the metaphor in their arguments for patronage of the sciences to particular case studies of individuals using the appeal to promote their specific areas of research in the biological sciences, and from the unreflective use of this metaphor by scientists to more thoughtful but ultimately unsuccessful attempts to thwart its influence by both a scientist and a nonscientist.

Chapter 1 begins with an etymological analysis of the term "frontier," drawing on different editions of American dictionaries over time to trace the development of its meaning as a metaphor for the limits of knowledge. That this metaphor is a relatively new development in the English language is evidenced by the fact that dictionaries did not identify a figurative use of the term until the middle of the twentieth century. To understand what led to this new meaning for the term "frontier," this chapter engages a study of significant uses of the frontier of science metaphor in early-to-mid-twentieth-century public address. It examines Frederick Jackson Turner's suggestion that science constitutes a new frontier for Americans to conquer, the competing uses of frontier metaphors for science by American political and intellectual leaders, a scientist's exultant classification of his colleagues as new frontiersmen in an epideictic essay, and Vannevar Bush's proclamation that the American government has a duty to support the exploration of science as an endless frontier for resource development. In each of these cases, the entailments of the metaphor as it becomes a conventional way of thinking about science are detailed.

Chapter 2 demonstrates that the frontier myth, firmly attached to science by the middle of the twentieth century, continues to guide the most recent public speeches of American scientists. In arguments for increased funding and support for science and science education, the frontier of science metaphor is used to promote a vision of the scientist as a model of hegemonic masculinity. Basic scientific research is privileged on the assumption that profitable applications will automatically follow the work of pioneering scientists just as resource flows back to the states followed the adventures of literal frontiersmen in the American western territories. And international collaboration between scientists is discouraged by a frontier metaphor that envisions science as a competition to plant the flag on intellectual territory, a zero-sum game in which individuals succeed by trampling those who get in their way. The texts examined in this chapter include speeches delivered from 1992 to 2006 by American scientists from various fields who hold leadership positions in educational and professional organizations or the business community. A counterexample to the assumptions contained in these speeches is presented at the end of the chapter in a look at the speech of a Chinese scientist who used the frontier metaphor when talking to an American audience, but then mentioned some of the more unfortunate implications of using this language and suggested an alternative way of thinking about our relationship to science.

In the next three chapters I offer case studies where I examine the use of the frontier of science metaphor in public arguments about particular subjects in the biological sciences. My aim is to examine not only what perspectives the metaphor selects and deflects but also what impact that filtering has on the rhetors who use the metaphor and the audiences who encounter it. The focus on biology in these case studies is deliberate. It is not just because the rhetoric of biology happens to be my own research specialty, or because, as I noted earlier, the impact of the frontier metaphor on public arguments for high-energy physics research has already been studied by other scholars. The justification for the selection of these case studies on the rhetoric of biology is the special relationship that exists between the biological sciences and the public. For example, members of the public make up the human bodies that are both subject to the research conducted by biologists and served by the medical technologies that biologists enable. And as I have already mentioned, the particular spatializations implied by the frontier of science metaphor can transform biological entities like people into territory to be explored and exploited. Because social, political, and moral issues are never far from the biological sciences, the rhetorician of science John Lyne has coined the term "bio-rhetoric" to talk about the way resources of language are drawn from the public sphere to be used by rhetors who occupy the technical sphere of the biological sciences, and vice versa.[68] The frontier of science metaphor as presented in the three case studies I have chosen is one type of bio-rhetoric, borrowing the myth of an American pioneering spirit from the public sphere to characterize the activities of biological scientists "in such a way that they mesh with the discourses of social, political, or moral life."[69] This cross-fertilization of spheres is built over a tension between the spheres, and both this association and this conflict are worthy of sustained critical attention.

In chapter 3 I examine Edward O. Wilson's use of frontier language in his popular books on biodiversity research. Despite Wilson's overall message that frontier lands, and the frontier forests of Amazonia in particular, require immediate protection from the assault of humankind, his books promote biodiversity studies as the profitable bioprospecting of wilderness territory by scientists who employ an American pioneering spirit to exploit natural resources for pharmaceutical development. This chapter offers a close reading of the frontier metaphors in Wilson's biodiversity books, as well as a reception study of book reviews published in English-language newspapers and scientific journals to demonstrate how his use of frontier language resulted in different readers interpreting his meaning in opposite ways, almost always countering his presumed intent. This chapter also examines how Wilson's books, which were translated into Portuguese, were received in Brazil, where the imperialist implications of his language choices ended up being counterproductive to his goals of promoting the global scientific

cataloging and preservation of biodiversity. The frontier of science metaphor thus helped to shape science in a way that ran against what the
rhetor using the metaphor in this case most likely wanted.

In chapter 4 I examine the appearance of the frontier myth in the
public discourse of Francis Collins, a leader of the Human Genome
Project who currently directs the National Institutes of Health. His use
of frontier rhetoric configures the scientific enterprise as an adventure
and the human body as a wilderness territory that biologists have a manifest destiny to survey, claim, and exploit. In addition to creating a divine
duty for the genome scientist to proceed with this research, and encouraging a competitive spirit between researchers from different nations,
a consequence of this figuration is a deflection of the ownership rights
of the human subject to his or her own genetic "territory." A recognition of how this metaphoric screen shapes Collins's discourse, even at
a remarkable moment when he explicitly tries to pull away from the
most troubling implications of the frontier myth, is the first step toward
rethinking the future use of frontier language in public discourse about
genomics research.

Chapter 5 differs from the other chapters in that I focus on the public speech of an American politician (rather than a scientist) in a case
where that rhetor makes a nationally broadcast attempt to counteract
the mythic appeal of the frontier as a metaphor for science. George
W. Bush used the metaphor briefly in his August 9, 2001, speech that
restricted federal funding for human embryonic stem cell research. In
using the metaphor, he was drawing on a long tradition of presidential
rhetoric that this chapter begins by tracing. This tradition assures Americans that scientists are modern frontiersmen, pathbreaking a better
future for the nation. However, Bush's speech was bucking that tradition because it announced the closure of a scientific frontier. By closely
reading this speech and the reception of its various audiences, I explain
how Bush was able to argue against the American impulse to cross that
frontier boundary. Even though most Americans disagreed with Bush's
policy, they approved of it immediately following his speech, in many
cases for contradictory reasons. I argue that the speech worked because
it deployed countermetaphors to reframe the frontier as a space that
Americans might want to avoid, it subtly created an ambiguity about the
president's stance toward forward movement across that frontier, and it
manufactured a controversy between ethicists and scientists that the
president could appear to resolve as a reasonable moderator balancing

conflicting opinions on a dangerous precipice. However, the president's rhetorical strategies to escape the power of the metaphor were unsustainable in the long term. This chapter ends by showing how his political opponents used the frontier of science metaphor to portray the president's policy as un-American and reinvigorate public opposition to it.

In the conclusion, I summarize the findings of my inquiry, assessing the growth, transformation, and subversion of the frontier of science metaphor since its introduction to American public address over 100 years ago. Many of the associated commonplaces for this metaphor are troubling, especially when one considers the contextual evidence that suggests this trope has shaped the thinking of scientists, deflecting their attention from ways of thinking that are alien to the frontiersman (such as, for example, the rights of indigenous peoples). We also find that in our globalized, nominally postcolonial world, what was once a useful appeal for American scientists is becoming a counterproductive move for them.[70] A consideration of the longevity, strength, and ubiquity of the metaphor suggests that simply removing it from our vocabulary is not a tenable solution to these rhetorical dilemmas. In the end, a thoughtful critique of the metaphor combined with an observation of the alternative inventional choices available to scientists and to their supporters and critics in the public sphere is what is most needed. That is what this book ultimately seeks to provide.

CHAPTER ONE

History of the Frontier of Science Metaphor

⌘

To begin a scholarly conversation about the "frontier of science" in American public address, a historical study of the metaphor is a logical starting point. As the rhetorical critic James Jasinski reminds us, "the words employed by any author are always already part of a performative tradition in which the author is situated and from which the author draws," and a "metaphoric structure" commonly used in a particular culture is one example of a performative tradition that rhetorical critics would do well to examine.[1] The frontier of science metaphor is this sort of performative tradition, an inventional resource appearing in the public address of many American scientists and politicians who seek to direct future trajectories of research when they make appeals to audiences who have the authority, the financial resources, or the potential energy and intellect to influence those trajectories. To develop a sense for how this performative tradition is used, extended, or destabilized by American rhetors today, a better understanding of its history is first required.

To that end, this chapter begins with an etymological study of the frontier of science metaphor, tracing its first appearances in English dictionaries around the middle of the twentieth century. To show how the metaphor came to be popular enough to be included in dictionaries, I examine some influential texts that helped to create, develop, or reproduce the idea of scientist as frontiersman. The first of these is Frederick Jackson Turner's frontier thesis, an argument introduced in 1893 that created an exigence for Americans to seek a new metaphoric outlet for the spirit of the frontiersman.[2] I then look to Turner's subsequent speeches and to other texts that extended or responded to Turner's thesis in the first three decades of the twentieth century with the idea of the frontier of science. Finally, I observe how the frontier became a guiding metaphor for science policy in 1945 with Vannevar Bush's *Science—The Endless Frontier*, a government report that set the stage for the National Science Foundation (NSF).[3] This look at the history of the frontier of science metaphor helps us to understand the context in which the term was inherited by scientists and political figures in the late twentieth and early twenty-first centuries, which is the subject of the rest of the book.

There are several critical findings about the entailments of the metaphor that emerge from this study of its history. For one thing, a metaphor evoked as a motivational appeal to link a scientific career with heroic and exciting work resulted in the transfer of an American pioneering spirit, warts and all, to scientists, molding them in the image of fiercely individualistic, authority-averse archetypes of virile white masculinity—coarse, competitive, and isolated from a fearful public. The frontier of science metaphor found purchase in the public imagination because it offered an assurance that the American Dream would continue despite the closure of the literal frontier, that expanse of land that once served as a safety valve for ambitious people whose hard work generated the flow of raw resources that turned the engines of the nation's prosperity. The new scientific frontier promised to serve this same function, providing a place for courageous risk-takers to seek their fortunes, an endless site for discoveries that could be turned to economic gain and thus ensure material progress. Another consequence of this belief that science would serve as a new frontier was a new duty for the federal government to fund science, and, more specifically, to fund basic science over applied science, discovery over refinement, while leaving the specifics of how that money would be spent up to the scientist-explorers whose independence from government control and from the oversight of a larger public was not only accepted in the context of the metaphor but expected and justified. These appeals, functions, duties, and characteristics are not the only ways of thinking about contemporary American science, but they are the rhetorical implications of the frontier of science metaphor as it was developed in an American context in the first part of the twentieth century. In subsequent chapters, I show that many of these associations continue to be carried along with the metaphor as it is used today.

Etymology of the Frontier of Science

The figure of the scientist as part of an advance force moving into intellectual territory is an old conceit, appearing as early as 1605 in *The Advancement of Learning*, where Francis Bacon suggested that we conceive of "two professions or occupations of natural philosopher, some to be pioneers and some smiths; some to dig, and some to refine and hammer . . . in more familiar and scholastic terms: namely that these be the two parts of natural philosophy—the inquisition of causes, and the production of effects; speculative and operative; natural science, and natural prudence."[4] Upon encountering the term "pioneer" in this passage, today's reader is likely to imagine an American frontier settler, but of course this was not the image of the scientist that Bacon was evoking in 1605. Rather, the term "pioneer" at that time referred to a soldier who moved ahead of an army or regiment to dig trenches for the main body of troops, or to dig mines during a siege.[5] Nevertheless, while drawing from an earlier martial metaphor rather than the image of an American pioneer, Bacon's vision of the natural scientist was equally focused on a person occupied in heroic work at the front edge of his community, doing the dangerous job of preparing the way for those who would follow with more refined applications or technologies. It is an image of the scientist that holds a certain appeal for its excitement, bravery, and importance. Bacon's metaphor creates this appeal by establishing a fundamental separation between the daring pioneers engaged in basic science research and the prudent smiths whose attention to applied research does not even warrant the label "science." The heroic allure of this image of the pioneer to those considering a career in science and the attendant denigration of applied research are themes that endure as the "pioneer" conceit gets transformed in a later American context and the term comes to refer to another type of hero traversing another dangerous frontier.

Just as the term "pioneer" has a different meaning for the modern reader than it did for Bacon's audience, so too has the term "frontier" evolved. The older and more central definition for frontier that still appears in every dictionary of the English language, usually as the first definition identified, is a "border between two countries," as in the Franco-German frontier. However, most dictionaries include another, more recent definition that is marked as an Americanism—that is, a word sense that first came into use in the United States. This sense of the frontier is "that part of a settled, civilized country which lies next to an unexplored or undeveloped region" or "the developing, often uncivilized or lawless, region of a country."[6] One dictionary of American English calls it "(esp. in the past in the US) a border between developed land where white people live and land where Indians live or land that is wild."[7] It is this meaning of the term that contributes the most to our current thinking about the frontier of science metaphor, where the scientist is imagined to work not as the advance front line of an army crossing the border into a hostile but sovereign nation, but as an explorer blazing sparsely inhabited territory to tame nature and lay claim to the resources he finds there.

The figurative stretching of the term "frontier" from meaning an unexplored geographical territory to denoting the extreme limits of knowledge, or *intellectual* territory, is a relatively new development in the English language, as evidenced by the first appearances of this meaning in dictionaries in the mid-twentieth century. The earliest instance I could find of this figurative meaning for the term "frontier" in a dictionary was in the fifth edition of *Webster's Collegiate Dictionary* in 1941, where one definition was "an advance or not fully explored region, as of thought, sentiment, etc."[8] This meaning for the term was not present in the fourth edition of the same dictionary, published in 1934, suggesting that it was sometime between these two dates that the figure of an intellectual frontier became common enough for these lexicographers to include it in their publication.[9] *Funk and Wagnalls New*

Practical Standard Dictionary of the English Language added a similar entry to its 1955 edition, identifying the primary meaning for frontier as "the part of a nation's territory that abuts upon another country," the secondary meaning as "that portion of a country bordering on the wilderness," and the tertiary meaning as "any region of thought or knowledge not yet explored; as, a *frontier* of science."[10] This third meaning was not included in an otherwise almost identical entry from the 1946 edition of this publisher's dictionary, indicating that it was only in the later edition that the lexicographers responsible for this dictionary considered this meaning well enough established to add it to the definition.[11] Oxford University Press dictionaries have been the slowest to take up this definition for the term. The *Oxford English Dictionary* still does not include this meaning in its most comprehensive listing of definitions, either in its multivolume 1989 print edition, or its supplements released in the 1990s, or its current online edition with ongoing draft updates.[12] However, some other smaller and more specialized dictionaries published by Oxford University Press do admit to a figurative meaning for the term as the extreme limits of knowledge or an underdeveloped area of scientific research.[13]

Many dictionaries are careful to mark this sense of the frontier as a derived or metaphorical meaning, either by their placement of this meaning of the term in an ordering system that lists figurative or transferred senses last or by explicitly identifying this meaning with the abbreviation "fig."[14] The fact that this meaning appears in dictionaries at all is evidence that the frontier of science might be considered by some people to be a dead metaphor, or at least a dying one. But the fact that it only began appearing in dictionaries in the middle of the twentieth century, is often marked as figurative, and still does not appear in all dictionaries suggests that the frontier of science is a fairly recent locution and that its historic resonances are not lost on the interpretive communities that encounter it. Certainly, in texts where the frontier of science appears as an extended metaphor rather than a fleeting reference, we would do well to consider those resonances.[15] The rest of this chapter examines some texts from the first half of the twentieth century that helped to call forth the image of scientists as explorers on a wild frontier so that the frontier of science could become a meaningful term appearing in dictionaries of the English language by midcentury. Later chapters examine texts from the late twentieth century and early twenty-first century where the frontier of science is used as an extended metaphor that draws, intentionally or not, on the meanings attached to the figure in these earlier years of its use.

Turner's Frontier Thesis

In a conference paper presented in 1893 to the American Historical Association, Frederick Jackson Turner argued for "The Significance of the Frontier in American History."[16] That this conference was held at the Columbian Exposition/World's Fair in Chicago, celebrating the 400th anniversary of the "discovery" of America, tells us something about the context in which Turner's frontier thesis was offered. Author and immediate audience were in a venue that asked them to look back to a past of geographic exploration by Columbus at the same time that they looked forward to the many technological marvels on display in the electrically illuminated "White City." As English professor Catherine Gouge has argued, the Columbian Exposition insinuated that "the future would be synonymous with 'progressing' in and exploring what would later be called technological and scientific 'frontiers'"; it was a setting that served as the perfect backdrop to transform Turner's thesis about the significance of the American frontier to American history into a call for the future exploration of "figurative frontiers."[17]

   The main point of Turner's paper was to get his fellow historians to recognize that "the American frontier is sharply distinguished from the European frontier," and to accept this difference as significant (3). Unlike "most nations" that expand "in a limited area" by conquering "other growing peoples" along "a fortified boundary line running through dense populations," American development has been along a wilderness frontier, an "expansion westward with its new opportunities" as settlers progress across "the meeting point between savagery and civilization" (2–3). Turner made it clear that he was using the term "frontier" in its Americanized sense, a sense that he argued was necessary to an understanding of American history. "The existence of an area of free land, its continuous recession, and the advance of American settlement westward, explain American development" (1), and, more important, "furnish the forces dominating American character" (3). In short, Americans had a frontier ethos, having been shaped by their experiences taming a new wilderness territory.

A critical reader might object that Indians occupied the "free land" that Turner described as an unpopulated wilderness, but his conflation of the aboriginal people of America with the savage environment itself was not unusual among historians of the time.[18] Rhetorical critics Mary Stuckey and John Murphy have pointed out that in Turner's text, the "Indian" is deflected, "identified with the wilderness, a part of the scene nurturing the process of Americanization."[19] In fact, this erasure of the native occupants of the American West is a constitutive part of the frontier myth, a narrative that treats "the land as unoccupied and untamed prior to the arrival of (White) frontiers*men*."[20] That Indians were agents in the American scene with their own varied interests, sometimes fighting and sometimes accommodating incursions on the territory that they had long occupied, is a truth that is deflected from our attention in Turner's account of the essential relationship between (white) Americans and a mythic American frontier.

Turner's paper argued that the frontier wilderness shaped the character of the (white) American who settled it, "developing the stalwart and rugged qualities of the frontiersman" (15) as he undertook the productive "exploitation" of beasts, grasses, and virgin soil (18); it also explains the American's democratic attitudes, his individualism, and his antipathy to government control (30). As rhetorical critic Timothy O'Donnell eloquently summarized, Turner's "rhetoric of encounter with the frontier created the notion of a unique national character that was fiercely individualistic, antipathetic to authority, ruggedly practical, savagely exploitative, and firm in its conviction that opportunity was boundless."[21]

Since Turner's thesis was presented at the turn of the twentieth century, it is possible to interpret it as an argument designed to promote a national anxiety; after all, the very thing that supposedly established his audience's national ethos had just come to an end. The structure of Turner's paper amplified this point. He began by reminding his audience that the "Superintendent of the Census for 1890" had just declared that the frontier of settlement in America no longer exists (1), and he concluded the paper with the pronouncement that "now, four centuries from the discovery of America . . . the frontier has gone" (38). That defining feature of a unique American character had come to an end.

But despite Turner's framing argument that the frontier era that shaped the heroic traits of an exceptional American character was over, the message he conveyed about the future of the American pioneer spirit was actually quite optimistic. Reception study shows that despite the fact that Turner's primary purpose was to persuade historians to stop neglecting the significance of the frontier, the impact of his thesis was wider, influencing not only scholars but also a broader American public that embraced the pioneer spirit as an enduring characteristic of American identity. Rhetorical critic Ronald Carpenter's detailed scholarship on reader response to Turner's essay demonstrated that the frontier thesis was taken up enthusiastically by a popular audience, not as an argument about historiography but "as a paean to pioneer attributes. Moreover, the urgency of Turner's proem and peroration about the closing of the frontier did not seem to suggest that those attributes were no longer useful but that they were all the more applicable in our new and different economic endeavors."[22] The result, said Carpenter, is that "a statement intended to alter the course of American historiography became instead the rhetorical source of a mythic, national self-conception," achieving "a rhetorical impact of mythic proportions upon our national psychology."[23] After Turner, Americans increasingly came to see their national identity through the screen of the frontier myth.

As Carpenter pointed out, the "dominant source of myth in the Frontier Thesis is a characterization of the frontiersman."[24] One passage of eighty-six words from Turner's essay was cited more than any other, a passage describing the intellectual traits that Americans had developed from the conditions of frontier life.[25] That passage reads as follows:

> To the frontier the American intellect owes its striking characteristics. That coarseness and strength combined with acuteness and inquisitiveness; that practical, inventive turn of mind, quick to find expedients; that masterful grasp of material things, lacking in the artistic but powerful to effect great ends; that restless, nervous energy; that dominant individualism, working for good and for evil, and withal that buoyancy and exuberance which comes with freedom—these are traits of the frontier, or traits called out elsewhere because of the existence of the frontier. (37)

It would not take much to see these characteristics in the eccentric, resourceful, and energetic scientists who were soon to be imagined as striking out across the metaphorical frontiers of science.

Turner hinted at this possibility when he followed his most evocative passage on the traits of the frontiersman with an assurance that he would not be that "rash prophet who should assert that the expansive character of American life had now entirely ceased." Rather, these traits would find a new outlet now that the physical frontier had closed: "the American energy will continually demand a wider field for its exercise" (37). Since the physical frontier was limited by geographic realities, a metaphoric frontier that expanded the field of endeavor for Americans would have to be developed to match their need for boundless opportunity. Here Turner was drawing on what Chaim Perelman and Lucie Olbrechts-Tyteca would call an argument from "unlimited development," a type of rhetorical appeal that will "insist on the possibility of always going further in a certain direction without being able to foresee a limit to this direction," an argument that is attractive to auditors because "this progress is accompanied by a continuous increase of value."[26] To continually demand a wider field for the exercise of a boundless American energy is to have faith in the promise of unlimited growth and to believe in the possibility of endless renewal, despite the fact that the literal frontier was no longer available to supply either.

Carpenter's analysis of four decades of correspondence with Turner and his family "reveals that people perceived the historian as having said that pioneer attributes were pertinent in the twentieth-century."[27] Rather than generate anxiety about the demise of these characteristics with the closing of the frontier, this "portrayal of frontiersmen, and similar descriptions, struck the responsive chords in readers that conduce to a persuasive myth," creating the second persona of a people "whose mythic character was capable of solving virtually any problem facing Americans, at any time."[28] The ingenuity of this indomitable frontier spirit would have to be put first toward imagining a new and wider field for the exercise of America's pioneering energy. Turner would soon show that he was up to that task.

In 1910, Turner elaborated on both the character stamped on Americans by the frontier and the new outlet for those traits now that the geographic frontier had closed. In a commencement address at the University of Indiana, reprinted as a chapter of his 1920 book *The Frontier in American History*, Turner characterized the pioneer as carrying "the ideals of conquest and of discovery" (271) as well as "ideals of individualism and exploitation under competition uncontrolled by government" (279). He then encouraged the "university men" in his audience to "conserve what was best in pioneer ideals" (281). Since democracy no longer "owns the safety fund of an unlimited quantity of untouched resources," science must lead the way in conquest and discovery: "scientific experiment and construction by chemist, physicist, biologist and engineer must be applied to all of nature's forces in our complex modern society. The test tube and the microscope are needed rather than the ax and rifle in this new ideal of conquest" (284). The tools of the frontier hero were thus replaced with the tools of the scientist as the role of the former was taken up by the latter. Of course, the frontier never truly offered the safety fund of an *unlimited* quantity of untouched resources, as evidenced by the fact that terrestrial frontiers always have physical limits. But science, as a metaphorical frontier, might just supply what the literal frontier could not.

In this speech, Turner went on to argue that the complementary frontier ideals of individual competition and fierce independence from government control also must be preserved by modern pioneering scientists:

> That they may perform their work they must be left free, as the pioneer was free, to explore new regions and to report what they find; for like the pioneers they have the ideal of investigation, they seek new horizons. They are not tied to past knowledge; they recognize the fact that the universe still abounds in mystery, that science and society have not crystallized, but are still growing and need their pioneer trailmakers. New and beneficent discoveries in nature, new and beneficial discoveries in the processes and directions of the growth of society, substitutes for the vanishing material basis of pioneer democracy may be expected if the university pioneers are left free to seek the trail. (287)

The aggressive determination of the frontiersman, his separation from ties to the past, and his righteous freedom from the control of the very government that supports his explorations were all transferred here to the heroic character of the university researcher, who acts as a new container for these purportedly essential American qualities. This connection of scientist to frontiersman develops a very specific ethos for the scientist, minimizing the collaborative quality of scientific work as well as its responsibility to a larger public by characterizing scientists as heroic individuals engaged in a competitive and fierce conquest of nature.

In another commencement address, presented in 1914 at the University of Washington and published as another chapter of his book, Turner told new graduates that "in the place of old frontiers of wilderness, there are new frontiers of unwon fields of science, fruitful for the needs of the race" (300). He thus confirmed that the frontier of science was an outlet for a uniquely American set of values that might otherwise be under threat of atrophy due to the previous success of Americans in taming the territory of the continental United States. Just as the heroic actions of American frontiersmen won the West for the benefit of the (white) race, so too would the heroic actions of scientists win the fields of unmapped intellectual territory for the continuing needs of the American people.

Science Steps Confidently into the Breach

The notion of a breach left in a people's national self-conception by the closing of a literal frontier, to be filled by scientists entering a new metaphorical frontier, was soon echoed by public figures supporting a broad range of conservative and liberal causes. Whether the frontier of science metaphor was being used to support the status quo or to argue for a new progressive agenda, it confidently aligned American scientists with values drawn from the frontier myth.

For example, former geologist and future Republican president Herbert Hoover evoked the frontier of science in a book called *American Individualism*, which was published in 1922 while he was serving as U.S. secretary of commerce.[29] This book sought to restore public confidence in American industry during a time of nationwide strikes by coal miners and railroad workers.[30] In an increasingly industrialized nation where the masses of people had little hope of bettering their condition no matter how hard they worked, progressive voices were calling for government planning to relieve their suffering; as a counter to these calls, Hoover assured Americans that new conditions did not warrant changes to the way they had done things in the past. Arguing that the pioneer spirit continues to thrive in America despite the fact that Americans no longer had a literal frontier to explore, Hoover insisted that the nation's future is bright since there will always be metaphorical frontiers to motivate achievement. "The days of the pioneer are not over. There are continents of human welfare of which we have penetrated only the coastal plain. The great continent of science is as yet explored only on its borders, and it is only the pioneer who will penetrate the frontier in the quest for new worlds to conquer."[31] According to Hoover, science would now serve as the substitute terra incognita to test the mettle of the American citizen and provide the natural resources for the nation's prosperity. Hoover addressed a nation that could no longer advise its young men to seek their fortunes by going west, so he assured his readers that the American's right to rise through individual effort would be preserved in new metaphoric fields of research that are sure to reward the energies of hard work, courage, and commitment—the frontier of science remains open for exploration.

In the same year that Hoover used the frontier of science metaphor to support his conservative argument defending American industry from progressive efforts at intelligent government planning, the progressive educational philosopher John Dewey embraced the frontier of science metaphor to support "intellectual radicalism in the United States" against the conservative's "attachment to stability and homogeneity of thought and belief." Dewey's essay "The American Intellectual Frontier" begins and ends by noting the success of the antievolutionist politician William Jennings Bryan "in his efforts to hold back biological inquiry and teaching" in the South. Dewey argued that the frontier town's "fear of whatever threatens the security and order of a precariously attained civilization" drives this sort of anti-intellectual conservatism in American education. Americans are "evangelical because of our fear of ourselves and of our latent frontier disorderliness," explained Dewey. This "frontier fear" has a "depressing effect upon the free life of inquiry and criticism." Making an analogy between unexplored intellectual territory and unexplored wilderness, Dewey diagnosed American anti-intellectualism as parallel to the town dweller's apprehension about venturing beyond the borders of civilization. "As the frontier ceased to be a menace to orderly life, it persisted as a limit beyond which it was dangerous and unrespectable for thought to travel." This metaphoric limit for the weak of heart can be seen alternatively as a challenge for the brave. If anti-science sentiment can be attributed to fear of the frontier by those who are conservatively settled in their ways, then the frontiersman's courage is required for the success of any "future liberal movement" based on "the insight and policy of intelligence."[32] The spirit of the American pioneer is thus inherited by scientists who stand up against religious fundamentalists and take the bold move of entering new intellectual frontiers despite the fearful containment efforts of those who would hold them back.

Thus did the metaphor of the scientist as new frontiersman function as part of Hoover's conservative defense of rugged individualism in response to economic unrest and as part of Dewey's liberal intellectual attack on the power of religious conservatives over public education. In both cases, Turner's seemingly pessimistic reminder that the frontier had closed is overlooked in favor of his positive suggestion that the frontier spirit will continue to thrive in the attitudes and actions of American scientists. The consequence of this metaphoric association is an image of scientists as rugged individualists competing for economic profit and separated from a timid public that seeks to restrain them (rather than, for example, the image of scientists as research communities working collaboratively to answer questions raised by a larger public of which they are a part). This imagined scientist takes on both the positive and negative connotations of the frontiersman ethos as the inventional possibilities for characterizing scientists in American public discourse are narrowed through the terministic screen of the frontier metaphor.

I have demonstrated the rise of the frontier of science metaphor in the early twentieth century public discourse of a historian, a politician, and a philosopher, so it should come as no surprise that it would also appear around the same time in the public discourse of a scientist. In 1930, the botanist and mathematician J. Arthur Harris published an article in the journal *Scientific Monthly* that introduced the frontier metaphor as a fitting way to advance the activity of American scientists.[33] Beginning with a Turnerian claim that "the geographic frontier has been until recently the most ever-present and compelling reality of our American history," Harris made the same argument as Turner about the difference between the European and American conceptions of that term. "In Europe they cross the frontier. In America we penetrate the frontier. In Europe they think of the defense of the frontier. In America we plan for its development. . . . To the American the term frontier implies the borderline between what is known and what is unknown. It can not be conceived of apart from those hardy, fearless and independent men who penetrated the wilderness and who by their daring made possible the development of a west and the regeneration of an east that was approaching decadence" (19). Continuing to echo Turner's thesis, Harris claimed that while it is true that "in a large way the forward movement of the frontier may be said to have until recently dominated our national life," it is also true that "geographically, our western frontier has passed into history" (19–20). Harris then set out the theme of his article. "The exploration of the West stimulated the imagination. The settlement of the west hardened the muscles and strengthened the moral courage of our forebears. The resources of the west made possible the development of independence of thought and action. It is the conviction that we must find some moral equivalent for the old frontier in our new social, intellectual and spiritual life that leads me to consider the frontiers of science" (20). Thus did Harris follow Turner in transforming myth into metaphor, binding a set of supposedly American characteristics drawn from a history of territorial expansion to the scientist's professional identity.

The inherent anxiety attached to Turner's construction of the frontier thesis at the very time that the frontier had closed was surely a motivation for Harris, as it was for others, to locate a new American frontier in the metaphoric space of intellectual territory. However, another motivation for a scientist like Harris to promote the frontier of science metaphor was the inspirational effect that such a characterization would have on those men who had chosen, or were considering, a career in science.[34] The portrait of the scientist created by the frontier of science metaphor was far removed from the unflattering image of a bespectacled weakling buried in books or hunched over lab equipment. "The frontiersman of science has in common with the true frontiersman of the American wilderness an unconquerable desire to penetrate the unknown, the courage to follow an individual vision and an exultation in doing the things which others know can not be done," proclaimed Harris (20). Harris warned that "not all men trained in the routine of scientific research can be frontiersmen of science, but only those who have the rare capacity to hear the one everlasting whisper," that irrepressible call of the wild. "To those who do hear and who are willing to make the necessary sacrifices the possible frontiers are boundless" (21). This appeal to "men" to show courage in penetrating a virgin land created the image of the scientist as the embodiment of virile masculinity; it is a vision of the scientific profession that seems to tell women of the time that they need not apply.

After making his inspirational call to young men considering a scientific career, Harris went on to describe several frontiers of science, from the literal frontiers of "the wildernesses of South America" that American naturalists have a responsibility to explore, to the figurative frontier of the laboratory where biological frontiersmen exchange "the old rifle or fowling-piece for the new microscope" (21–22). In each case the frontiersman of science is characterized as heroic, meeting a great challenge with the courage of an explorer, and ready as a path breaker to reap the rewards of new opportunities. By the end of the article, a patriotic American male reader can be expected to long for a career as a new frontiersman of science. "Our western frontier has passed into history. With it has gone one of the forces which developed our national character. For it we must find some equivalent. . . . We await only frontiersmen to create the new frontiers beyond the foothills where the trails run out and stop. I venture to think that in the manifold frontiers of science we shall find one of the means of meeting the moral needs of our time" (32). According to Harris, to be a good American frontiersman in these modern times, one must explore the unknown in remote fields of science; and to be a good scientist, one must adopt the heroic characteristics of the American frontiersman. Tenor and vehicle thus interact to reshape our understanding of both.[35]

Vannevar Bush's Endless Frontier of Science

Although Harris brought his enthusiastic deployment of the frontier of science metaphor to the pages of an American scientific magazine in 1930, there is little evidence that his argument was directly taken up by scientists or policy makers. Instead, it was Vannevar Bush's 1945 report, *Science—The Endless Frontier*, that became the definitive statement metaphorically linking the work of American scientists to frontier exploration. O'Donnell's scholarship on the rhetoric of the Bush report points out that this document "was so enormously influential in shaping our ways of thinking and talking about science policy that its rhetoric has become inescapable": a generation of scientists raised during the golden age of American science "trace their heritage to the Bush report, and pay it homage for laying the groundwork for their careers"; the NSF ties the roots of its institutional identity to this report by reprinting it to mark its anniversaries; and its symbolic importance is manifest in the fact that "hardly a word is written about science policy today without making reference to Bush and his report."[36] According to O'Donnell, much of this influence can be attributed to the report's pervasive "use of frontier rhetoric."[37]

The production history of the Bush report locates multiple points of origin for the guiding frontier metaphor of its title. The metaphor first appeared in an eloquent passage near the end of the letter signed by President Franklin Delano Roosevelt on November 17, 1944, that initially requested that Bush, then director of the Office of Scientific Research and Development (OSRD), report on his recommendations regarding the government's postwar science policy: "New frontiers of the mind are before us, and if they are pioneered with the same vision, boldness, and drive with which we have waged this war we can create a fuller and more fruitful employment and a fuller and more fruitful life."[38] It is hardly surprising that the report that responded to this request would pick up on the frontier metaphor. Of course, the request letter was not personally written by Roosevelt; the historian Daniel J. Kevles attributes this line in the letter to government lawyer Oscar S. Cox, who drafted and polished the request with the help of others, including Bush himself, Bush's aide James B. Conant, OSRD general counsel Oscar M. Ruebhausen, and Roosevelt advisers and speechwriters Harry Hopkins and Samuel I. Rosenman.[39]

That the metaphor was in Bush's mind long before either the letter of request or the responding report was conceived is demonstrated by the fact that he had used it in 1937 in an essay in which he titled a section of his argument "Frontiers of Science Still Remain" and wrote: "It was independence of thought, freedom of action, the opportunity of a vast untamed domain that built this country and gave it the highest standard of living in the world. The geographical frontiers have disappeared, but the frontiers of science and technology still remain. Those qualities which built a trail into the wilderness can still build trails in the technological advance. The same qualities of courage, resourcefulness and independence which opened the nation are as necessary to-day as ever."[40] There is also documentary evidence that Ruebhausen, writing memos during the drafting of the 1945 report on March 15 and April 23, made special note of the importance that the frontier metaphor should have to the overall argument.[41] Since the frontier of science metaphor was not unique to any of these thinkers, the origin of this language in the contributions of Cox, Bush, Ruebhausen, and others to *Science— The Endless Frontier* is difficult to untangle. What can be said with confidence is that the figure of the frontier was recognized by all to be an important rhetorical tool in the production of this document.

The U.S. Government Printing Office published the final report in 1945.[42] It includes a "Letter of Transmittal" signed by Bush (v–vi), a reproduction of the presidential letter that requested the report (vii–viii), an epigraph in which the "frontiers" line from the presidential request letter is repeated in isolation on a page of its own (ix), a "Summary of the Report" written by Bush and others at OSRD (1–4), the six chapters of the report itself (5–34), and four committee reports by scientists assigned to offer advice on different aspects of postwar science policy (35–184).[43] Two of those committee reports repeat the "frontiers" line from the presidential request in their introductions (71, 135). As if the publication's quadruple repetition of the "frontiers" line from the request letter were not enough, Bush's "Letter of Transmittal" presents the same thesis using slightly different words in his peroration: "The pioneer spirit is still vigorous within this nation. Science offers a largely unexplored hinterland for the pioneer who has the tools for his task. The rewards of such exploration for both the Nation and the individual are great" (vi). With these references and the "endless frontier" of the title, the frontier of science metaphor could be seen as the text's principal message.

A close look at several other instances of frontier rhetoric in the report helps to reveal the many functions this metaphor served and the consequences, both intended and unintended, of this language choice. *Science—The Endless Frontier* justifies government funding of basic scientific research with a frontier analogy that demands that America compete with other nations to claim open territory that is rich with natural resources in anticipation of the profitable extraction of those resources; it simultaneously promotes the independence of scientist-frontiersmen from the government (and the larger taxpaying public) that funds those explorations. The character of the scientist subsequently recruited through this analogy is consistent with the myth of an American hero whose aggressive and single-minded pursuit of the unknown isolates him from the larger community.

Let us start with a look at the document's argument that a postwar American government should devote tax dollars to scientific research. The belief that the government should fund scientific research was not commonly held at the time the Bush report was written. Before World War II, the federal government played little role in supporting American science.[44] The NSF did not yet exist, and the OSRD was only a temporary agency, created in the emergency of war with the limited mission of supporting the application of scientific research to military use. In a nation that had no tradition of devoting large sums to basic scientific research, the Bush report used the frontier metaphor to make the idea of federal funding for science sound reasonable. By connecting scientific research to frontier exploration, Bush set out the argument in his "Summary of the Report" that "the Government should accept new responsibilities for promoting the flow of new scientific knowledge and the development of scientific talent in our youth" (4). Just as the American frontier myth tells the story of the federal government once granting new land out west to the most courageous and industrious citizens who would initiate the resource flow from west to east that fueled the nation's prosperity, Bush was telling Americans that so too should talented young scientists be given government support to promote the flow of intellectual capital that would fuel the nation's continued prosperity; after all, it has always been "basic United States policy that the Government should foster the opening of new frontiers and this is the modern way to do it" (4). Bush elaborated and emphasized this analogy so that the point of the argument could not be missed. "It has been basic United States policy that Government should foster the opening of new frontiers. It opened the seas to clipper ships and furnished land for pioneers. Although these frontiers have more or less disappeared, the frontier of science remains. It is in keeping with the American tradition—one which has made the United States great—that new frontiers shall be made accessible for development by all American citizens" (6). A clearer statement of the implications of the frontier of science metaphor could not be made; imagining science as a frontier requires that the government support these new scientific frontiersmen in exploring and developing promising but as yet uncharted fields of research.

A corollary to this claim that the federal government has a responsibility to fund research on the "frontiers" of science is the idea that science is an "endless" frontier that can relieve any post-Turnerian anxiety that might be created by the nation's current geographically limited borders. Americans knew that the full employment of the war years would soon come to an end, and their young men would be returning to a nation that no longer had a frontier outlet of free land to guarantee the right to rise for those with the ambition and industry to take advantage of it. The appendix reporting the conclusions of the Committee on Science and the Public Welfare sought to alleviate any such anxiety when it imagined a new frontier where the "flow of new scientific knowledge" would replace the flow of resources from the now closed literal frontier. Even if a nation's "geographical frontiers become fixed, there always remains one inexhaustible national resource—creative scientific research. In view of the importance of science to the Nation, the Federal Government, by virtue of its charge to provide for the common defense and general welfare, has the responsibility of encouraging and aiding scientific progress" (68, see also 71). This was the argument from unlimited development set out in unambiguous terms. The literal frontier might *seem* endless, but terrestrial space will always run out eventually; in contrast, metaphorical fields of research hold an inexhaustible supply of new knowledge.

Another corollary to the argument that the federal government has a responsibility to fund research on the frontiers of science is the idea that science should be seen as a competition between nations vying to stake a claim to new intellectual territory. According to the Committee on Science and the Public Welfare, Americans must win priority claims and thus own the stream of scientific knowledge if they are truly to benefit from its flow because "a nation which borrows its basic knowledge will be hopelessly handicapped in the race for innovation. The other world powers, we know, intend to foster scientific research in the future" (72–73). Although the report gives lip service to the notion that science involves international cooperation and benefits all of humankind, the appeal to a competitive national spirit prevails, and the analogy with frontier exploration helps to make this happen. Readers are told that American science deserves to prosper since "it is part of our democratic creed to affirm the intrinsic cultural and aesthetic worth of man's attempt to advance the frontiers of knowledge and understanding. By that same creed the prestige of a nation is enhanced by its contributions—made in a spirit of friendly cooperation and competition—to the world-wide battle against ignorance, want, and disease" (73). The implication is that Americans, known for their frontier spirit, would be shamed if they were to fall behind in the international race to occupy new territory on the frontiers of science; the federal government must fund scientific exploration to ensure that the American flag is planted in as many promising new intellectual fields as the flags of other nations that cooperate *and* compete with America to make discoveries in that open territory.

The type of research that should be funded is also implicit in the report's deployment of the frontier of science metaphor. The metaphor suggests that Bacon's pioneers should be supported over his smiths; those who undertake cutting-edge basic science research should be

funded over those who seek to apply existing knowledge in the production of new technologies. Bush's report makes this point when it
contrasts those involved in the mere "application of existing scientific
knowledge to practical problems" with those who "devote most of their
research efforts to expanding the frontiers of knowledge" (2). Those
who deserve government funding belong to the latter group, working in
"colleges, universities, and research institutes" upon which government
and industry are dependent "to expand the basic scientific frontiers and
to furnish trained scientific investigators" (15). This remittance of limited financial resources to basic science might seem more risky than
the targeted funding of a specific application that promises immediate
results, but just as risky frontier exploration led to profitable discoveries,
so too will investments in fundamental research reward the nation in
the long term. As the attached report of the Medical Advisory Committee explains, "Discoveries in medicine have often come from the most
remote and unexpected fields of science in the past; and it is probable
that this will be equally true in the future" (49–50). The report of the
Committee on Publication of Scientific Information makes a case for
supporting the pioneers of science over its smiths when it complains
that during the war, "we have been living to a considerable extent on
our scientific capital, as scientists who would normally be extending the
frontiers of knowledge have instead devoted their efforts to the application of our scientific knowledge to the development of new and better
equipment, processes, and materials for war purposes" (181). That must
change in the postwar years. "The frontiers of science must be thrown
open so that all who have the ability to explore may advance from the
farthest position which anyone has attained" (181). The image of basic
science as a wilderness territory that the government has the power
to open for exploration, and of the scientist as an explorer advancing
where no man has gone before, comes into focus through this extended
metaphor.

It is important to recognize that the economic appeal of applied science is not dismissed when the frontier metaphor is evoked. Indeed,
the financial reward of technical application is highly valued. But it
is assumed to follow inevitably from the funding of basic scientific
exploration, so that no special attention to the applied aspects of tech-
noscientific work is required. Just as the flow of resources from the
frontier guaranteed the accumulation of capital in the more settled parts
of the developing American nation, so too will the flow of profitable

applications from basic scientific research follow inevitably and swiftly from the discoveries made on the frontier of science.

A corollary to this argument about the desirability of funding basic scientific exploration over applied science is that the public must trust scientists to choose the paths that this research should take and the nature of the research conducted; there is no legitimate role for public oversight. "We must remove rigid controls which we have had to impose, and recover freedom of inquiry and that healthy competitive scientific spirit so necessary for expansion of the frontiers of scientific knowledge. Scientific progress on a broad front results from the free play of free intellects, working on subjects of their own choice, in the manner dictated by their curiosity for exploration of the unknown" (7). This passage from the "Summary of the Report" imagines the scientist as independent, competitive, and driven by the desire to explore unknown territory. The qualities of the American frontiersman as described by Turner seem to carry over to the American scientist here, culminating in the scientist's fierce resistance to government control even when that very same government finances the research. What might otherwise seem like an outrageous demand for a blank check from the government becomes, in the context of the frontier metaphor, a reasonable investment in those courageous, unconventional, and independent souls whose explorations of the unknown will most assuredly result in the return of great treasure to the national coffers.

This characterization of scientists might seem wholly positive for them, but it separates them from the public, just as explorers find themselves isolated by their attitudes and conduct from those lesser souls who settle down in towns and cities on the safe side of the wild frontier. As O'Donnell affirms, the report's "utilization of frontier imagery played upon and further developed an emerging popular image of science as an adventure and scientists as heroic explorers."[45] This identity surely encouraged some to pursue a career in basic scientific research. But it also might have contributed to an antagonistic relationship between risk-taking scientists and those supposedly inferior and timid nonscientists who are expected to fund scientists' research while otherwise keeping out of their way. It additionally promoted a particularly macho vision of who should aspire to be a scientist, possibly discouraging some who otherwise might have pursued a career in scientific research.

Conclusion

By the time John F. Kennedy's 1960 Democratic National Convention speech envisioned his American audience standing "on the edge of a New Frontier" beyond which lie "uncharted areas of science and space," the frontier of science metaphor had already taken hold in the public imagination. His call "to the young in heart, regardless of age—to the stout in spirit, regardless of party" to "be pioneers towards that New Frontier" was an effective motivational appeal not because it was unique, but because it participated in a dawning understanding of American scientists as new frontiersmen. His call for Americans to compete with "the Communist system" in "a race for mastery of the sky and the rain, the oceans and the tides, the far side of space and the inside of men's minds" was doubtless the inspiration for many who would take up the post-Sputnik challenge to advance science in this country.[46] But it was merely one of a number of other such appeals in twentieth-century American public address that equated science with frontier values in order to invent a challenge for Americans to embrace, construct an ostensibly desirable identity for American scientists, and promote government support for scientific research.

Recalling Turner's inventory of the striking characteristics of American intellect that were nurtured by the frontier experience, we should not forget that there were negative as well as positive traits listed there—coarseness as well as strength, a lack of aesthetic sensitivity, a restlessness and nervousness, a dominant individualism that can work for "evil" as easily as it can work for "good" (37). The transfer of frontier traits to American scientists can pass on a great deal of baggage at the same time that it carries over heroic and patriotic values. A focus on what is missing when the scientist is characterized as a new frontiersman is another way of coming to recognize not only the positive but also the negative connotations of this metaphor. For example, science can be imagined as a collaborative activity undertaken by citizens who are tasked with resolving problems that are raised by the larger community of which they are a part. Or science can be seen as a human endeavor to understand the natural world, rather than an international race to be the first to discover and lay claim to new territory in anticipation of extracting valuable resources from it. I do not offer up these characterizations as ideal alternatives to replace the frontier of science metaphor and its negative entailments; each representation of science has its own blind spots. These complementary descriptions are merely offered to illustrate that the characterization of science as frontier exploration is a rhetorical screen, filtering out some aspects of science while highlighting others. Recognizing this helps us to see how the use of this metaphor can influence our understanding and decision making about priorities for scientific research. The performative tradition of the frontier of science metaphor has a historical origin and a very specific set of associations that we should consider when coming to better understand its contemporary use as an available means of persuasion in the invention of public discourse about science.

CHAPTER TWO

The Frontier Metaphor in Public Speeches by American Scientists

⌘

At the beginning of the twentieth century in America, when the western frontier had disappeared because the citizenry had sufficiently spread out to fill the empty places on the nation's maps, Americans came to believe that it was a pioneering spirit that most distinguished their national character. As the preceding chapter documented, the "frontier of science" was introduced by Frederick Jackson Turner and others as a promising new metaphor to meet the American citizen's need for an unlimited space in which to employ that characteristic spirit. As this chapter demonstrates, at the beginning of the twenty-first century American scientists continue to be presented in the public imaginary as pioneers and explorers who preserve the American way by venturing into challenging new territory to open it for profitable development. Today, appeals for government funding of basic scientific research are still grounded on the assumption that technological applications will inevitably follow the discoveries of scientists engaged in pioneering basic research, just as the discoveries of risk-takers traversing the geographic frontier resulted in resource flow out of the new territories. An attitude of individualism and a disposition that delights in competitive struggle for personal, corporate, and national advantage continue to flourish as entailments of this frontier metaphor in American public address about science.

In our contemporary postcolonial era, the forces of globalization recommend a different idealized image of science, one that promotes cooperation across borders by men and women working together to resolve the dilemmas facing all of humanity. But even as the modern problems of worldwide epidemics and global climate change call for international knowledge communities to work together, the frontier of science metaphor persists in attaching the imperialist motives of an earlier era to American science. Influenced by a familiar terministic screen, contemporary American scientists characterize themselves in a way that promotes science but also insensibly restricts the possibilities for reshaping the future of science in America.

In this chapter I examine a corpus of recent public speeches by scientists, each of which utilizes the frontier of science metaphor as a central organizing theme in making arguments for increased funding and support of scientific research and education.[1] Speech texts were chosen as the object for analysis because they allow us to see how scientists present their profession to others when putting their best foot forward in arguments to recruit acolytes and financial backing. Speech texts also were chosen because they are such understudied artifacts in the rhetoric of science. Although rhetoric as a field of study was first developed in ancient times to investigate the persuasive design of public speeches, the more recently developed subfield of "rhetoric of science" has rarely taken the public speech texts of scientists as objects for analysis.[2] As I indicated in the introduction, the more typical discursive artifacts selected for scrutiny by rhetoricians of science are scientific monographs or journal articles and their transformation through popularization or public controversy.[3] These more typical choices of objects for study are appropriate when the purpose of the rhetorician of science is to better understand the specialized discourse of scientific communities or the transformations of that discourse by journalistic science writers. But the purpose of this study is different. This chapter calls attention to speech texts by scientists who are directly addressing public audiences about the value of science, and the purpose of studying these texts is to better understand how scientists are conceptualizing and characterizing their profession.

Rhetorical criticism of these speeches tells us a great deal about how the frontier of science metaphor shapes the character of scientific research in America. The assumptions about science that accompany the frontier metaphor in these speeches are that scientists are heroic risk-takers, that basic scientific exploration deserves to be funded over applied research, and that scientists are engaged in a competitive race to claim new territory for profitable development. Each of these is a theme introduced in the previous chapter, a part of the performative tradition of the frontier of science metaphor that is preserved and extended in the contemporary public address of American scientists.

The Frontier of Science as a Heroic and Exciting Space

In 1992, Nobel prize–winning physicist Leon Lederman used the frontier metaphor extensively in his presidential lecture for the American Association for the Advancement of Science (AAAS).[4] The previous year, he had used the same metaphor in his widely circulated report for the AAAS titled "Science: The End of the Frontier?"[5] In both the report and the speech, Lederman argued that there was a crisis of morale among scientists, not because they were lacking exciting new frontiers of knowledge to explore but because the federal government was not keeping up with its responsibility to supply the necessary financing to those who wanted to do such research. Expressing outrage at the relative decline of funding for American scientists, Lederman's speech called forth testimony from a New York financier who, after a trip to Europe, complained that ironically, "returning to the United States was like coming to the old country from the new world" (1122). Other nations were marshaling resources to claim new frontiers of science and leaving American scientists behind.

To reverse "the malaise eating at American society," Lederman argued that Americans need "to forge anew a vision of a dynamic society in which children can once again expect to do better than their parents" (1123). The promise of unlimited growth that had been established with the American frontier would have to be renewed. Just as those who responded to Frederick Jackson Turner had done a century earlier, Lederman used the frontier of science metaphor as a rhetorical tool to reinvigorate a nation foreseeing its imminent decline. As Lederman explained, "some kind of an endless frontier is really an essential need of humankind—we need the challenge, we need the frontiers" (1120). The need for boundless opportunity, to escape a decadent past and reinvent oneself through sheer will and effort, is especially intense for Americans. "As a nation," Lederman said, "our old frontiers have been converted to shopping malls and used car lots, our old adversaries, which contributed so much to national purpose, are gone. Science research and scholarship offer new horizons, new wealth, an inherent and contagious optimism, and the possibility of restoring the planet and also restoring our own society via the immense power of rational thought molded by aesthetics, compassion, and wise self-interest" (1123). The nation no longer advises young men to "Go West" to make their fortunes, but as Lederman suggests, it can now advise them to go to the university and the research park.

According to Lederman, the best way to reverse the malaise plaguing America is to provide increased federal funding to researchers who want to explore the frontiers of science. The following year, eulogizing the Superconducting Super Collider, he scolded Congress for its decision to not fund such an ambitious scientific research facility. "After all, we live in a nation that grew rich by exploring and settling its frontiers. We learned that the bolder the thrust, the greater the returns. Isn't the supercollider a sort of wagon train into the frontier of our comprehension of the universe? How could we not continue?"[6] The failure of the American government to support its new pioneers on the frontier of physics was an abandonment of American values, according to Lederman. If this trend continues, it will lead inevitably to the end of American exceptionalism. The language that Lederman chose was freighted with chauvinistic undertones; by not making the bold thrust that can result in productive issue, by not funding the provisioning of the supercollider wagon train, Congress was being both unmanly and un-American.

Another contemporary scientist who uses the frontier of science metaphor to appeal to the American spirit while arguing for increased funding for scientific research is Arden Bement Jr., a professor of nuclear engineering who was director of the National Science Foundation (NSF) when he gave a speech in 2006 to a group of leading technology companies. In America, Bement proclaimed, we have always "kept our eyes on the frontier—on the unexplored territory." Just as "the National Science Foundation remains focused on the frontier," so too should American industry help support basic scientific research. The excitement of providing such support comes from recognizing that researchers are analogous to the nation's heroic frontier explorers. "As we explore the frontier, we hone future generations of explorers. Through cutting-edge research opportunities, students grow into world-class scientists, engineers, technologists and mathematicians, becoming the Lewis and Clark of the laboratory and the classroom."[7] The fact that Lewis and Clark were funded by taxpayer dollars, not industry sponsorship, likely did little to undermine Bement's argument to industry leaders. The Corps of Discovery expedition was an explicitly imperialist endeavor funded by the government to expand the nation's borders, to secure the riches of the Northwest Territory before other European nations could solidify their claims to it.[8] But that disconnect would not have made the analogy any less appealing to business leaders who covet the resources that modern explorers of that stature could secure for their companies. By metaphorically linking Lewis and Clark to modern scientists, the associated commonplaces of material gain and competitive success surfaced, creating a powerful appeal for businessmen motivated by the bottom line of profit for their companies.

Note that Americans were not being asked to imagine scientists as the Sacagawea of the laboratory and the classroom. The archetype of the frontier explorer to which scientists are invariably compared is a white male risk-taker, eager to isolate himself from society for long stretches of time as he makes a bold thrust forward into dangerous territory. The feminist science studies scholar Evelyn Fox Keller would have us consider the implications of this sort of comparison. "Would not a characterization of science which appears to gratify particular emotional needs give rise to a self-selection of scientists—a self-selection that would, in turn, lead to a perpetuation of that same characterization?" The "connotations of masculinity and conquest" that our typical language choices attach to science have a real impact on both the structure of science and the uses to which it is put in society.[9] If young women have difficulty identifying with Lewis and Clark, they could be discouraged from pursuing a career in science, while those men and women who do become scientists are encouraged to think of themselves as risk-takers who are most heroic when separated from the larger community, a perception that could exacerbate tensions between scientists and the public that regulates and funds them.

When scientists like Bement talk about science education, the language they use can help shape not only the public's perception of scientists but also how scientists themselves come to be shaped through recruitment and training. Another example of a scientist who draws on the frontier of science metaphor to convey excitement about cultivating the future Lewis and Clark of the laboratory is Shirley Tilghman, the president of Princeton University and an accomplished molecular biologist who gave a speech in 2006 titled "Science: The Last Frontier."[10] Although her professional success stands as evidence that science is not exclusively a masculine endeavor, Tilghman adopted the same heroic frontier rhetoric in her speech, language that could unintentionally deter young women considering a career in science.

Speaking at a prestigious K–12 private school in Washington, D.C., Tilghman compared science to "the geographic frontiers that have always captured the popular imagination" and urged her audience "to see science as one of the most exciting and rewarding callings imaginable." To enter the "last frontier" that is science is to enter "a place of profound change and infinite possibilities." To underscore her claim about the excitement of being an explorer on that last frontier, the word "challenge" appeared five times in the speech, signaling the adventurous ethos Tilghman would attach to the scientific researcher. Arguing that "there is a pressing need in the United States for children to be instilled with a passion for discovery" as they are being prepared to enter the nation's research universities and government laboratories, Tilghman described science as "enormously rewarding for those involved." She elaborated on the thrill-seeking character of the scientist when she argued that "the excitement to be found on the frontiers of science springs from three primary sources: the lure of the unknown, the extraordinary rush at the moment of discovery, and the satisfaction that comes when scientific progress transforms the lives of our fellow men and women for the better." The adventure narrative suggested by the lure and rush of the frontier metaphor makes science sound like an exciting career choice, a natural calling for Americans seeking fame and fortune; science thus takes the place of the old geographic frontier on which, in an earlier era, young men were sent to test their mettle. Her portrayal of scientists as heroes who should be admired and thanked for their contributions to the prosperity of a larger public was likely meant to be inspiring to scientists, however presumptuous it might sound to nonscientists in that larger public. But whether received as inspirational or arrogant, it did the work of drawing a line separating scientists from everyone else.

What is striking about these speeches is that each of these American leaders of science could just as easily have been speaking in the early years of the twentieth century as at the beginning of the twenty-first. The frontier metaphor was equally compelling in both time periods as a way of characterizing the excitement and promise of scientific research to American audiences. Significantly, what continues to lie just beneath the surface of the metaphor is the assumption that scientists are risk-takers, fiercely individualistic and competitive, seeking glory for self and nation. Also just beneath the surface is the assumption that basic scientific research should be financed to broadly expand the borders of our knowledge (rather than applied research that is designed to meet a particular public need), since such fundamental exploration will inevitably result in resource flow back from the front just as an earlier generation's financing of geographic exploration resulted in profit for the nation.

Financing the Pioneers of Basic Scientific Research

In her study of print popularizations of scientific articles, the rhetorician Jeanne Fahnestock established that two types of appeal are used to introduce science to the public: "the wonder" appeal, which makes reference to the amazing things that scientists have discovered, and "the application" appeal, which points to the spin-offs that will follow a scientific research project.[11] One of the few published rhetorical studies of scientists' speeches argues that these two appeals appear in the oral remarks of scientists as well.[12] In my own corpus of public speech texts by scientists, the wonder appeal can be found in the statements discussed above that claim that the frontier of science is an exciting place for adventurous souls to unleash their pioneering spirit. An examination of these speeches shows that the application appeal is also prevalent, appearing frequently in the articulation of a belief that basic science on the frontiers of knowledge will result in new technologies or resource flows that will reap profitable returns for investors. This appeal serves the ideological function of privileging research into basic science over applied science, and deferring to the research priorities of scientific frontiersmen rather than allowing those priorities to be set by a larger public.

Lisa Keränen and her colleagues pointed out the use of the application appeal, which they identify with a problematic "linear model" of science, in their rhetorical study of a public speech by physicist and presidential science adviser John Marburger III at the University of Colorado at Boulder in 2005. They showed how Marburger's speech promoted science by asserting "a unidirectional relationship between 'basic' or 'pure' research and societal benefits."[13] Keränen et al. identified this as the same linear model that Vannevar Bush used in *Science— The Endless Frontier*, in which it was assumed that scientific research conducted in universities will result in the discovery of a reservoir of knowledge from which applied research will inevitably draw to develop technologies that lead to national prosperity. To develop this "predominantly entrepreneurial model" of science in his speech, Marburger deployed the same frontier metaphor that Bush used. Other models of science that recognize the influence of social and ethical concerns on funding priorities have much to recommend them, according to Keränen and her colleagues, but those models are elided by the dominance of an application appeal that envisions investment in the basic research of pioneering scientists as leading invariably to resource development and profit.[14]

As Keränen et al. suggested, and my own study of similar texts confirms, the frontier metaphor is particularly well suited to the promotion of this linear model of science. We can see this alignment between metaphor and model in several of Arden Bement's speeches as director of the NSF. For example, in the speech where he invoked the spirits of Lewis and Clark to inspire students to become scientists, he also used the figure of these legendary explorers to persuade his American audience that "frontier" research results in profitable application.

> Early American explorers revealed that the frontier can yield surprising discoveries with unforeseen results. Lewis and Clark discovered new species and natural resources that we enjoy and take for granted today. Likewise, who could imagine that the discovery of a magnetic property—a quirk—of hydrogen atoms would lead to development of magnetic resonance imaging? NSF-sponsored scientists weren't looking for a huge medical imaging breakthrough. They were examining the basic properties of the smallest atomic element. This type of frontier exploration—fundamental research

leading to diverse development—is a hallmark of innovation. It continues to be the key to our future.[15]

In this passage, Bement linked the heroes of early American frontier exploration with fundamental physics research that leads to lucrative technologies. By analogy, the riches of the geographical frontier are equivalent to the riches that result from the study of fundamental questions in science; the natural resources that Lewis and Clark "discovered" are parallel to the profits that come from magnetic resonance imaging technology. In both cases, societal benefits result when the nation equips pioneering explorers and sends them out to do what they do best, trusting in their leadership to "yield surprising discoveries with unforeseen results." This is the American way of doing things, both the key to the nation's past and to its future.

The privileging of basic scientific research and the linear and certain link between such fundamental research and its profitable application were also made clear in another speech that Bement gave a few months earlier before the Senate Commerce, Science and Transportation Subcommittee on Technology, Innovation and Competitiveness. In this speech, he defined the mission of the NSF as funding the pioneers of basic scientific research, not funding those smiths who are merely "tinkering on the sidelines."[16] In all of the NSF's endeavors, he said, "we focus on the frontiers of knowledge and beyond—the fertile territory where new ideas are born, nurtured and eventually bear fruit in economic and social returns."[17] The image of nature as a fecund female is a familiar one in frontier rhetoric, deployed here to reinforce a frontier of science metaphor in which male scientists enter a new form of fertile intellectual territory where their ideas can be nurtured into valuable new assets.

In another speech that Bement gave the previous year, he made it clear "what the frontier is and what it is not. The frontier is risky, so if it's 'safe science,' NSF should not fund it. The frontier is murky and without definition, so if there are no big unanswered questions in a proposal, NSF should pass it up." Only "fundamental" research questions are worthy of support. "If we wind up enmeshed in the nuts and bolts of these activities, then we've strayed from our purpose. Our primary task must be to tenaciously dog the frontier. The frontier is our bull's eye. We can't dally in the outer circles; we have to stick to the very heart of the matter." To "stop short in our pursuit of high-risk endeavors" is "to divert our focus from the frontier" and, in doing so, to "put the nation at peril."[18] Once again, the figure of the metalworker that Bacon once imagined as tinkering with the nuts and bolts of what we might call applied scientific research was dismissed by Bement as unworthy of financial backing; NSF must only support the basic scientist that Bacon had labeled with the figure of the courageous pioneer. Notice also how the predicates that Bement used to describe the action of that figure are drawn from the idiom of the hunt: to dog, to aim for the bull's-eye, to aim for the heart. The adjectives and adverbs are likewise evocative of life on the frontier: "risky," "murky," "high-risk," "tenaciously." According to Bement, the NSF-funded scientist is a tough guy who tenaciously dogs the frontier, aiming for the bull's eye, aiming for the heart, unafraid of the murkiness, pursuing the highest of risks while penetrating the most fertile of territory to reap the greatest of economic and social returns.

It is taken for granted that rewards will come out of the endeavor. The assumption that profitable applications will effortlessly follow the courageous forays of fundamental scientific research is an entailment of the frontier of science metaphor that justifies resource allocation to basic rather than applied research. The identification of scientists with the most manly of character traits, as fiercely competitive and daring, suggests that scientific discovery is only achieved by individuals engaged in a brutal contest with each other and with individuals from other nations for the right to claim profitable new territory. This too is an entailment of the frontier of science metaphor with significant consequences for how Americans think about science.

Frontier Science as a Race for Territory

The characterization of scientists as rugged individuals competing with each other in an international race to lay claim to limited new intellectual territory is common in these speeches, flowing naturally from the frontier of science metaphor. Turner added competitiveness to the traits of the pioneer in one of his earliest elaborations of his frontier thesis, and he made much of this competitive character in his first explicit call to American scientists to act as new frontiersmen.[19] So it should come as no surprise that competitiveness continues to be a major theme in contemporary speeches that link science to the frontier myth. Historically, this competitiveness was inspired by the "Doctrine of Discovery" used by people of European descent to claim property that was previously unknown to them; according to European international law, those who were the first to "discover" and occupy "new" lands could secure a title to that territory, regardless of any claims made by non-European peoples who were already living there (and regardless of the refusal of some of those non-European peoples to recognize the rights of *any* people to claim land as property to be owned).[20] In the history of the Americas, this Doctrine of Discovery was behind the scramble for land that colonial powers embarked upon as they raced each other in voyages of exploration to be the first to lay claim to New World territory and thus own the natural resources that might be extracted from it. Metaphorically linked to scientific research, this feature of the frontier myth encourages international competition for new knowledge "territory" on the assumption that only the first to discover and lay claim to it can ultimately benefit from it.

Tilghman articulated this image of science as a contest between nations for new territory when she quoted from a National Academy of Sciences report that warned Americans that their scientific and technological leadership is "eroding at a time when many other nations are gathering strength"; the report she cited urged her audience to "fear the abruptness with which a lead in science and technology can be lost—and the difficulty of recovering a lead once lost, if indeed it can be regained at all." Imagining American scientists as striving to remain at "the forefront of global scientific progress," Tilghman told her auditors that they had to maintain "international competitiveness" by reinvigorating American knowledge institutions; this "will be the only way to compete in our new flat world."[21] Facing more rivals that ever before in the race for scientific territory, and enjoying no geographical advantage on this metaphoric frontier, Americans would have to redouble their efforts to remain at the front of the race.

Bement offered a similar fear appeal based on the perception that Americans are falling behind in a competition with scientists from other nations. He argued that America has always had "an eye on the next unmet challenge, the territory unexplored by other nations. That is becoming increasingly difficult with the prospect of nations like China and India building powerful economic momentum through a burgeoning science and engineering workforce and strong research capacity. There is fierce competition for ideas and talent, for comparative advantage and

market opportunities worldwide." Only a focus on research and education will "keep America at the forefront of science and engineering."[22]
Bement was suggesting that with other nations now eying that unexplored territory across the frontiers of knowledge, Americans will have
to do more to generously sponsor their scientists; to do less would be to
relinquish their American identity as victors in the contest over frontier
territory. In an earlier speech where Bement used the same line about
China and India, he said, "The challenge for the U.S. is always to make
the gigantic leap beyond where other nations are looking. . . . This is a
high-powered, high-stakes endeavor that will be determined by several
factors, not the least of which will be securing ample resources on our
part."[23] In both of these speeches, the new knowledge territory that is
imagined to lie just across the metaphorical frontier is portrayed as a
delimited space that scientists from different nations must race to claim
as their own, and that America will have to leap out ahead of its competitors to possess.

A different way of thinking about science is to imagine it as a collaborative endeavor in which researchers, irrespective of national
background, work together to solve the problems that face humankind.[24]
In this view, knowledge is not a finite territory that can be owned only by
the winner of a global competition, but a conceptual product of shared
effort that is unlimited in its potential for distribution. Regrettably, such
an ideal is not encouraged by texts that ground an argument for science
funding on the frontier of science metaphor. By imagining individuals
from different nations as vying with each other to plant their flags on
profitable new land before it has been divvied up by their competitors,
these texts portray science in a competitive and nationalistic vein.

August Watanabe, vice president of science and technology at the
pharmaceutical company Eli Lilly, gave a speech in 1996 that is cen-
tered around this theme of frontier competitiveness. In his speech,
Watanabe connected the scientist to figures from the frontier myth
that are "ingrained in the American character" as a part of "America's
blood"—the frontiersman who was so adept at "taming a continent" and
the heroic voyager of the Age of Exploration. Like the other American
scientists whose speeches I have analyzed in this section, Watanabe
used a fear appeal to argue that the U.S. government should increase its
funding for scientific research and development. As "our global competitors are aggressively pursuing an edge through science," he warned that
America's national investment is shrinking. Making a historical analogy

between early geographical explorers and modern scientists, an analogy that he attributed to "distinguished cell biologist George Palade," Watanabe reminded his audience of the fate of the Renaissance Italian city-states that withered when they lost their drive for leadership. "They were content to ply Mediterranean trade lanes while the Portuguese, Spanish, English, and Dutch were exploring the world and reaping the rewards of that exploration. You either push the frontiers or fall behind. The choice is ours." Assuming that his audience did not want to fall behind in this imperialist contest, that they wanted to remain true to their "legacy," he encouraged them to support their country's scientists so that they could continue to win the race for new frontier territory.[25]

In a world where global networks of communication, transportation, and commerce have increased the ease of international scientific collaboration, and where there is heightened need for scientists from different parts of the world to work together to resolve global challenges to the environment and public health, the frontier of science metaphor continues to divide American scientists from their "competitors" in other nations. It also encourages Americans to think about knowledge territory as a bounded space to acquire in anticipation of its subjugation and exploitation.

Some scientists seem to recognize the incongruity of these entailments for the frontier of science metaphor in our postcolonial era, as new interpretations of history have taken some of the sheen off of the frontier myth. But the metaphor persists nonetheless. For example, Robert Gagosian, chemist and director of Woods Hole Oceanographic Institution, gave a public speech in 2004 that included an acknowledgment that the frontier metaphor is problematic, even while he used that frontier myth to make the case that America is losing an international race for promising new knowledge territory.[26]

In the speech, Gagosian cited a *New York Times* story on how the United States is losing its dominance in the sciences, with Asia and Europe ascendant, to ground an argument that funding for science in America should increase. Centering his speech on an analogy between the funding Columbus was able to secure and the need for more patronage of the sciences, he called on Americans to reverse their recent decline in support for science. "If we answer this call, our ships—literally and figuratively—may continue to depart for uncharted waters. . . . Our 'crews' . . . will bring back word from new territories. And our modern versions of gold—knowledge and understanding—will enable us to make wiser decisions in the stewardship of our planet. . . . The voyage is hazardous; the pay is low and the return uncertain. The risk of the voyage is high, but the risk of not taking the voyage, and the cost of ignorance, I hope you will agree, are even higher." Although Gagosian explicitly defined "gold" as a metaphor for idealized states of knowledge and understanding, in the context of the speech "the cost of ignorance" is more accurately interpreted as loss of material wealth for "our" nation. Without financial backing, "the best of American science—will falter, and the dividends it pays in technology and commerce . . . will decline," according to Gagosian.[27]

However, while Gagosian used an analogy to the Age of Exploration as his central argument in the speech, there was also a point where he explicitly acknowledged his discomfort with drawing on this component of the broad American frontier myth to talk about science. He admitted that Columbus "was an agent of economic imperialism, out for gold, and the conversion of native populations," and he argued that these facts made his analogy "inexact" since "we like to think of science as serving all of humankind, in the pursuit of knowledge."[28] For a brief moment in the speech, a postcolonial critique of the frontier of science metaphor seemed ready to emerge.

But this critical perspective toward the frontier metaphor was rejected almost as soon as it was introduced. Rather than abandon the comparison of modern scientists to explorers like Columbus, because of the analogy's conflict with our idealized understanding of science, Gagosian chose to shift our understanding of science to more closely match the vehicle of a colonizing force. While briefly acknowledging that "Columbus was an agent of European colonialism, one of the darker periods of human history," Gagosian nonetheless claimed that "Columbus has taken a bad rap lately," thus summarily dismissing revisionist histories of the heroic explorer. In the end, Gagosian praised Columbus for his ability to scare up financing for "an incredible voyage" that saw an "incalculable" return on investment for the government that sponsored him.[29] In this speech, Columbus ultimately served as a model that American scientists should emulate. Gagosian recognized that something was distasteful about the nation's mythic past, but the lesson of history was lost once lip service was paid to a critique of the heroic story. The thesis of Gagosian's speech is that American scientists should get private and public funding so that they can win the race to establish profitable disciplinary colonies on the new worlds of knowledge discovered by scientific exploration.

If, in fact, we like to think of science as serving all of humankind, as Gagosian claims, then logically it should not matter if Americans lose their dominance in science to other nations that explore the same knowledge territory as long as that knowledge territory is being adequately explored. But the national identity of who wins the race to colonize the frontier of science matters a great deal to Gagosian and the other scientists whose speeches I have examined in this chapter. The frontier metaphor encourages us to think of science as an international competition to claim (intellectual) property, rather than as a puzzle-solving collaborative activity that can benefit all of humankind, and a brief acknowledgment of the darker side of the Columbus story does little to obscure this nationalistic and competitive vista from the terministic screen. The frontier of science metaphor, when used as a central theme to guide the public speech of American scientists, pushes the altruistic motives of scientists and those who would fund science to the background, and discourages international collaboration by envisioning science as a race for territory, a zero-sum game in which one nation must win its place by pushing out others who get in the way.

Science studies scholar Sheila Jasanoff argues that different nations have different "civic epistemologies" that mark their culturally specific ways of thinking about science. Her comparative study of biotechnology politics and policy in three nations concluded that the civic epistemology in Britain can be best described as communitarian, in Germany as consensus-seeking, and in the United States as contentious.[30] The historically grounded cultural meaning of the frontier myth to Americans may help to explain the last part of this finding. If the activity of scientists is seen as a fierce competition to claim ownership of territory on a "frontier" before others claim it, and if it is assumed that profitable resources will swiftly flow from the discoveries of this basic "frontier" research, then it is reasonable to take on a contentious stance toward potential rivals and to exist in an uneasy relationship with a larger public that is skeptical and fearful of your frontier-breaching ways. Likewise, if one has a contentious civic epistemology, it is reasonable to characterize science through a frontier metaphor that envisions scientists as engaged in a fierce contest to claim profitable new knowledge spaces.

One way to recognize a culturally specific way of thinking about something is to look at it through the eyes of someone who is a visitor to that culture. The public speech of mechanical engineering professor and university administrator Choon Fong Shih, visiting the United States in May 2008, illuminates both the power and limitations of the frontier metaphor for science.[31] Praising American science before an American audience, Shih took time in this speech to reflect on his childhood in China, when he watched Americans meet John F. Kennedy's challenge to send a man to the moon. "The U.S. was audacious. The U.S. was irreverent. And preposterous. And bold. And imaginative. And all of that was absolutely inspiring." According to Shih, the "quintessence of the West's greatness," the "magic of America" at its best, "has come from two journeys toward two types of frontiers. The first journey was to discover new geographical frontiers; the second, to break new grounds in science and technology." To elaborate on this point, Shih narrated a story of the European explorers of the fifteenth century, "motivated by a desire for glory and gold . . . to explore and exploit new lands"; Shih then marveled at "what appeared to be a scientific mind at work in Columbus." This contrasted with the myopia of Chinese sailors who had superior navigation equipment a hundred years before Columbus sailed, but who did not discover America because they preferred "control over knowledge." The same American attitudes that drove frontier explorers allowed American science to ascend, according to Shih. "While the geographical frontiers were conquered, other knowledge barriers were being breached, not in sailboats, but in laboratories. This emboldened intellectual inquiry led to the emergence of science as we know it today. Science in the centuries following Columbus proliferated into multiple disciplines, leading the way in exploring, exploiting and explaining nature, whether atoms and stars, or genes and brains, or black holes and light." Calling upon a mythic American pioneering spirit, Shih praised his auditors for their daring, competitive national character.

But the congratulatory message that Shih seemed to offer in this speech took an abrupt turn when he pointed out the "unintended consequences" of scientists' attempts to bend nature to their wills. "As the frontiers of scientific knowledge are pushed back, we find ourselves coming full circle. . . . We are now compelled to confront the consequences of choices we have made. The consequences of colonization, of climate change, of global security. We have come full circle." It is at this point in the speech that Shih recommended a third journey for Americans, a journey that takes its cue from a sixteenth-century Chinese novel rather than from an American frontier myth. This would be "a journey toward achieving understanding," which "includes empathy and compassion," a "quest for wisdom" rather than just "fortune and knowledge." It is a decided shift away from the frontier journeys that Shih described earlier in the speech as both the characteristic strength of American science and the source of a number of undesirable consequences. Only by moving away from the frontier myth toward another myth, this one taken from a Chinese adventure story, can an alternative vision of the future of science be introduced.

Conclusion

This chapter has offered a critical analysis of the contemporary use of the frontier of science metaphor. The intent has not been to argue that this rhetoric is wholly inadequate to the purposes toward which it is being put in speeches that seek to increase government or industry support for scientific research. Scientists reading this analysis will confirm that their profession can be an exciting space for bold and ambitious young men, that funding of basic research can lead to discoveries that are swiftly translated into profitable applications, and that international competition for intellectual property rights can be fierce. But if pressed, they will also confirm that science can be other things as well. In the first two chapters, I pointed out that the frontier of science metaphor is a terministic screen that concentrates our attention on some focal themes while deflecting other possibilities from our view. A critical analysis reminds us that there are other, equally accurate depictions of science that we might want to consider as well, and that in some situations, we might prefer those alternatives.

For example, the frontier of science vista turns our attention away from the fact that there are often lengthy and nonlinear links between basic research and profitable applications, with increased funding for the former never a guarantee of revenue return from the latter. Given this fact, it is sometimes the case that funding for research in applied science is a more desirable choice for a democratically organized public, even if that prospect seems ludicrous when one's vision is constrained by an account that privileges basic "frontier" science. Also dropped from our field of vision when we are blinkered by this metaphor is the necessarily collaborative nature of most modern science, where interpersonal skills can be more valuable than the will to conquer nature, and international cooperation can be more productive than a competitive race to claim knowledge territory. The frontier metaphor constructs scientists as masculine risk-seekers, isolated from the rest of civilized society, eager to claim knowledge territory for self and nation, and driven by a desire for conquest. This construct shapes the American public's perception of science, for better and worse, and if individuals choose to pursue a career in science based on this perception of what it entails, it can shape the vocation itself in ways that are not desirable.

I demonstrate in the next two chapters that there are some other unintended consequences that follow the application of this terministic screen to contemporary characterizations of American science. When audience members who carry negative associations for the frontier myth encounter the metaphor being used positively and triumphally to describe American science, their reception of the proposals made by the scientific rhetors using such language can be unfavorable, even hostile. In a postcolonial transnational context, the metaphoric alignment of science and the American frontier myth can be especially problematic. In those cases, frontier rhetoric does much to undermine the specific purposes of the scientists who use it.

CHAPTER THREE

The Dangers of Bioprospecting on the Frontier: The Rhetoric of Edward O. Wilson's Biodiversity Appeals

⌘

One scientist whose use of the "frontier of science" metaphor has resulted in some unintended consequences for his own work is biologist Edward O. Wilson. For example, his 1998 national best seller, *Consilience: The Unity of Knowledge*, drew on the metaphor while arguing for the construction of a bridge between the natural sciences and the social sciences and humanities. A review of his book by the historian of science D. Graham Burnett captured the skeptical response of many scholars of the social sciences and humanities to that call. "Here is a kind of bridge one might eye with suspicion, for the message comes through clearly: the humanities and the social sciences represent science's last frontier. Let us build a bridge, he effectively proposes, and take over your island."[1]

I have argued elsewhere that one of the reasons Wilson's *Consilience* met with so much resistance from its readers was Wilson's pervasive use frontier-era images of exploration and conquest to characterize the proper attitude of natural scientists to the subject matter of the social sciences and humanities, a "self-conscious language of imperialist expansion" that worked to anger or embarrass many of those who reviewed the book, both those readers who were positioned as the natives to be civilized by natural science and those who were being imagined as the colonizers with a manifest destiny to conquer territory that was not being productively developed by its current occupants.[2] I suggested that Wilson used this language because his sociobiologically inspired theory of persuasion holds (incorrectly it seems) that people are most effectively influenced by appeals to deep-seated impulses such as our Paleolithic desire for territorial expansion.[3]

Given the prevalence of these metaphors of frontier conquest in Wilson's *Consilience*, I wondered whether he used the same language in other popular books he wrote, especially in those texts that are not explicitly focused on popularizing his sociobiology theory but are focused instead on his second major line of public argument about science—namely, his environmentalist plea that we preserve and catalog biological diversity in the last remaining literal frontier spaces. Are the same metaphors for natural science as an expansionist advance on the frontier of knowledge present in the very texts where his main argument is that we should protect nature by renouncing our frontier-expanding ways? If so, that can tell us a great deal about the power and peril of the frontier metaphor for scientists today.

The Paradox of Protecting and Exploring the Wildlands

The first of these biodiversity books, Wilson's best-selling 1992 *The Diversity of Life*, ends with a call for "an enduring environmental ethic."[4] His passionate appeal for "the stewardship of environment" (*D*, 351) was advanced throughout this book with his presentation of "evidence that humanity has initiated the sixth great extinction spasm, rushing to eternity a large fraction of our fellow species in a single generation"

(*D*, 32). Wilson was especially concerned about the "flood of new immigrants now pouring into" the North Region of Brazilian Amazonia, who will, for the most part, seek income "by advancing the agricultural frontier," a practice that is "responsible for most of the devastation being visited upon Amazonian rainforests" (*D*, 324). Recognizing the alarming speed with which species are disappearing, Wilson pleaded for a halt to the destruction: "every scrap of biological diversity is priceless, to be learned and cherished, and never to be surrendered without a struggle" (*D*, 32). Repeating this call at the end of the book, Wilson argued that "the ethical imperative" demands that we "judge every scrap of biodiversity as priceless" (*D*, 351).

But even in this most straightforward statement of Wilson's thesis about the need to protect and study the biodiversity of frontier forests and other wilderness regions, we can see signs of tension between his purpose and the means of persuasion he selected to achieve that purpose. His treatment of biodiversity in economic terms (priceless even in small amounts) and his positioning of the audience in a martial stance (they must not surrender without a struggle) point to the "strong and multifarious links between a style and an outlook" that the rhetorical criticism of metaphor can reveal.[5] These economic and martial metaphors are contextual cues that activate the frontier of science metaphor that lies at the heart of his book. Wilson, in *The Diversity of Life*, used metaphors to represent biological organisms as profitable treasure and scientists as frontier adventurers, even while he argued for an environmental ethic that would protect biodiversity from the destructive power of humanity's adventurous and profit-driven encroachment on undeveloped frontiers.

The same contradictory set of appeals is present in another popular book about biodiversity that Wilson authored ten years later.[6] In *The Future of Life*, Wilson argued forcefully for a new "global land ethic" (*F*, xxiii). As he explained: "The European conquest of the New World established the concept of wilderness as a frontier region waiting to be rolled back. The image was most clearly formed in the United States, whose early history is geographically defined as a westward march across an undeveloped and fertile continent" (*F*, 144). But a "tipping point" has been reached, and we must now recognize wilderness as "a scarce resource" that is worth saving (*F*, 144); we must abandon the frontier mentality that "pushed back virgin land" (*F*, 143). In this same book, however, Wilson wrote a chapter titled "To the Ends of the Earth," which depicts scientists doing field research as enjoying high adventure on the frontier, and he portrayed biological organisms as a "pharmacological bounty" (*F*, 119) that can be productively mined through "bioprospecting" (*F*, 124). A close reading of both *The Diversity of Life* and *The Future of Life* can reveal the entangled strands of Wilson's paradoxical repudiation of the frontier mindset and simultaneous use of language that appeals to that very same mindset.

Metaphor and Myth in Wilson's Biodiversity Books

Since the subject matter of Wilson's biodiversity books often demanded that real frontiers be discussed, a close reading is required to distinguish his literal references to current and future frontier exploration from his use of metaphorical language to conjure a standard frontier myth replete with conquistadors, prospectors, and frontiersmen, in which nature is a repository of riches to be exploited and indigenous people are elided, along with any ownership rights they might claim to literal or intellectual property. When Wilson recalls an evening doing field research in the Amazon rain forest in Brazil, for example, his reference to the use of a headlamp to search for insects on the forest floor is literal. But his exclamation after lighting up wolf spiders that he had "found—diamonds!" and his expressed desire to then "hunt for new treasures" are metaphors, envisioning biological organisms through terms that symbolize the accumulation of wealth that inspired an earlier era of frontier adventure on the South American continent (*D*, 4).

Wilson did not *have* to invoke frontier metaphors to develop his appeal for the preservation of wilderness regions and the scientific study of those areas. The fact that he chose to do so is significant, suggesting the influence of frontier imagery in public discourse about science. By examining his language choices in some detail, and tracing the reception of this rhetoric in reviews of the books and in the response of those who control the lands he was seeking to preserve, we see evidence that Wilson's rhetorical invention had consequences that he likely did not anticipate.

Throughout these books, Wilson connected vehicles that signify a frontier mythos to two tenors: the organism that is the subject of the biological scientist's study, and the process of scientific research itself.

As an example of the former, consider his treatment of wolf spiders as "diamonds" (D, 4). Through this metaphor, he transformed living organisms into minerals, figuratively killing them and making them subject to an ethic that treats them as precious materials to be collected, preserved, displayed, and used as a means of economic exchange. This language of organisms as mineral treasure appears in both books. That it was influential is demonstrated by the way it seeped into the writing of those who read the books. For example, reviewers echoed Wilson's word choice when they commented on the "disproportionate concentration of the earth's biological wealth in the tropical belt," a place where "biological treasures" and "evolutionary relics" are in need of "salvaging," and where one can find "treasure . . . [that] has barely been tapped"; they accepted his language when they spoke of "the earth's biological riches" and affirmed that "the environment is a treasure."[7] In each case, the metaphors of colonial wealth that Wilson employed were appropriated by his readers without quotation marks, accepted as natural terms for the living things being referenced. Copying Wilson, they metaphorically transformed organisms into material objects with high economic value.

With regard to the second tenor, Wilson's description of scientific practice drew on a broader metaphor that imagines science itself as a frontier, and scientists as frontiersmen in search of elusive ideas on an unexplored field of knowledge. Consider, for example, his description of "scientific exploration as a whole" in the beginning of *The Diversity of Life* (D, 8). Here he used a familiar spatial metaphor that imagines knowledge production as the exploration of new territory: "We search in and around a subject for a concept, a pattern, that imposes order. We look for a way of speaking about the rough unmapped terrain" (D, 8). Scientists, by this account, are explorers making maps of a harsh land that was previously unknown to them. Their relationship to what they find there is prefigured as violent. In this metaphorical frontier territory, "ideas" are the "quarry" for the scientist-explorer to hunt: "These whispering denizens of the mind are sensed but rarely seen. They rustle the foliage, leave behind a pug mark filling with water and a scent, excite us for an instant and vanish" (D, 8). This passage portrays the scientist as a hunter on the frontier who "can hope to capture" only several ideas in a lifetime and who pursues the "hunt" because the "value of the quarry" is so high (D, 8). Wilson described the "best of science" as springing from "the hunter's mind," and he recalled his own efforts to "move forward" with the help of some new image that "might propel me past the jaded

76 Chapter Three

puzzle to the other side, to ideas strange and compelling" (*D*, 8). With similar language in *The Future of Life*, Wilson promoted the cause of biodiversity studies as an exciting pursuit, rather than a dull taxonomic chore. "Now the renewal of the Linnaean enterprise is seen as high adventure," he proclaimed (*F*, 15). By entering the "the open frontiers in biodiversity exploration," scientists and amateur collectors can undertake "the full and exact mapping of all biological diversity" (*F*, 15–16). Scientific frontiersmen who embrace the heroic work of charting a mysterious land and hunting what they find there are imagined to be on an exhilarating expedition. As one postdoctoral fellow in conservation biology put it in a review of *The Diversity of Life*, right before she appreciatively quoted the passage that metaphorically treats the scientist as a hunter on the frontier, "Wilson takes us on a sensuous journey . . . [with] energy and excitement."[8] If young people are looking for a career that runs high on thrills, the science of biodiversity studies is set out as the profession to choose.

Many American readers noted Wilson's frontier language in their reviews of his book, often adopting it themselves, and in some cases they showed enthusiasm for the promise of adventure it offered to scientists who undertake the study of biodiversity. If it helped to draw the interest of his target audience, what is wrong with Wilson's use of the frontier metaphor and myth in these texts? As I suggested in previous chapters, the martial and material valences of frontier language can construct a scientific vocation that values attributes that have been traditionally marked as male, treating knowledge as property to be conquered and owned, emphasizing competitiveness over cooperation, and generally devaluing other perspectives toward science that can be more useful to the profession in the long run. Beyond these general problems, an analysis of text and reception indicates that there are two very specific problems for Wilson that arose when he chose to use frontier language in these biodiversity books. First, some of his language choices were interpreted by readers as a call for colonizing nations to renew the exploitation of other countries, and, as a result, Wilson's laudable appeal for the study of biodiversity was resisted as a neocolonialist message by those who control the very territory that he would have scientists enter to do this research. Second, Wilson's paradoxical swings from rejection of the frontier mindset to passionate appeals to the frontier spirit led to a confusion of meanings, with readers interpreting his texts in contrary ways, to the detriment of his larger message.

Reading Wilson in a Postcolonial Transnational Context

It is not difficult to see why Wilson's use of frontier appeals might be seen by some as objectionable, especially when his texts are encountered outside of mainstream America by audiences familiar with postcolonial narratives of European conquest. For example, consider the first pages of *The Diversity of Life* where Wilson recalled having discovered the wolf spider "diamonds" and where he compared "scientific exploration as a whole" to a hunt on the frontier (*D*, 3–8). In the context of the literal setting he established for himself in a Brazilian rain forest, this evocative metaphor of scientists as explorers who hunt the valuable denizens of an unmapped terrain carries with it the associated commonplace of imperialist conquest. Assisting with this association is Wilson's explicit comparison of the Amazon forest in which he works to "wilderness in the sixteenth-century sense, as it must have formed in the minds of the Portuguese explorers, its interior still largely unexplored and filled with strange, myth-engendering plants and animals" (*D*, 7). Recalling the excitement that first led him to study tropical rain forests, "to look for something hidden, as Kipling had urged, something lost behind the Ranges," Wilson encouraged his readers to conflate current scientific discovery with stories of colonialist adventure (*D*, 7).[9]

It is not unusual for rhetors to "become accustomed to routine extensions of images no longer serving their original purposes," allowing underlying metaphors to limit the possibilities for rhetorical invention.[10] In this case, the grip of a powerful metaphor undermines Wilson's argument when it encourages him to promote the mining of frontier regions by American scientists. Wilson's literary allusions to frontier adventure stories align with his characterization of biodiversity as wealth to create the image of American scientists as treasure-seekers eager to exploit another country.

Chapter 13 of *The Diversity of Life*, titled "Unmined Riches," depicts biodiversity with an abundance of vehicles signifying the colonialist desire to discover untapped wealth in the hidden wildlands. Readers are introduced to biodiversity as a "treasure house of the wild" (*D*, 281); they are informed that wildlands can be "mined for genetic material" because wildlands contain "the richest deposits of biological diversity" (*D*, 282); they are told of the "dilemma of the stewardship of the world's biological riches by the economically poor" (*D*, 283); and they are encouraged to think of the "mostly unwritten archives of native peoples" as "a wealth of information about wild and semicultivated crops" (*D*, 291). By the end of the chapter, Wilson would triumphantly evoke the frontier spirit: "The riches are there, fallow in the wildlands and waiting to be employed by our hands, our wit, our spirit" (*D*, 310). The character traits of the American frontiersman listed by Turner in 1893 are the very traits that Wilson was attaching to scientists who agree to engage in the study of biodiversity. At the same time, he characterized native peoples and others who occupy the territory to be mined by those scientists as incapable stewards who leave the land fallow rather than developing it, and he dismissed native cultures as nothing more than a source of information about where the largest deposits of biological wealth are to be found. In Wilson's view, it is the manifest destiny of scientists to mine those riches.

At the beginning of the next chapter, Wilson defined biological diversity as "a potential source for immense untapped material wealth in the form of food, medicine, and amenities" (*D*, 311). He urged scientists to engage in "*chemical prospecting*, the search among wild species for new medicines and other useful chemical products" (*D*, 311). Working with "Merck and other research and commercial organizations" that "are increasingly inclined to take on chemical prospecting," scientists can consider natural products from the wildlands "a potential shortcut" to discovery at the frontiers of science, "a Columbus-like journey west, for those willing to acquire the essential skills" (*D*, 321). If the reference to a company like Merck extracting profitable resources from a South American forest sounds a bit too much like the exploitative qualities of Columbus's literal voyage to the New World, Wilson took no notice. "Wildlands and biological diversity are legally the properties of nations, but they are ethically part of the global commons," he argued (*D*, 326). The "biological wealth" of the wildlands must be cataloged and preserved (*D*, 311, 319, 342, 347, 351). This appeal to scientists to consider their work equivalent to the exploration of Columbus brings to mind the Doctrine of Discovery, which puts ownership of wealth found on the frontier into the hands of the foreign adventurers who "discover" it, rather than the people who have long been living with it. The prospecting metaphor helps to reinforce this profit orientation of Wilson's appeal to scientists who might want to "discover" wealth in the wildlands.

The practice that Wilson called "chemical prospecting" in 1992 got taken up by others the following year under the name of "biodiversity prospecting."[11] This was shortened further over time into the term "bioprospecting," which is the word Wilson used in 2002 in *The Future of Life* as he again promoted the exploitation by "industry strategists" of "Nature's pharmacopoeia" (*F*, 126). As in *The Diversity of Life*, he used Brazil as one of his examples, but he appeared to dispense with geopolitical borders when he linguistically expanded the ownership of wilderness territory through a globalized possessive, claiming that the rain forests of Brazil contain "the world's store of biodiversity," a "pharmacological bounty" that must be retrieved by scientific explorers (*F*, 118–19). Wilson explicitly defined bioprospecting as the "exploration of wild biodiversity in search of useful resources" (*F*, 124). Like their namesakes who mine precious metals, biological prospectors could take one of two approaches: "Sometimes bioprospectors screen many species of organisms in search of chemicals with particular qualities," while on "other occasions bioprospecting is opportunistic, keying on one or a few species that show signs of yielding a valuable resource. Ultimately, entire ecosystems will be prospected as a whole, assaying all of the species for most or all of the products they can yield" (*F*, 124). The goal in each case is the "extraction of wealth from an ecosystem" (*F*, 124). The motives that drove extraction of wealth on the frontiers of the New World are thus mapped directly onto the present endeavor.

To be fair, Wilson's proposal to save the rain forests by protecting them as "extractive reserves" (*D*, 303) is an argument with a certain logic; it was presented as a pragmatic appeal that aligns economic benefit with the larger moral imperative of preserving nature for its own sake. Wilson made it clear that he was calling for bioprospecting "with minimal disturbance," the kind of prospecting that is not "destructive" but "benign" (*F*, 124–25). "Bioprospecting can serve both mainstream economics and conservation when done on a firm contractual basis," he insisted (*F*, 127).

However, Wilson's orientation toward the human occupants of the land to be bioprospected is troubling because it mirrors the orientation of Europeans toward the native peoples of the Americas in an earlier age of imperialist conquest. For example, Wilson acknowledged that "the richness of biodiversity's bounty is reflected in the products already extracted by native peoples of the tropical forests, using local knowledge and low technology of a kind transmitted solely by demonstration and oral teaching" (*F*, 125). To establish this rich bounty, Wilson listed "a small selection of the most common medicinal plants used by tribes of the upper Amazon" (*F*, 125). But when he then went on to identify some praiseworthy examples of bioprospecting "on a firm contractual basis," none of the cases he mentioned includes native peoples as signatories. He listed contracts such as those between Merck and Costa Rica's National Institute of Biodiversity, between Diversa Corporation and Yellowstone National Park, and between Glaxo Wellcome and a Brazilian pharmaceutical company (*F*, 127–28). In these cases, Wilson made it clear that "mainstream economics" is served by the named multinational corporations (Merck, Diversa, Glaxo Wellcome), and conservation is served by local scientists in research institutes who use the funds that are contractually provided by the corporations to support "basic scientific research" (*F*, 127–28). Wilson never mentioned the interests of the native groups whose indigenous knowledge is being mined.

That he was aware of these interests is confirmed by the fact that two of the articles he cited as his sources for information about particular "bioprospecting efforts" made a point of commenting on the "heated debates" taking place over proper compensation for the communities whose indigenous knowledge is being mined.[12] But perhaps because he was carried along by the promise of mutual benefits for science and commerce in these mining efforts, Wilson made no note of the concerns that local communities might have about their ecosystems or biological knowledge being excavated.

As one Peruvian critic of "bioprospecting" points out, we would do well to remember that gold and silver mining in Latin America in the sixteenth and seventeenth centuries exploited the people of these lands to the point of extinction.[13] The call for a new campaign in which monied Western powers employ science to extract the wealth from other nations is not likely to be heard positively by the people of those nations being mined. "The new invasion looks remarkably like a second coming of Columbus to some of us," says one activist.[14] From the point of view of indigenous peoples, the parallel between the Industrial Revolution's destructive extraction of inanimate nonrenewable matter such as mineral ores and the Biotechnology Revolution's proposed extraction of genetic materials is a troubling one.[15] Vandana Shiva, a respected environmental activist and philosopher, has argued that the mining metaphor is not only inappropriate because of the history of exploitation it evokes but also because of its fundamental assumptions. "The metaphor of prospecting suggests that prior to prospecting the resources lie buried, unknown, unused, and without value. However, unlike the case with gold or oil deposits, local communities know the uses and values of biodiversity. The metaphor of bioprospecting thus hides the prior uses, knowledge, and rights associated with it."[16] Drawing on the values of individualism, progress, and capital accumulation that have long been a part of frontier exploration, bioprospecting ventures promote the interests of industry strategists and the scientist-prospectors who assist them, but not the indigenous people whose knowledge traditions are being tapped. As Shiva explains, "The bioprospecting perspective reflects the commodification and privatization paradigm, which only protects the rights of those who appropriate people's common resources and turn them into commodities."[17]

In the era in which Wilson writes, it should come as no surprise that audiences more sensitive to the destructive aftermath of frontier prospecting would respond with alarm to his metaphoric imagination. One case in point is the Brazilian response to his books. Wilson's 1992 and 2002 biodiversity books were both translated into Portuguese and sold in Brazil.[18] But Brazilians have not embraced Wilson's call for bioprospecting in the Amazon. In fact, Brazil has passed legislation that significantly restricts scientific study in the Amazon by foreigners "to protect the country's sovereignty and biodiversity" against what it calls "biopiracy."[19]

Not all Brazilians who are opposed to bioprospecting are concerned about the rights of indigenous tribes. Some who speak out against foreign influence are themselves the privileged descendents of colonizers, motivated by a desire to exploit this wealth for their own benefit rather than allow foreign corporations to steal what they see as their own nation's property. But no matter what the motive, whether it is to protect the rights of native tribes or to protect Brazil's national heritage, the perceived enemy is the same. Wilson's language of bioprospecting unifies (in opposition) a diverse coalition of Brazilians, including those with indigenous or nationalistic sympathies, liberal or conservative leanings, and environmentalist or antienvironmentalist sentiments—all speak out in defense of the Amazonian rain forest and against the encroachment of foreign scientists on these frontier lands.

In fact, the belief that arguments like Wilson's for biodiversity conservation are driven by an imperialist agenda is widespread in Brazil. Brazilian environmentalist Marina Silva reminds us of the context in which arguments like Wilson's are received. "Historically, Brazil always assumed a position of colonized country, in which its natural resources are removed indiscriminately."[20] In this context, retired Brazilian judge and amateur ornithologist Antonio Silveira R. dos Santos points out that the popularization of biodiversity by Wilson's *Diversity of Life* led to legitimate fears of exploitation on the part of Brazilians. "Brazil is considered the country with the greatest diversity of life on the planet, and therefore is the target of greediness." Biodiversity, which is "considered a treasure," is subject to the "exploitation" of "bioprospecting." According to this judge, Wilson's book neglects the "legal aspects" surrounding who owns the resources being studied and used. But "we must not forget that biodiversity, which is the cause and the bone of bioprospecting, is not a resource without an owner, on the contrary, it belongs to the country that carries it."[21]

Whether the resource belongs to the country that carries it, or the tribe that has been using it for countless years, or to no one at all, what Brazilians can agree about is that it does *not* belong to the scientists who would bioprospect it. Some environmentalist nongovernmental organizations have tried to answer Wilson's call to protect biodiversity by preserving forests, but their efforts have been interpreted by many Brazilians as a nefarious plot to exploit Brazilian land. Some, like Lorenzo Carrasco, the editor and coauthor of a popular tract against environmentalism, believe that when environmentalist organizations are engaged in "creating and controlling these reserves, which are full of mineral and other valuable resources," they are engaged in "a new form of colonialism."[22] Brazilians are quick to point to American portrayals of the Amazon as an "international reserve" that belongs not to Brazilians, but to the world, as proof that foreigners do not respect their territorial borders.[23] When Wilson makes statements that characterize biodiversity studies as a part of a "bioprospecting" venture and the Amazon forest as part of a "global commons," he confirms their worst fears. Comments like this "have reignited old attitudes of territorial protectionism and watchfulness for undercover foreign invaders (now including bioprospectors)."[24]

Such fears are not confined to the fringes of Brazilian society. A Brazilian military intelligence report claimed that environmentalist groups are merely acting as arms of "the hegemonic powers [that] are engaged to maintain and augment their domination."[25] A weekly newsmagazine that is the Brazilian equivalent of *Newsweek* or *Time* has compared scientific researchers to the "European colonizers" of 500 years ago, seeking "to steal the richness of the biggest biodiversity in the world."[26] It reports that "foreigners have felt for years that they own the region," and the coveting of Brazil's "biodiversity richness" is merely the most recent case "of international greediness."[27] Such sentiments are widely shared by Brazilian citizens. According to Brazil's leading polling organization, in 2005, 75 percent of Brazilians said that they thought their nation's natural riches could provoke a foreign invasion, and nearly three out of five distrusted the activities of environmental groups.[28]

When Wilson waxes poetic about "biophilia," his sociobiological term for "the connections that human beings subconsciously seek with the rest of life" (*D*, 350), or when he criticizes those shortsighted souls who assume humanity should look to the stars for the next frontier and "let species die if they block progress, [since] scientific and technological genius will find another way" (*D*, 348), it is clear that he loves nature, that his plea to preserve it is genuine, and that his ultimate goal is laudable. But the metaphoric entailments of frontier exploration and exploitation through which his argument is framed carry a heavy burden in a postcolonial transnational context. Wilson portrays the biologist as a special sort of scientist who metaphorically explores the territory of new ideas and literally explores and exploits those spaces that have not yet been sufficiently mapped by the industrialized world. When it comes to the preservation of biological diversity, it is up to "science to blaze the path by research and development," according to Wilson (*D*, 336). "Enchanted by the continuous emergence of new technologies and supported by generous funding for medical research, biologists have probed deeply along a narrow sector of the front. Now it is time to expand laterally, to get on with the Linnaean enterprise and finish mapping the biosphere" (*D*, 346). But since this mapping project is done in the service of opening the global commons to bioprospecting by large corporations that seek to profit by extracting the natural resources of a land that is characterized as not being profitably used by those who currently occupy it, it is neither innocent nor pure. Instead, it participates in the exploitative heritage that is the worst part of a history of Euro-American frontier exploration.

Reading Wilson's Contradictory Treatments of the Frontier Myth

If the exploitative rhetoric of the frontier myth is troubling to Brazilians and/or indigenous peoples and their allies reading Wilson in a

postcolonial transnational context, then how are his books received by
those who are presumably his primary audience? Would the excitement
created in a typical American reader by Wilson's use of the frontier myth
outweigh any disadvantage created when another audience reads these
books? A close reading of text and reception shows that a mainstream
American audience encountered an entirely different problem with
Wilson's frontier language than the issue identified by those who see
themselves as the potential victims of a new campaign of colonization.
Rather than reject the books outright as part of a colonialist agenda,
these readers found themselves buffeted in different directions by
Wilson's paradoxical denunciation and simultaneous adoration of the
frontier myth.

According to Esa Väliverronen and Iina Hellsten, the most common
metaphors that are used in popular scientific discourse about biodiversity loss promote two opposite environmental narratives: "an apocalyptic
view of species extinction and a view that stresses the economic benefits
of biodiversity conservation."[29] Wilson's language of frontier development, or bioprospecting, is an example of the latter view, a "positive
popular image of biodiversity" that appeals to Euro-American audiences
who are excited by the prospect of searching for biological "gold and
treasures" in the untapped ecological repositories of tropical lands.[30]
What is strange about Wilson's rhetoric is that in the same books where
he made these appeals, he also employed the frontier myth to create
what Väliverronen and Hellsten identify as the opposing environmental
narrative, an "elegiac rhetoric" that mourns the worlds lost by humankind's apocalyptic destruction of natural environments.[31] The result is
an odd clash of pro-imperialist and anti-imperialist narratives.

For example, the anti-imperialist narrative in *The Future of Life*
depicts the colonization of frontier lands as a wave of mass destruction:
"As a rule around the world, wherever people entered a virgin environment, most of the megafauna soon vanished" (*F*, 92). A chapter titled
"The Planetary Killer" employs words like "serial killer of the biosphere"
(*F*, 94), "slaughter" (*F*, 94), "sweep of a scythe" (*F*, 94), "waves of invasion" (*F*, 96), and "progression of megadeath" (*F*, 96) to paint a picture of
humankind as butchers of all they survey. The chapter immediately preceding it, titled "Nature's Last Stand," describes the loss of biodiversity
in Latin America as "a war against nature" and a "massacre" (*F*, 57–58)
perpetrated by settlers who use up the land and then "move on to occupy
land closer to the frontier" (*F*, 63). Wilson embraced a romantic elegiac

nostalgia for what was lost when he imagined precolonial Hawaii as "a ghost that haunts the hills" and pronounced that "the planet is poorer for its sad retreat" (*F*, 44–45). Since the image he was referencing was Hawaii before the very first *Polynesians* arrived, he made it clear that it is not just modern humans who are responsible for the massacre. In *The Diversity of Life*, Wilson was equally clear on this point. He said that the "Paleo-Indian hunter-gatherers" who first entered North America 10,000 years ago and spread throughout the New World "demolished most of the large mammals during a hunter's blitzkrieg" (*D*, 249). In fact, he said, whenever "human colonists arrived, not only in America but also in New Zealand, Madagascar, and Australia . . . a large part of the megafauna—large mammals, birds, and reptiles—disappeared soon after" (*D*, 249). Wilson concluded that the truth of "the whole melancholy situation" is that whenever "the human wave rolled over the last of the virgin lands like a smothering blanket," they carried with them the "mindless horsemen of the environmental apocalypse" (*D*, 253). In the context of his simultaneous characterization of nature as overflowing with biological treasure in need of bioprospecting by adventurous scientist-explorers, this apocalyptic scene of desolation is incongruous, to say the least.

Readers facing this mixed message might be forgiven if, in an effort to relieve cognitive dissonance, they were to ignore one message and focus on the other, even to the point of misinterpreting Wilson's thesis. For example, consider the reading that James Lovelock produced in his review of Wilson's *The Diversity of Life*.[32] Lovelock approached the book from an antienvironmentalist stance; this independent scientist has long been known for opposing what he calls the environmentalists' "idiotic" desire for curbs on economic expansion, and he argues that we are being misled by environmentalists who "look for trouble in the wrong places."[33] Seeing an opportunity for fellowship in Wilson's eloquent catalog of the diversity of life, Lovelock completely ignored the apocalyptic rhetoric of Wilson's warnings about biodiversity loss, and interpreted the book as fully supporting his own fight against the alarmism of the environmentalists' message. According to Lovelock, "[Wilson's] theme is the fruitful superabundance of creatures, not 'biodiversity,' the banner word that marching environmentalists shout with fervour but little understanding." Lovelock claimed that Wilson's book was committed to proving that things are not as bad as those shouting environmentalists would have us believe, and he offered a creepy simile to make his point: "Species richness is like a blush of embarrassment on the cheeks of a young girl. Flustered she may be but not distressed. Girls do not blush when raped." Although Lovelock acknowledged that he cannot claim "the chainsaw enrich[es] the creatures of the forest," he did not seem overly concerned about the number of recent extinctions that Wilson identified, extinctions that Lovelock failed to even mention in his review. Lovelock ended his review by thanking Wilson for "a beloved book" that cherishes the multitude of "rare" species that "signify a healthy world."[34] Could it be that Wilson's portrayal of frontier forests as teeming with biological treasure encouraged Lovelock to produce a resistive reading of the meaning of the book? If so, then one unintended consequence of Wilson's use of a "positive" frontier myth to promote a narrative of economic benefits was to allow an interpretation of his book that directly counters his main message that "humanity has initiated the sixth great extinction spasm," and we must do everything we can to stop it (*D*, 32).

Most other readers were unable to follow Lovelock's lead in so completely ignoring Wilson's depiction of human colonists as an apocalyptic force, but since this depiction appeared in the context of Wilson's more romantic frontier narrative, readers oriented toward the contrary themes in various ways. Some reviewers who approached *The Diversity of Life* from an antienvironmentalist stance remained skeptical of "the apocalyptic nature of Wilson's warnings" and were quick to dismiss the book as "one more woolly paen [*sic*] to environmentalism."[35] As Gunther Stent dismissively put it, Wilson "has joined the environmentalist campaign to save mankind from itself." This is the main reason Stent disliked the book, because Wilson "was unable to find one kind word about mankind, which is mentioned only as an unmitigated natural disaster." According to Stent, Wilson demonstrates a "hatred of one's own biological species," an attitude that Stent sees "in the environmental movement" and that he disdains as an "egghead-inspired species self-hatred."[36] Stent completely overlooked Wilson's admiring characterization of the adventurous scientist who uses his hunter's mind to discover treasure in unexplored realms. For Stent, Wilson's use of the apocalyptic frontier narrative drowned out Wilson's allusions to a more "positive" Euro-American romantic vision of the frontier myth.

Diametrically opposed to Stent's reading was a reading produced by Stephen Jay Gould; the difference between the two demonstrates the confusion inherent in Wilson's dual frontier narratives. A vocal critic of

Wilson in the debate over sociobiology, Gould saw his own scientific theory of punctuated equilibrium gratuitously savaged in Wilson's *The Diversity of Life*.[37] But despite this, Gould judged the book positively, mainly because he appreciated Wilson's apocalyptic environmental rhetoric, "a deft and thoroughly successful mixture of information and prophecy" at a time when "we need prophets to shake the souls and grab the attention of those who have eyes but see not" the alarming "wave of extinctions unleashed by human depredation of our earthly environment." According to Gould, "if ever there were a subject for beating the swords of professional dispute into ploughshares of joint action, then preservation of biodiversity is our common strength and shield." But unlike Stent, who thought the book was too hard on humankind, Gould actually thought Wilson was too soft on humans. One of Gould's main criticisms of the book was that Wilson privileged humans too much, seeing humankind as the apex of a great chain of being. "I confess that I do get cross. . . . This, after all, is the very enshrining of arrogance and exaggerated self-importance that we must avoid if we are ever to take fellowship with nature seriously—and thereby avert the biodiversity crisis."[38]

Stent and Gould were each critiquing different versions of the frontier narrative in Wilson's book. Stent oriented negatively toward those parts of the text where Wilson railed against immigrants in Brazil, Paleo-Indian hunters, and British colonists whose encroachment on the frontier destroys species; in contrast, Gould oriented negatively toward what he called the "romantic nonsense" of Wilson's description of the human spirit yearning for wilderness as a pioneer yearns to enter a place of "unlimited opportunity." For Gould, insofar as "we are the huntsman," we must admit that "the enemy is us"—that *we* are "the destroyers of habitat, the blight upon former plentitude."[39] In other words, Gould embraced Wilson's use of the apocalyptic entailments of the frontier myth, while rejecting his romantic vision of modern scientists emulating explorers who discover treasure in the wilderness. In contrast, Stent rejected Wilson's apocalyptic version of the frontier myth as misanthropic environmentalism, and failed to even notice Wilson's romantic vision of scientists as heroic figures on the frontier.

Wilson might have preferred that environmentalists like Gould recognize that he was critiquing the human species for its frontier-encroaching ways, and that those skeptical of environmentalism like Stent be enticed to support biodiversity research through arguments that championed the frontier spirit of scientists who explore the remaining wilderness spaces to catalog the species there. But these two readers got their wires crossed. The contrary treatments of the frontier narrative that Wilson employed allowed each reader to take from the book what he brought to it, and this resulted in judgments that ran counter to his presumed intent.

Similar interpretations are found in the Euro-American reviews of Wilson's other popular book on biodiversity, *The Future of Life*. For example, consider a review of this book that was printed in the pages of *Commentary*, an American magazine that describes itself as "the flagship of neoconservatism."[40] Praising Wilson for his "eloquent summary of the earth's biological riches" and for refusing to dismiss those who disagree with him "as redneck frontiersmen," this reviewer nonetheless found the book "not entirely persuasive." Because Wilson's argument corresponded "to the dire and highly questionable pronouncements of the radical Environmental Left" by "reciting a litany of disasters" and describing human beings as "an unmitigated disaster for the biosphere," the reader judged the book nothing more than "an environmentalist tract immodestly titled." In his opinion, the argument of *The Skeptical Environmentalist* is more compelling, a book that criticizes Wilson "for alarmism (and arrogance) on the subject of biodiversity."[41] For a reader with these sympathies, the apocalyptic frontier story that Wilson told overpowered any nods made to a more "positive" frontier narrative, and the result of this focus was the reader's rejection of Wilson's message.

Another disapproving reviewer of *The Future of Life* treated Wilson's "apocalyptic visions" as "alarmist speculation" and chose instead to reaffirm his own "faith in human beings, and in science . . . to conquer all frontiers."[42] Although both a horrific vision and a romantic vision of humanity's frontier exploits are present in Wilson's biodiversity books, most of those who remain unpersuaded by Wilson's argument for environmental conservation seemed either to ignore or respond in anger to his narrative of human destructiveness, and in most cases, his more romantic "positive" vision of the frontier spirit did little to temper their anger at his treatment of humans as invaders who massacre all that they encounter.

Conclusion

After reviewing the reception of Wilson's books, an obvious question arises. Why did he make the rhetorical choices he did? One explanation for Wilson's paradoxical characterization of the frontier spirit as both something to embrace and something to reject is a growing American ambivalence about the frontier myth. Limerick reminds us that recent histories have pointed out that "the idea of the frontier is ethnocentric, placing Anglo-Americans at the center of the story and placing everyone else at the edges." As a result, two contrary frontier narratives vie with each other for dominance in American public address, one that recognizes that "the frontier was, in fact, a place where violence served the causes of racial subordination" and another that "says that the frontier is where people of courage have gone to take a stand for the right and the good."[43] It is possible that Wilson's paradoxical treatment of the frontier myth is a result of this cultural ambivalence being played out in the public address of an American rhetor.

But another explanation is also likely. It is possible that Wilson included positive references to the frontier spirit in books that were otherwise designed to quash the frontier-encroaching nature of destructive humanity because he was operating under a theory of persuasion that encouraged this rhetorical choice. As I mentioned at the beginning of this chapter, Wilson's sociobiological theory recognizes the impulse to colonize as fundamental to human nature. So when writing books that seek to stimulate what he thinks are our evolutionarily Paleolithic brains, it is not unreasonable for Wilson to draw on an appeal to the passion for conquest.

As evidence for this explanation, consider Wilson's final chapter in *The Diversity of Life*, titled "The Environmental Ethic," where he explicitly acknowledged his metaphoric treatment of the frontier as a symbol of opportunity. "Into wilderness people travel in search of new life and wonder. . . . Wilderness is a metaphor of unlimited opportunity, rising from the tribal memory of a time when humanity spread across the world, valley to valley, island to island, godstruck, firm in the belief that virgin land went on forever past the horizon" (*D*, 350–51). Wilson's characterization of scientists as explorers hunting for new ideas in a virgin knowledge terrain and his characterization of biologists as prospectors of biological wealth were both contextualized here as part of his sociobiological belief that people are most effectively persuaded by appeals to their human nature, and that our human nature is most accurately defined by a specific Western vision of what our Paleolithic ancestors did in prehistoric times—namely, act as destructive coloniz- ers who drove native big mammals to extinction as they swept across a virgin land (*D*, 246–47).

Believing the spirit of colonization to be a fundamental characteristic of human nature, sociobiologically engrained in our Paleolithic brains, Wilson made an appeal to the frontier myth as a way to excite readers about the prospect of undertaking a study of biodiversity. By encourag- ing readers to imagine themselves (or the scientists they are asked to finance) as explorers and prospectors, he might have hoped to trigger something deep in their psyches to excite them about the idea of under- taking or funding the taxonomic study of biodiversity in the remaining wilderness regions, even though the central message of these books was to persuade readers to do all they could to ensure that those wilderness regions would be left intact. Unfortunately, the image of the scientist as colonizer put these two purposes in competition with each other, as the most obvious way to protect biodiversity from the encroachment of destructive colonizers is to block the access of frontier-exploring sci- entists to such wilderness regions. So Brazilian legislators, intent on protecting the Amazon rain forest from bioprospectors who want to mine the global commons, voted to shut out the very scientists that Wil- son might have hoped to inspire through his rhetorical appeals to their legendary frontier spirit. Brazil decided to block the bridge between sci- entists and the objects of their study for fear that such a bridge was going to be used to conquer their land, a territory that stands as the final frontier for explorers from other nations to exploit. In the next chapter, I identify a similar incompatibility between the deployment of a frontier of science metaphor and the rhetorical intent of a biologist who, like Wilson, is known for promoting his research priorities in public address.

CHAPTER FOUR

Biocolonialism and Human Genomics Research: The Frontier Mapping Expedition of Francis Collins

⌘

E dward O. Wilson's appeal to the frontier spirit of American read- ers backfired on him when Brazilian readers encountered his arguments; it also was counterproductive with American readers insofar as his celebration of frontier attitudes contradicted his central argument that we should preserve biodiversity by halting our advance across frontier lands. In a similar way, Francis Collins drew on the fron- tier myth to excite American readers about the accomplishments of genomic scientists, but in doing so, he created an appeal that backfired with some Native American critics of genomic research; it also resulted in a conflict between his central message about the international cooperation of altruistic genomic scientists and an image of frontier scientists as fierce competitors racing each other to claim profitable genomic territory. The entailments of the "frontier of science" metaphor in the public address of Collins replicate the patterns discussed in previous chapters regarding this metaphor's tendency to commodify living organisms and characterize scientists as competitive risk-takers seeking profit for themselves and their nation, while ignoring the rights of people who arguably have a greater claim to ownership of the "territory" being explored. A limited retraction of the frontier of science metaphor in an essay by Collins suggests his dawning ambivalence about the negative effects of frontier rhetoric in public discourse about science, but a close reading of the terms of that retraction reveals that the metaphor continues to limit the imaginative possibilities of a scientific rhetor even when that rhetor explicitly makes an effort to turn away from it.

I begin this chapter with an overview of the frontier appeal in the public address of Collins. I then take a closer look at one of his speeches, tracing the implications of his language choices and focusing in particular on how they work against some of the specific goals that he set out to accomplish with that speech. I end the chapter with an analysis of his failed attempt to escape the pull of the frontier myth. This case study confirms the powerful influence of the frontier of science metaphor and illustrates some of the ways that influence can work against the interests of the rhetors who use it.

Frontier Rhetoric in the Public Address of Francis Collins

In June 2000, a White House ceremony was held to announce "the completion of the first survey of the entire human genome project." President Bill Clinton and genome scientists Francis Collins and Craig Venter gave speeches at the event, as did Prime Minister Tony Blair, who was speaking by satellite from England. On first glance, this media event seems premature, announcing what really amounted to just an initial "draft" of the survey, which Collins admitted included "97 percent of the human genome" for which only "85 percent" had actually been sequenced.[1] Why not wait until the sequencing was complete (as it would be three years later)? In his brief personal history of the Human Genome Project, Collins explained that an effort to counter an image of competitive scientists scrambling for financial advantage was the reason for the timing of the White House ceremony. By 2000, a sense had developed that a "patent gold rush" was under way in genomic science as 1,000 gene patents had already been granted in the United States for sequences from the human genome.[2] It was decided that a joint announcement from the publicly funded human genome sequencing project that Collins led and the privately funded company run by Venter that was simultaneously sequencing the genome, Celera Genomics, would serve to visibly "call a truce" between the teams of scientists whose presumptive race to sequence the genome was "becoming unseemly."[3]

If the exigence calling forth this media event was a need to offset the image of genomic science as a fierce race to claim genomic territory, then the speeches given at that event would have to be designed to present an alternative vision of what it means to be a scientist in today's world. There is evidence to suggest that Collins attempted to do just that, arguing in his speech that the great accomplishment being celebrated that day could be attributed to "an international team of more than a thousand," and was the result of a "dedicated partnership" between public and industry scientists.[4] This characterization of science as a massive team effort that transcends national boundaries and economic self-interest in order to create limitless knowledge for the benefit of all of humankind was the stated purpose of his speech, as well as the talking point that motivated the media event itself; it was present in some form in each of the other speeches that day. But it was a vision of science that ultimately was undermined by the frontier of science metaphor that also appeared in those speeches.

Before Collins spoke, President Bill Clinton introduced the frontier theme that would come to dominate both his speech and the speech that Collins gave on that day.

> Nearly two centuries ago, in this room, on this floor, Thomas Jefferson and a trusted aide spread out a magnificent map—a map Jefferson had long prayed he would get to see in his lifetime. The aide was Meriwether Lewis and the map was the product of his courageous expedition across the American frontier, all the way to the Pacific. It was a map that defined the contours and forever expanded the frontiers of our continent and our imagination. Today, the world is joining us here in the East Room to behold a map of even greater significance. We are here to celebrate the completion

of the first survey of the entire human genome. Without a doubt, this is the most important, most wondrous map ever produced by humankind.[5]

According to Clinton, this wondrous genome map sketched the future contours of our divinely inspired destiny of scientific expansion, giving us "ever more awe for the complexity, the beauty, the wonder of God's most divine and sacred gift." In celebrating the map-making achievement of these new genomic explorers, Clinton looked forward to their continued advance "toward the next majestic horizons." While he recognized that there are "ethical, moral and spiritual dimensions" to be considered when undertaking such research, he concluded that the promise of the future "diagnosis, prevention and treatment of most, if not all, human diseases," a future in which "our children's children will know the term cancer only as a constellation of stars," warrants sustained and vigorous support for the genome scientist's frontier expeditions. "We must not shrink from exploring that far frontier of science," said Clinton. This "first survey" was just a beginning, a "triumphant expedition" in "the greatest age of discovery ever known."[6]

As the director of the National Human Genome Research Institute, Collins was, by the terms of Clinton's analogy, the Meriwether Lewis who had just figuratively set the genome survey map in front of the president in the East Room. Collins later acknowledged that he had "worked closely with the president's speechwriter in the frantic days just prior to this announcement," and had strongly endorsed the language selected for the president's speech.[7] In his own speech that morning, Collins demonstrated his approval by repeating the frontier metaphor that Clinton had introduced at the beginning of the ceremony. "Science is a voyage of exploration into the unknown," Collins confirmed. "We are here today to celebrate a milestone along a truly unprecedented voyage, this one into ourselves."[8] He would repeat the word "milestone" four more times in his short speech, emphasizing forward progress in the continuing trek of the scientists who had made this triumphant genomic expedition.

Ten years later, in a popular book that Collins wrote about genomics, he recalled the president's Lewis and Clark analogy and jubilant predictions at that White House ceremony. Upon reflection, Collins admitted that "politicians are prone to exaggeration, so perhaps these stirring sentences might be considered a bit overblown."[9] But as his assessment of Clinton's speech continues in this reflection, it becomes clear that this acknowledgment (with its unnecessarily redundant qualifiers—"perhaps," "might be," "a bit") is nothing more than a procatalepsis on the part of Collins, a statement anticipating what some readers *erroneously* think prior to his own refutation of such thinking. To prove that Clinton was *not* exaggerating on that occasion, Collins would call forth the testimony of popular science writer (and zoology Ph.D.) Matt Ridley, who "only a month after the White House event" wrote: "'I genuinely believe we are living through the greatest intellectual moment in history. Bar none. . . . Until now human genes were an almost complete mystery. We will be the first generation to penetrate that mystery. We stand on the brink of great new answers, but, even more, of great new questions.'"[10] In choosing this passage to excerpt, with its image of explorers who "penetrate" strange new territory to stand "on the brink," where they can sight new discoveries that lie beyond where they have already traveled, Collins once again embraced the stirring frontier imagery that he feared readers might have initially dismissed as overblown.

Elsewhere in his 2010 book, to establish the legitimacy of the triumphant rhetoric of the Human Genome Project, Collins recalled his own keynote speech at Cold Spring Harbor, New York, in May 2000, a month prior to the White House event, when he used the Lewis and Clark analogy prior to Clinton's introduction of it in the East Room. Collins informed his readers that he began that earlier speech as follows:

> We have been engaged in a historic adventure. Whether your metaphor is Neil Armstrong or Lewis and Clark, your metaphor is at risk of falling short. There is no question that the enterprise we have gathered here to discuss will change our concepts of human biology, our approach to health and disease, and our view of ourselves. This is the moment, the time when the majority of the human genome sequence, some 85 percent of it, looms into view. You will remember this. You will tell your future graduate students, perhaps even your future grandchildren, that you sat, stood, or sprawled in Grace Auditorium, in the presence of the intellectual giants of genomics that fill this hall right now.[11]

In setting the scene for this speech, Collins characterized the audience as so excited to hear the tales of these returning heroes that the room is filled past its capacity, with the alliterative *incrementum* of "sat, stood, or sprawled" creating an image of listeners so eager to come close to greatness that they fill every space available in the lecture hall. Notice also the correctio at the beginning of the fourth sentence of this passage, in which the immediacy of this "moment" is transformed into the more expansive impression of the historic "time" in which we live, a time when the majority of the human genome sequence "looms into view" like the vast expanse of the Pacific Ocean sighted at long last by frontier explorers.

The only critique Collins offered of the Lewis and Clark analogy was that the historic import of that earlier frontier survey was not sufficient to capture the significance of this one. As Collins said in a 1998 interview, it is his belief that the Human Genome Project is not only greater than Lewis and Clark's journey, it is "more significant than even splitting the atom or going to the moon," and he is fortunate to have had the "chance to stand at the helm" of this "most significant undertaking that we have mounted so far in an organized way in all of science," this "adventure into ourselves."[12] Comparing the triumph of the Human Genome Project at the turn of the twenty-first century to an earlier era of frontier exploration, his 2010 book proclaims, "We had climbed to the top of one big mountain, and we were about to start rushing down the other side, into a valley full of potential discoveries."[13] As frontier heroes, genomic scientists had accomplished the most difficult of ascents and were ready to scramble down to the fertile plain to reap the rewards of their effort.

Other speeches that Collins has given over the years celebrate genome scientists who have been "working at the frontiers for many years" to "narrow the hunt for genes" and produce maps and atlases of what they find, scientists who undertake "trailblazing research" as they "continue to forge ahead into new frontiers of biomedical research."[14] This type of language is not unusual in public discourse about genomic science. One study of the metaphors used by scientists to promote the Human Genome Project predicted a shift in imagery after the 2000 White House announcement, from "a wilderness to be conquered by genomic settlers" to a landscape undergoing development, as suggested by a 2003 essay where Collins used an architectural metaphor to describe the future of genomic research.[15] However, further analysis of that 2003 essay by Collins demonstrated to the authors of that metaphor study that, counter to their expectations, "the metaphorical foundations of genomics were not seriously shaken between 2000 and 2003"; in fact, the landscape vista that Collins envisioned in his 2003 essay continued to promote "metaphors of science as an adventurous journey, in which scientists venture forth onto a new 'plain.'"[16]

Mapping metaphors like the ones employed by Collins are also common in public discourse about genetics, contributing to the broader frontier of science metaphor that guides our thinking about this subject. Two years before that "first survey" was declared complete in a White House ceremony, media studies scholar José van Dijck observed that the mapping language of the Human Genome Project lends itself particularly well to frontier language, with nonfiction popular books about the research replete with analogies to Columbus, Balboa, and Lewis and Clark. As she put it, "genomics seems to revive old colonialist notions of discovery and conquest. The 'discoveries' of America or the American West are presented not as an interpretation of history, but as uncontroversial historical facts. By means of analogy, the basic benevolence and economic pay-off of neo-colonialist expeditions is projected onto the 'genetic frontier.' The neo-colonialist myth is remarkably similar to the old, as the need to discover and own dark continents is presented as a 'natural' impulse."[17]

Science studies scholar Alice Domurat Dreger made a similar point in her study of the language that proponents of the Human Genome Project used in the late 1980s and early 1990s to win moral and financial support from Congress and the lay public. She found that the most common trope employed was the "genetic frontier," a metaphor that "situated the Project rhetorically as part of the great American tradition of manifest destiny; it made the project 'American' in style and gave Congress an imperative to beat other nations." Scientists effectively argued that the Human Genome Project "was simply part of the great American tradition of bold exploration and settlement." In addition to seizing the lay imagination with "the excitement of the journey to map a new land," this metaphoric construction allowed "Project scientists to argue for their freedom as paradigmatic brave American 'pioneers' to journey out and 'map' the 'genetic frontier.'" Unfortunately, it also carried the implication that the genome was something to own, "a prized commodity—real estate." It was not long before both individuals and organizations "sought the deed to the land they claimed to have found, a deed in the name of their nations or in their own name," and other nations began to "question the imperialism of the U.S. in the land of the genome."[18]

In 1995, feminist rhetoricians Mary Rosner and T. R. Johnson pointed out that metaphors associated with the Human Genome Project "invariably cast the researcher as one who dominates and exploits the Other." Genome mapping metaphors that envision nature as unexplored territory, and scientist as explorer, frame the enterprise as one of conquering and controlling mysterious lands. "Like imperialist maps, these genome maps are claims to ownership, not only of the specific sites of genes that scientists have identified (with fortunes that can come from patents) but also of the power and status associated with making sense of what has been unknown, with imposing order on chaos."[19]

A closer look at how Collins used the map metaphor in his 2000 White House speech, and at some of the scholarship that analyzes both his speech and the media response to it, reveals the significance of this particular treatment of genome science as a frontier mapping expedition. In short, his use of the frontier map metaphor carries all the troubling entailments that scholars identified in earlier examples of public discourse about the Human Genome Project. Collins not only configures the scientific enterprise as an adventurous journey but also imagines the human body as a wilderness territory, a shared inheritance that scientists have a manifest destiny to survey and exploit, a territory that explorers from different nations or in different research teams must race each other to occupy and thus claim as their own. This set of associated commonplaces works against the presumed purpose that called forth the speech, undermining Collins's attempt to portray science as an international cooperative endeavor that disregards economic self-interest to serve the needs of all.

Manifest Destiny

As the philosopher of science Hub Zwart concluded in his close reading of the metaphors that "enter[ed] and exeunt[ed] the East Room stage" in that 2000 ceremony, "the dominant metaphor that won the day . . . was the *map* metaphor." Clinton's speech might have introduced the image of the frontier map with its extended Lewis and Clark analogy, but the speech that Collins made offered a significant elaboration on the trope when it established that the map was the result of a voyage *into ourselves*.[20]

> Science is a voyage of exploration into the unknown. We are here today
> to celebrate a milestone along a truly unprecedented voyage, this one into

ourselves. Alexander Pope wrote, "Know then thyself. Presume not God to scan. The proper study of mankind is man." What more powerful form of study of mankind could there be than to read our own instruction book? . . . Today, we celebrate the revelation of the first draft of the human book of life.[21]

By making the tenor of the genomic voyage metaphor explicit—that is, by pointing out that the genetic material in the human body explored by genome scientists is the analog to the literal frontier territory explored by Lewis and Clark—this text draws the critical thinker's attention to a disturbing associated commonplace. We are uncomfortable thinking about ourselves, our physical interiors, as territory that can be penetrated, conquered, claimed, or mined by explorers, as was done with literal frontier land. Yet this is exactly what the genome-as-frontier-territory metaphor implies.

Of course, most audiences were unlikely to recognize this implication, at least on a conscious level. One study of the White House speeches and their aftermath pointed out that "the rhetorical strategies adopted by the politicians and scientists involved in the announcement" tended to suppress such upsetting thoughts by evoking the discourse of promise rather than the discourse of concern. The speakers urged audiences to imagine the future "eradication of illnesses and diseases such as cancer, heart disease, sickle cell anaemia and other physical and mental health problems."[22] With this utopian vision, the manifest destiny of the American frontiersman was effectively transferred to genomic scientists, whose heroic ability to improve the territory of the human body seemed to give them a divine right to enter and create order out of that chaotic wilderness.

For those who harbored a concern that genomic science might tamper with God's creation, the manifest destiny association could dampen that apprehension. Scholarly reflection on the genomic frontier metaphor shows that for the theologically inclined, it encourages the perception of genomic science "as the fulfilment of Divine Purpose, another way of marvelling at the Creator's skills."[23] The metaphor of genome as instruction book that ends this passage from Collins helps to promote that perspective. On its own, the "instruction book" vehicle can be seen as part of a cluster of informational metaphors that compare the genome to text, language, or code, a completely different set of metaphors than the mapping, surveying, and exploring cluster of metaphors.[24] But in the context of Collins's refiguring of the human body ("ourselves") as a frontier wilderness territory, the demand to study humankind by reading our instruction book has a more complicated layer of meaning as well. Clinton's speech earlier that morning introduced an analogy between Galileo, who had, upon understanding celestial mechanics, "learned the language in which God created the universe," and genome scientists today, who are "learning the language in which God created life."[25] With the reference to Alexander Pope bringing to mind the natural theology of that era, in which scientists sought to comprehend the magnificence of God's creation not just by studying the book of God (the Bible) but by studying the book of nature (a metaphor for the natural world) as well, one might view the "instruction book" metaphor that Collins uses here as an extension of his comparison of "ourselves" to frontier territory. He seems to be suggesting that the inner territory of the body *is* the book of nature, a metaphoric book of life written in God's language that scientists are morally obliged to explore, just as earlier naturalists were obliged to explore an exotic wilderness that told the story of God's magnificence.[26]

Collins supported this interpretation later in his speech when he admitted that it "is humbling for me and awe-inspiring to realize that we have caught the first glimpse of our own instruction book, previously known only to God."[27] The worldview being promoted here tasks genomic explorers with the modern version of natural theology. As Collins elaborated a few years later when writing about his religious beliefs, the "elegance behind life's complexity is indeed reason for awe, and for belief in God," but not in the simplistic way that William Paley argued for intelligent design in the natural theology of an earlier era. "To examine the complexity of life and our own origins on this planet, we must dig deep into the fascinating revelations about the nature of living things wrought by the current revolution in paleontology, molecular biology, and genomics. . . . If God is truly Almighty, He will hardly be threatened by our puny efforts to understand the workings of His natural world."[28] According to Collins, the genome that exists inside the human body is the natural world that modern scientists on the frontiers of knowledge must explore, the book of nature that they must read, to reveal the truly awe-inspiring wonders of God's creation.

In the context of the American frontier myth that frames the White House speech in June 2000, one might conclude that modern genome scientists have two divine purposes—a duty to read the book of ourselves (the inner territory of our bodies) to reveal the glory of God's natural world, and a manifest destiny to explore, map, and settle this genomic territory to eliminate disease and create order. What seemed on first glance to be the two very different metaphoric vehicles of book and territory turn out, in the context of the specific case, to resolve into a single image, a mixing of metaphors that refracts the book of life through the territory of the human body to create a new figurative space for scientists to explore.[29]

A Race for Ownership of Genomic Property

Another entailment of the genomic map metaphor used by Collins that might be troubling upon closer reflection is the claim to ownership of the body-as-territory that the comparison implies. As the philosopher of science Cor van der Weele put it, "the Lewis and Clark map was very much about the ownership of the land, and the introduction of the human genome map took place in a similar property-oriented atmosphere."[30] Recall that Collins saw his purpose in this speech to be to convey to the public the image of scientists from multiple nations and from both publicly funded and privately funded ventures working together without rancor to create new knowledge that would then be shared by all of humankind. He wanted to disabuse the public of the unseemly notion that genomic scientists were engaged in a patent gold rush.

In that context, the trope of the frontier survey in these speeches was especially counterproductive. One scholar examining the impact of this East Room media event pointed out that the use of the map metaphor in these speeches is evidence of an orientation that makes "a distribution of the promised genomic land through patents possible."[31] Another scholar elaborated on this point, reminding us that the "map-making endeavour of Lewis and Clark was a gesture claiming ownership. . . . Therefore, the conscious and deliberate decision, on June 26, 2000, to present the human genome sequence as a revivification of the Lewis and Clark map, a map that was as notorious as it was famous, was a rather telling and problematic decision, a remarkable gesture. . . . What kind of practices would be supported and made possible by this new 'map'? Was a second gold rush awaiting us?"[32] To this scholar, the links seemed inevitable between making maps in a voyage of discovery and using those maps to support ownership claims, then mining that territory for the riches to be found there.

In his East Room speech, Collins hinted at the starkly competitive atmosphere in which scientists were operating when he identified those working on the project as having "entered the fray." When he announced, as a transition to his introduction of Venter's speech, how happy he was "that today, the only race we are talking about is the human race," the tension between his publicly funded project and the privately funded Celera team rested just below the surface, held in check only by the truce of a joint announcement to share this claim to the (near) completion of the first survey of the entire human genome.[33]

Scholars who examined the media response to the White House announcement found that the desirability of owning profitable genomic territory is a theme that many took from the event. For example, "the charting of an unknown territory, which will lead to the discovery of treasure, is an image triggered by many of the metaphorical expressions employed by Greek journalists" who reported on the media event, including the comparison of genomic knowledge to "a gold mine."[34] Press coverage in the United Kingdom also spun the territorial metaphor in economic directions, describing the genome as "a human goldmine" and the "gene frontier" as a place where profits must not be outlawed and where competing scientists fight with each other for ownership of valuable territory.[35] In German press reports, the White House map metaphor "leads to associations with the conquest of the West and the drawing up of the map of America two hundred years before," but journalists also drew associations that resonated with their own country's imperialist experiences. A German news report six months after the White House press conference talked about the "conquest in the genome desert," a particular "fight" to sequence one human chromosome that "Germany won this time."[36]

The genomic frontier metaphor thus worked against the putative goals of the media event. Each of the speakers in the East Room that morning praised the collaboration that occurred between scientists from different nations as well as the cooperative efforts of the publicly funded and privately funded scientific research teams. Some of the speakers repeated this point several times. In fact, the whole event was "substantially a device for avoiding the production of a 'winner' and a 'loser'" from the competition between scientists in different countries and from different organizations.[37] It was meant to be a celebration of mutual action, a ceremony signaling the praiseworthy scientific sharing of resources and credit. Yet the characterization of the genome as frontier territory to be mapped by scientist-explorers worked against this purpose, implying that genomic territory was property that could be surveyed as part of staking a claim and then extracting profitable materials from it. Winners and losers are implicit in this metaphoric terminology, so it is no surprise that journalists who reported on the speeches continued to tell the story of a competitive race to claim profitable territory, rather than just dutifully repeating the explicit paeans to scientific cooperation that the speakers offered that day.

Genomic Territory as Federal Property

Ironically, at the same time that the notion of genomic research as a frontier mapping expedition directs our attention toward a competition between scientists who discover and lay claim to the inner territory of our bodies, it operates under an assumption that ownership of that territory cannot be claimed by the individuals or groups who physically possess it. Recall that the Lewis and Clark map was "a first decisive step toward the colonization and usurpation of the North-West *territories* by the eastern *States*, not least by presenting the landscape as if it were uninhabited and unclaimed (virgin territory)."[38] Under the terministic screen of the genomic frontier, scientists are the explorers discovering and claiming genomic territory, and the rights of the people whose genomes are being studied become as invisible as the rights of American Indians were to those Euro-Americans who staked claim to the Northwest territories. Groups of people whose bodies contain specific genomic sequences are imagined to hold no significant ownership claim to that genomic territory, in the minds of the scientists engaged in mapping it.

This implication is revealed by Collins's statement at the White House media event that "the human genome is our shared inheritance."[39] Like the Louisiana Purchase being mapped by Lewis and Clark, it is territory held in common for the citizens of the nation by the federal government, which operates as a legal entity with the power to give out deeds to portions of that territory that it believes will be improved by pioneers who have the courage and fortitude to stake a claim to it. Clinton made this association possible with his introduction of the Lewis and Clark analogy. Prime Minister Tony Blair of England seconded it with his speech that celebrated this breakthrough of progress "across a frontier and into a new era" where "the common property of the human genome" is being explored.[40] Craig Venter agreed with this vision of the human genome, calling for "the wise use of our common heritage" and imagining a future "in our lifetimes" where the efforts of genomic scientists to improve genomic territory would result in no one dying of cancer anymore.[41] The idea that the entire complement of human genes is property held in common, not owned by the individuals or groups of people who possess the specific genetic variants being studied, and yet still subject to being claimed through the patents of pioneering scientists, is a strange idea made to seem reasonable through the frontier metaphor.

Of course, for those who think about the fact that the territory being explored is *ourselves*, and for those who recall the history of forced migration of indigenous people, which operated on the belief that a territory is not owned by the people who possess it but by a government holding it in trust for its citizens and parceling it out to pioneers and developers, there is something particularly unsettling about the genomic-as-frontier-territory metaphor. In fact, by 2000, the most serious public critique of genomic science had come from indigenous communities who "were able to mount some very effective campaigns" against a research effort known as the Human Genome Diversity Project (HGDP), a proposal that would extend the Human Genome Project by sequencing the genomes of American Indians and other so-called vanishing populations.[42]

Critics of the HGDP identified it as nothing short of biological imperialism and demanded "an immediate moratorium on collections and/or patenting of genetic materials from indigenous persons and communities."[43] As Leota Lone Dog put it, "A new frontier is developing in the medical community at the expense of indigenous people," indigenous populations that "have been continually exploited in the name of progress."[44] Indigenous critics of the HGDP argued that this scientific research "will enable prospectors to stake legal claims on the natural genetic resource base of Indigenous peoples."[45] Gene patents would take the place of land deeds, but the territory would similarly be "considered vacant and therefore open to exploitation" by those who have formal structures for ownership and improvement of the property

in question, property that in this case is the internal genetic complement of human bodies.[46] In short, critics feared that with the "promise
of profits in the genetic resources of our bodies," the shameful history
of colonizers exploiting the resources of indigenous people would be
repeated.[47] In an American context where the government continues
to drag its feet about repatriating the remains of American Indians on
display in national museums, the notion that biological resources might
be removed from indigenous peoples and exploited by scientists is not
difficult to entertain.[48]

The criticism of the HGDP by Native activists was powerful, and
ultimately successful. By the time scientists and politicians gathered
to celebrate the (near) completion of the first survey of the entire
human genome, the HGDP was struggling for survival.[49] Not long after,
it would lose that struggle. By refusing to participate in the studies,
and publicly critiquing the project with terms like "biocolonialism" and
"biopiracy," indigenous critics of the HGDP managed to effectively shut
down this line of scientific research. As a result of their criticism, the
United Nations refused to endorse the project, the National Research
Council produced a report that questioned the project's planning and
ethics, and funding agencies that had previously been interested in the
HGDP backed away.[50]

In June 2000, the Human Genome Project was not explicitly linked
to the HGDP and its troubles by the speakers at the White House celebration. According to science studies scholar Jenny Reardon, as soon
as the HGDP became mired in controversy, "US government administra-
tors of human genome research made every effort to distance themselves
from it."[51] But where an explicit connection between the Human Genome
Project and the HGDP was lacking, implicit links were made in the frontier map-making imagery of the White House media event. In the context
of indigenous critiques of biocolonialism that were powerful enough to
result in the abandonment of a line of research (the HGDP), a set of
speeches that imagines genomes as common property to be explored
and cataloged by government and industry agents seems particularly
shortsighted. Whether the subject of future genomic research was to be
a "vanishing" indigenous community, a group of people with a so-called
disability, or an individual with a genetic variant that holds promise in
the war on cancer, the metaphor of the genome as frontier territory carries the implication that scientists, not the humans who possess those
genomes, will own the genetic material discovered there. For public

critics of genomic science, the rhetorical resources to characterize such research as yet another form of colonialism in a purportedly postcolonial world is readily available in the frontier language used by scientists like Collins.

Limited Retraction of a Metaphor

The troubling implications of the frontier map metaphor in the White House media event were considerable; through this metaphor, scientists embraced their manifest destiny to explore, claim, and exploit the human body as if it were a wilderness territory. Given those implications, and the continued appearance of frontier metaphors in the subsequent discourse of Collins, one text of his stands out as an anomaly worthy of further study. Five years after the White House media event, in a *Seattle Times* opinion editorial, Collins offered a slightly more nuanced treatment of the relationship between genomics research and the frontier metaphor.[52]

A rhetorical critic would not suspect that anything different was going to be said in this text by looking only at its title or its accompanying illustration. "Exploring the Frontiers of Life: Northwest at the Forefront of Pioneering Effort to Mine the Secrets of the Human Genome" starts with two columns of text framing the sketch of an oversized DNA double-helix, which tiny explorers carrying backpacks are using ropes to climb. As one might expect from the headline and Collins's previous rhetorical choices, the essay begins with the triumphalism of the frontier of science metaphor. The central theme of the introduction is a positive analogy between "the Lewis and Clark Expedition" and the "pioneering work" of genomic scientists; the essay references and repeats the analogy that Clinton had used five years earlier in the White House ceremony and celebrates current efforts to "mine the genome's freely available information."[53]

But then, about halfway through the essay, Collins stepped back from his typical rhetoric to briefly acknowledge that we also "need to learn a lesson from an aspect of the Lewis and Clark expedition that did not go so well." Recognizing that the land that Lewis and Clark opened and that the pioneers settled "was not vacant," because "American Indians already lived throughout the region," Collins expressed regret that "when the white settlers came" to the Northwest, "many indigenous peoples were pushed aside." He said: "We must ensure that we do not push anyone aside as genomic exploration proceeds. We need to make sure that unjust actions, such as those inflicted upon the American Indians 200 years ago, are not repeated as we strive to build a new life in this rapidly expanding genomic frontier."[54]

The fact that Collins acknowledged in this essay that there is something troubling about his use of the genomic frontier metaphor is remarkable. The significance of this statement retracting the frontier imagery was emphasized by the editors of the newspaper, who repeated it as a pull-out quote on the second page of the essay. This critical statement seems to reflect a postcolonial ambivalence with the frontier myth in contemporary America, an attitude that was evident in the debate over the HGDP but lacking in most other public discourse concerning genomic research. Collins appeared here to be thoughtfully examining his own rhetoric and explicitly distancing himself from its most disturbing implications. Such a withdrawal from the American exceptionalism that typically accompanies the genomic frontier metaphor suggests that the meaning of the frontier myth is shifting as the nation's history is rewritten over time. It is no longer quite as easy to embrace the narrative of manifest destiny that is implied by the Lewis and Clark analogy since we know so much about how populations of people were "pushed aside" in the nation's frontier-conquering past.

However, a look at the rest of this essay by Collins shows that the shift in attitude only went so far. After setting out the problem created by efforts to model the current exploration of genomic frontiers after the actions of earlier frontiersmen (namely, pushing people aside, just like the white settlers "pushed aside" American Indians), Collins concluded his essay with a solution to this future injustice that completely missed the point of his own analogy. He went on to argue for legislation that protects the privacy of individuals who fear their genomic information will be used against them by insurers or employers. This is a laudable cause (achieved three years later when Congress passed, and President George W. Bush signed, the Genetic Information Nondiscrimination Act). But a moment's reflection reveals that this solution does nothing to address the issue of injustice to groups like American Indians that might result from a new eagerness to explore the genomic frontier. Instead, it is a solution to the *use* of genomic information *after* it is discovered by scientists. It does nothing to resolve the issue of who owns the genomic territory being explored by scientists or who should have a say over whether it should be explored. By 2005, the most serious criticism of genomic research had come from those who wanted some types of genomic exploration to *stop* because they did not accept the premise that their genomes should be thought of as common property open to mining by scientists or anyone else. These people were not primarily concerned with how genomic resources would be used against individuals by those who buy the goods carried out by the frontiersmen-scientists, like insurance companies or employers. They wanted something more fundamental; they wanted their genomic resources to be left alone by the scientists who are so eager to explore them.[55]

This failure on the part of Collins to fully digest the implications of an analogy that recommends restraint on scientific research is not unexpected. The philosopher of science Laurie Anne Whitt has pointed out that although the Human Genome Project had a critical component in its commitment to devote 3–5 percent of its budget to ethical, legal, and social issues (ELSI) research, the ELSI charge only specified that scholars should attend to the *consequences* of having increased ability to obtain genetic information on individuals. "The ethico-political question which ELSI was not charged with addressing is whether such knowledge should be produced in the first place."[56] According to rhetoricians Marouf Hasian and Emily Plec, when the HGDP was critiqued as a neocolonialist endeavor, the leader of the project replied that he "knew about the 'history of human destruction' that accompanied 'western colonialism,'" but he claimed that his project's goals were being misunderstood, and he insisted that there would be "no tolerance of the ideas of any moratoriums" on the research; the scientists simply "assumed the scientific and social legitimacy of their pursuits."[57] Reardon found a similar sentiment on the part of those who designed the subsequent HapMap project: "the possibility for critique was limited by the overarching assumption that the project would move forward in a form that matched the interests of the genome scientists who proposed it."[58]

In each of these cases, the logic of the frontier continues to guide the scientist's value system. Even when scientists begin to shy away from the more obvious negative connotations of the frontier metaphor, their discourse continues to be marked by the commodification of the natural world and a commitment to always pushing back the frontiers of science. Paying lip service to a critique of the frontier myth does not demonstrate that a scientist has truly learned "a lesson from an aspect of the Lewis and Clark expedition that did not go so well."[59] That lesson teaches that just as the land that Lewis and Clark opened "was not vacant," so too are genetic materials owned by the people whose bodies contain those materials, and treating genomes as valuable territory for scientist-explorers to survey in anticipation of frontier development continues to "push aside" those people and inflict "unjust actions" against them. Collins might have briefly pulled away from the rhetoric of the frontier metaphor, but he remained tied to the value system that accompanies the frontier mythos in American public life.

CHAPTER FIVE

Reframing the Frontier of Science: George W. Bush's Stem Cell Rhetoric

⌘

Like Francis Collins, President George W. Bush tried to pull away from the rhetorical force of the "frontier of science" metaphor when addressing an American audience about new and promising scientific research. But unlike Collins, Bush chose not to offer an explicit critique of the troubling implications of the metaphor. Instead, he chose other rhetorical strategies to subtly call into question the intrepid boundary-crossing that the myth promoted. Bush's attempt to pull away from the influence of this terministic screen was similar to Collins's in another respect though; it was not entirely successful.

In this chapter, I continue the project set out at the beginning of this book, to answer questions about the entailments of the frontier of science metaphor, its effects on the rhetors who use it, and efforts to counteract its influence. But this chapter is different from the others in one significant respect. In the preceding chapters, I focused for the most part on how the frontier of science metaphor is used in the public address of scientists. This chapter turns to an investigation of its use in the popular speeches of politicians. A study of presidential speeches from the twentieth century shows that the "frontier spirit" was a topos used by almost every modern American president to praise what they saw as an exceptional national character. Americans are consistently represented as having a driving force to move forward with courage as they strive to discover or make a better future for themselves, and the frontier of science metaphor is a trope that is often used by presidents to evoke this topos. In fact, language conflating promising new scientific research with an American pioneering ethos has become so ubiquitous that it is hard for presidents to avoid it when talking about science.

On August 9, 2001, George W. Bush demonstrated this point when he identified "human embryo stem cell research" as "the new frontier" in a widely viewed, nationally televised speech.[1] But this was the very same speech in which he announced a policy that would effectively halt American scientists who wanted to pursue such research, keeping them from "crossing a fundamental moral line."[2] How could a president use a metaphor that associates scientists with a praiseworthy American pioneering spirit in the same speech where he offers a justification for shutting off a promising new area of scientific research? To answer that question, in this chapter I undertake a close reading of Bush's speech and its reception history. Rhetorical analysis discloses how Bush reframed the frontier from a place of heroic American discovery into a place that should be avoided; Bush also created a productive ambiguity of meaning around a manufactured controversy to temporarily persuade an American audience to support his policy to close this new frontier of scientific research. The persuasive effect was fleeting though, as the identification of Americans with a heroic frontier spirit soon reasserted itself to counter Bush's rhetorical reframing.

To get a better sense for the performative tradition that Bush was attempting to counter, before analyzing the way he attempted to counter it, I begin this chapter with a closer look at the frontier of science metaphor in presidential speeches. Rhetoricians have produced a great deal of research on presidential uses of the frontier myth, detailing the ways in which it has defined an exceptional American identity in administration arguments about such subjects as immigration, war, and space flight.[3] What is lacking in the existing scholarly literature is a sustained look at how presidents connect the myth to science. My analysis of presidential speeches shows that narratives attaching the frontier myth to the scientific profession are not always told in precisely the same way; different rhetors emphasize different aspects of the myth to support different political ends. But the broad frontier story persists. Almost all American presidents have used the frontier of science metaphor to create a positive association between the nation's scientists and its frontier heroes.

Prior Presidential Uses of the Frontier Metaphor for Science

Long before a figurative meaning that connected the term "frontier" to new scientific knowledge began appearing in American dictionaries in the 1940s and 1950s, the frontier of science metaphor had found its way into the speeches of American presidents. The first uses of this metaphor reflected an attempt to allay anxiety about America's future. Before long, the metaphor became a standard epideictic appeal, employed whenever the speaking occasion called for praise of American scientists, whether to honor specific individuals, to establish that a president's policies supported science and technology, or to make Americans feel good about themselves and their future. Elaborated with explicit comparisons between modern scientists and the frontier heroes of American history, the frontier of science metaphor was often linked to a mythic "frontier spirit" that established Americans as having a special identity. With the dawn of the space age, the frontier myth began appearing as part of a literal analogy between terrestrial and extraterrestrial exploration. But the metaphoric alignment of science and the frontier did not disappear with the rise of the moon and planets as a real "new frontier" for Americans to conquer. The frontier of science metaphor continued to be used, often in concert with references to the "frontier of space." With regard to both space exploration and scientific exploration, the frontier myth was deployed to favor those who are bold enough and strong enough to venture forth across boundaries in order to make discoveries that benefit them and the nation as a whole.

Responding to a Turnerian Anxiety

As early as 1928, President Calvin Coolidge used the frontier of science metaphor to counter any anxiety that might have followed Frederick Jackson Turner's thesis that the nation's character had been uniquely shaped by a wilderness frontier that no longer existed.[4] Rather than bemoan the loss of the frontier and voice dread about the diminution of character that was likely to accompany that loss, Coolidge argued that the American pioneering spirit continues to be strong as Americans venture forth into new metaphorical territories.

> One of the great sources of the strength of our country has been the pioneering spirit. It was characteristic of those who first settled on our shores and was the cause of a resistless march to the Pacific Ocean. Our people have ever been going forth into the forest and over the plain to establish themselves in the region of the unknown. They have sought for new fields to conquer. They have been pioneers, however, not only in the physical world, but in the realm of ideas. In science and invention, and especially in the art of government and of social relations, they have taken a dominant part. The frontier has long since disappeared, the opportunity for exploration into unfrequented lands is gone, we seek no additional territory, but the ambition to enter uncharted regions of industry, of enterprise, of social relations, and of thought continues with increasing fervor.[5]

As Turner hinted when he said the American spirit will *continually* demand a wider field for its exercise, and as Vannevar Bush would later argue with his notion of an *endless* scientific frontier, so too did Coolidge imagine a realm of ideas that, unlike the terrestrial realm, enjoys the virtue of being truly unending. In making his point about uncharted regions of thought, he drew on the argument from unlimited development to present the frontier of science as more filled with opportunity than the literal frontier had ever been.

Coolidge completed his reflection on the persistence of an American pioneering spirit in this speech with special praise for the consequences of that frontier attribute of unlimited opportunity, a characteristic of the nation that is treasured by its people because it allows them to escape the doctrine that "all persons were born to a certain station" that they must hold throughout their lives.[6] The 1928 outlet for ambitious young Americans might be "science and invention," rather than the western territories, but that metaphoric frontier promised to serve the same salubrious function for them and their nation as the literal one had.

Fellow Republican president Herbert Hoover used the same metaphor, a frontier of "science and invention," to attack the campaign rhetoric of his Democratic rival in the election of 1932.[7] Pointing to Franklin Delano Roosevelt's Commonwealth Club address of the previous month, Hoover interpreted its reference to the end of the frontier in America as nothing short of a "counsel of despair for the future of America."

> That is not the spirit by which we shall emerge from this depression. That is not the spirit which has made this country. If it is true, every American must abandon the road of countless progress and countless hopes and unlimited opportunity. I deny that the promise of American life has been fulfilled, for that means we have begun the decline and the fall. No nation can cease to move forward without a degenerating spirit.

According to Hoover, Roosevelt's pessimistic announcement about the end of the frontier failed to recognize that science is a new frontier that will revitalize the spirit of America. Extolling scientific "discoveries in electricity, the internal-combustion engine, the radio" as the "greatest advances made in America," Hoover predicted a bright future for the nation since "we are yet but on the frontiers of development of science and of invention."[8]

Three years later, President Roosevelt tried to wrest interpretive control of the frontier myth back from Hoover. The rhetorical critic Davis Houck has argued that the imagery of the frontier's closing had been inserted into Roosevelt's Commonwealth Club address by its primary authors, Adolf and Beatrice Berle, and that Roosevelt and his regular speechwriter, Raymond Moley, made a blunder by failing to excise it from the final draft of that speech.[9] Roosevelt would correct that rhetorical error in a radio address to America's young people in 1935. In this speech, he repeated his argument that "we can no longer escape into virgin territory," but this time he agreed with Hoover that there yet exists metaphoric territory for the American spirit to conquer. "The youth of this generation finds that the old frontier is occupied, but that science and invention and economic evolution have opened up a new frontier— one not based on geography but on the resourcefulness of men and women applied to the old frontier."[10] The same terms used by Hoover, a "new frontier" of "science and invention," were now being embraced by Roosevelt.

In this speech, Roosevelt made the same central argument as in his earlier Commonwealth Club address, that Americans needed a prudential modification of "the American spirit of individualism" to "adjust our ideas to the facts of today."[11] But this time, rather than countering the frontier myth, he voiced his approval of it, while carefully adjusting it to meet his own needs. Speaking out against "the Tories of the world" who are "united in standing still on the same old spot and, therefore, never run the danger of getting lost on divergent trails," Roosevelt encouraged the youth of America to avoid that danger themselves by working together to advance as a group upon the new frontier, always remembering that "the spirit of America is the spirit of inquiry."[12] Young American pioneers of science were thus placed in cooperative alignment with each other and set in opposition to the staid townsfolk whose conservative ways can be attributed to their fear of venturing out in new directions.

President Roosevelt and his speechwriters had learned their lesson well.[13] The frontier myth is an American commonplace that the nation's leaders are expected to embrace. Leroy Dorsey has identified other cases of presidents who, like Franklin Delano Roosevelt, effectively adjusted the frontier myth to support their policies, including Theodore Roosevelt's praise for the frontier's yeoman farmer rather than the trapper or miner in his public address supporting conservationism, and John F. Kennedy's reframing of frontier warriors as fighters of poverty and disease in speeches to promote the Peace Corps.[14] In all such successful cases, the frontier myth is enthusiastically intoned, while being subtly retuned to support the specific political arrangements required by the rhetors using it. This is equally true when a president is attaching the frontier myth to the metaphor of science. Whether it is used as Hoover did to praise the scientist-inventor as a rugged individualist with faith in unlimited opportunity for advancement or as FDR did to celebrate young scientists who demonstrate the helping-hand spirit of the wagon train united in pursuit of a common goal, the one universal is that an appeal to a mythic narrative of frontier advancement must be made. The frontier of science metaphor has become a convention through which American presidents are expected to show faith in the endurance of a pioneering spirit, patriotically insisting that the nation will always make forward progress toward a brighter future.

SPACE, THE (NOT SO) FINAL FRONTIER

Science was not the only new outlet for a pioneering American spirit. Space also came to fill this rhetorical niche for American presidents. But a close look at how space was set out as the final frontier for Americans to exercise their exceptional virtues shows that a metaphoric frontier of *science* was often intoned as a natural accompaniment to this rhetorical vision.

For example, John F. Kennedy recognized the rhetorical power of the frontier myth when he famously adopted the symbol of the "New Frontier" as the slogan for his administration. In his 1960 Democratic National Convention nomination acceptance speech, he described what he meant by the term. Reminding his West Coast audience that "the pioneers gave up their safety, their comfort and sometimes their lives to build our new West," Kennedy demonstrated his ability to meet the expectations for patriotic presidential oratory when he rejected those pessimists who "would say that those struggles are over, that all the horizons have been explored, that all the battles have been won, that there is no longer an American frontier." Kennedy countered such naysayers by introducing the frontier as a metaphor for "a set of challenges" that will take Americans to "uncharted areas of science and space."[15]

His naming of two alliterative frontier areas in this speech was significant. He envisioned America's new heroes conquering both real and figurative frontiers to achieve a future that would bring us breakthroughs in "a race for mastery of the sky and the rain, the ocean and the tides, the far side of space and the inside of men's minds."[16] Notice how each couplet of terrains breached in this "race for mastery" includes first a literal spatial territory that is being explored (the sky, the ocean, the far side of space) and then a subject of scientific research that promises a technology of control (of the rain, the tides, and the inside of men's minds). This melding of literal spatial frontiers with metaphorical scientific ones is characteristic of Kennedy's rhetoric, and key to understanding the power of his "New Frontier" theme.

According to rhetorical critic James L. Kauffman, Kennedy's presidential administration skillfully depicted the space program with a frontier narrative because that made it impossible for critics to refute him; such critics "did not wish to suffer the adverse political consequences of maligning such a nationalistic, patriotic story."[17] This is an important point that helps to demonstrate the power of the frontier myth for American presidential address. What Kauffman does not note though, but is equally important, is that the *literal* analogy Kennedy established between old frontier narratives and the new frontier adventure of a manned mission to the moon was being rhetorically linked to a *figurative* analogy between frontier exploration and scientific discovery.

As Kennedy told a Houston, Texas, audience in his Rice University speech on the space program in 1962, their location, which "was once the furthest outpost on the old frontier of the West, will be the furthest outpost on the new frontier of science and space." Once again, the alliterative naming of both metaphoric and spatial frontiers signals that the development of "space science" is a primary goal of this great adventure. As rhetorical critic John Jordan established in his close reading of this speech, Kennedy invited his audience to view themselves as "a unique blend of frontier adventurer and scientist."[18] A broad frontier of science metaphor was developed in this speech with an allusion to the Age of Exploration: "We set sail on this new sea because there is new knowledge to be gained, and new rights to be won." A Cold War competitive impulse is evident here; the literal new frontier of space promises the traditional reward that awaits any explorer: "new rights to be won" as the nation plants its flag on land that it reaches before its rivals do. But the way the speech phrases its announcement of this new journey also suggests that a metaphoric new frontier *of science* promises that is just as lucrative as those land rights in the long run: "new knowledge to be gained" through scientific inquiry into "the vast stretches of the unknown and the unanswered and the unfinished."[19] Such scientific knowledge is what would presumably supply the rich resource flow back from the frontier that an advance into new territory has always promised the nation supporting such a venture.

Other presidents would imitate Kennedy's alignment of literal spatial frontiers and metaphoric scientific frontiers. In a speech at the dedication ceremony for the National Air and Space Museum, President Gerald Ford described a progression of frontiers that have "shaped and molded our society and our people." He claimed that the American spirit of adventure pushes always across the edge of the unknown, "across the oceans, across the continent, across the solar system, across the frontiers of science, beyond the boundaries of the human mind."[20] The metaphoric "frontiers of science" coming at the end of this anaphoric sequence is the one item in the list that warrants elaboration ("beyond the boundaries of the human mind") and the only true provider of boundless opportunity, the epitome of frontier expansiveness that fulfills the American Dream of unlimited development. President George H. W. Bush made a similar appeal when he placed space exploration along a continuum of eternal voyages for Americans, with high-energy physics as the metaphorical new frontier for his time: "Centuries after Columbus set sail, our forebears tread this soil in wagon trains, and two centuries after that, scientists at Johnson Space Center watched as brave Americans set sail for the stars. Today, new frontiers beckon; new discoveries await; new progress lies before us. . . . Our vessel is not called Santa Maria, it is the super collider."[21] Once again, an American president set out a metaphorical voyage to unexplored fields of science as the culmination of American progress. In presidential rhetoric, it is part of the American's national character to make that unending push forward across the current boundaries of scientific knowledge.

After Kennedy, perhaps the most eloquent narrator of the frontier myth in presidential rhetoric was President Ronald Reagan, who likewise aligned space and science as literal and metaphoric frontiers. We can see this in the speeches he gave eulogizing the *Challenger* space shuttle crew. Mary Stuckey's rhetorical analysis of Reagan's speech to the nation on the day of the *Challenger* explosion identified the frontier myth as central to its power, a theme that worked well for both occasion and purpose, and perfectly fit the speaker's personal style.[22] In that speech, Reagan memorably identified the astronauts as "pioneers" whose dedication to "expanding man's horizons" was as complete as that of "the great explorer Sir Francis Drake." As Reagan explained, the brave souls who crewed this modern voyage had "a special spirit," "a hunger to explore the universe and discover its truths." Devoted to "exploration and discovery," they were "pulling us into the future."[23] This link between exploration and discovery of the universe's truths hinted toward a connection between space and science, a connection that would be repeated in Reagan's longer speech at the memorial service three days later.

In that later speech, he again summoned the frontier spirit when he called forth the image of "the pioneers of an earlier century, the sturdy souls who took their families and their belongings and set out into the frontier of the American West. Often they met with terrible hardship. Along the Oregon Trail, you could still see the grave markers of those who fell on the way, but grief only steeled them to the journey ahead." After setting out this frontier narrative, Reagan offered a comparison in both literal and figurative directions. "Today the frontier is space and the boundaries of human knowledge."[24] Because the frontier of science had already become such a powerful and ubiquitous trope in American presidential speech, the final frontier of space would become, for Reagan, only the final literal voyage in America's eternal scientific journey across the metaphoric boundaries of human knowledge.

Shared in all of these presidential expressions of America's frontier spirit is a patriotic commitment to envisioning the nation as moving forward, always progressing across scientific boundaries toward a brighter future. As President Dwight D. Eisenhower put it in a 1956 speech, the American character is unique in being "able to look upon change, the ever-unfolding future, with confidence rather than doubt, hope rather than fear. We, as a people, were born of revolution. And we have lived by change—always a frontier people, exploring—if not new wilderness— then new science and new knowledge."[25] In a speech twenty years later, President Ford voiced the same theme, telling Americans that the "frontier shaped and molded our society and our people," developing in us a "spirit of adventure" that drives us now to "find out even more about the forces of nature, how to harness them, preserve them"; America is "a place where men and women try the untried, test the impossible, and take uncertain paths unto the unknown."[26] A little more than two decades later, President Clinton repeated this refrain in arguing that Americans must not "step off the path to progress and scientific research" since the nation was "built by bold, restless, searching people. We have always sought new frontiers. The spirit of America is, in that sense, truly the spirit of scientific inquiry."[27] In each of these speeches, a praiseworthy American frontier ethos is patriotically connected to the forward movement of the nation's scientists across existing boundaries of knowledge.

For over seventy years, from Coolidge to Clinton, American presidents insisted that it is a national duty for citizens to face the future with hope and courage as they venture across the frontiers of science. In this context, how can a president make a case for slowing down or even stopping the forward momentum of Americans across the latest frontier of science? President George W. Bush did just that with his August 9, 2001, speech on human embryonic stem cell research. A close reading of the speech in which he first drew "a fundamental moral line" across which American scientists were not to trespass shows both the power of the frontier metaphor and the rhetorical strategies that a rhetor can deploy in an effort to counter that power.

George W. Bush's Stem Cell Speech of August 9, 2001

A review of George W. Bush's presidential speaking career establishes that he was familiar with the frontier of science metaphor, and often used it in predictable ways. In a speech honoring recipients of the National Medals of Science and Technology, Bush lauded "America's spirit of innovation" and identified the scientists being celebrated on that day as "pioneers" who have "the same passion for discovery that drove Lewis and Clark."[28] In a speech confirming his support for expanded investment in basic scientific research, Bush promised to fund "our Nation's most creative minds as they explore new frontiers in nanotechnology or supercomputing or alternative energy sources."[29] In a speech reassuring Americans that their economy would remain strong, Bush offered the evidence that "our scientists continue to push forward the frontiers of technology and science."[30] In these speeches, Bush used the frontier of science metaphor in all of the ways it is typically used in presidential speech: to honor praiseworthy scientists, to establish that the administration's policies support science and technology, and to make an audience of Americans feel good about themselves and confident about their future. That he used it in each of these ways is a testament to the lasting strength of this modern topos in American presidential rhetoric.

It should come as no surprise that in the speech where he first announced his policy on stem cell research, he also used the frontier of science metaphor, declaring that "the genius of science extends the horizons of what we can do," and identifying human embryonic stem cell research as "the new frontier."[31] But a close reading of this speech reveals something different about his use of the metaphor here; the image that we might expect of a heroic pioneer moving toward a horizon of promise was replaced with the image of an evil genius entering a blighted zone. Bush never directly countered the traditional American frontier topos in this speech, but he subtly reframed the frontier from a place of hope and glory to a place that should be avoided. Unlike Roosevelt's adjustment of the frontier myth to emphasize one characteristic (wagon train cooperativeness) over another (rugged individualism),

Bush actually transformed the frontier itself from a place that heroic Americans are expected to enter into an undesirable space that lies beyond a border that should remain closed.

IMMEDIATE CONTEXT OF BUSH'S STEM CELL POLICY SPEECH

To understand Bush's speech and how it accomplished this transformation, it is necessary to briefly review the legal and political context in which it was inserted. The history of federal funding for embryonic stem cell research in the United States is part of this context.[32] In the 104th U.S. Congress, with a Republican majority in both houses, a rider that came to be known as the Dickey-Wicker Amendment was added to the 1996 budget bill that funds the National Institutes of Health (NIH); it prohibited federal funding of research that creates, destroys, or knowingly risks the destruction of human embryos. Congress included the same rider in each subsequent budget bill for the NIH, so that when stem cells were first isolated from human embryos at the University of Wisconsin in February 1998, it was with research that had not been federally funded. But once that research made studies of human embryonic stem cell lines possible for scientists, intense interest in the promise of the research inspired the general counsel of the Department of Health and Human Services to interpret the Dickey-Wicker Amendment as only prohibiting federal funding for the *derivation* of human embryonic stem cells; federal funding for research that used cell lines that had already been produced through privately funded research would be allowed. As President Clinton explained to the press, "the potentially staggering benefits of this research," which promises cures for "everything from birth defects to Parkinson's to Alzheimer's to diabetes . . . to certain kinds of cancers, spinal cord injuries, burns," creates an imperative for federally supported research. According to Clinton, "we cannot walk away from the potential" that has been opened by this breakthrough in the development of human embryonic stem cell lines.[33]

The NIH took pains to create ethical guidelines to accommodate this new reading of the law; they stipulated that federally funded research on embryonic stem cell lines could use only those cell lines developed from excess frozen embryos that had been donated from fertility clinics after a rigorous process of informed consent.[34] But before any funding could be awarded under these new guidelines, a change in presidential administration resulted in a moratorium on the grant application process. For several months after President George W. Bush took office, the prospect of funding for this research was in limbo as scientists waited to learn what the new administration's policy would be. Afraid that the new pro-life president would bring embryonic stem cell science to a standstill just after a "significant milestone" had been reached, eighty Nobel Laureates signed a letter urging him to retain the newly developed NIH guidelines so that this new area of research could move forward.[35]

Rhetorical critic John Lynch, who has written an extended analysis of Bush's stem cell speech, has argued that in addition to knowing the history of federal funding for research on early embryos, another important factor that should be considered in the immediate context for this August 9, 2001, speech was the political exigence faced by the early Bush administration. Having lost the popular vote in the presidential election, Bush faced a divided nation. The president also struggled with the damaging perception that he lacked the intellectual ability to handle the complex issues that he would face in office. Some of the spin produced by administration sources prior to the speech indicates that this was on their minds, as they were quick to emphasize the care that the president was taking to research the complexity of the issue with various experts before reaching a decision.[36]

However, given the administration's motivation to emphasize the president's participation in intellectually sophisticated meetings where he was deliberating with eminent specialists, it is interesting that the public relations campaign designed by Bush adviser Karen Hughes for the days immediately preceding the speech positioned the president with an entirely different image, making him out instead to be a solitary cowboy doing manual labor on the edges of civilization. Hughes was a primary author of Bush's stem cell policy speech, writing it with the help of policy expert Jay Lefkowitz and the president himself.[37] According to administration insider David Frum, Hughes also took charge of shaping the president's public image immediately prior to his delivery of the speech, crafting the president's August vacation to Texas as a carefully orchestrated photo op. "Hughes called it a 'Home to the Heartland' tour," and "released White House photographs of Bush striding the range like the Marlboro Man: clearing brush in the early morning hours."[38]

This PR campaign was yet another sign of the power of the frontier of science metaphor. Anticipating a need to remind Americans that

President George W. Bush shared the values of the American pioneer even as he effectively closed off a frontier of research, Hughes had Bush perform that role on his Crawford, Texas, ranch for maximum visual impact in the media. She also selected the ranch as the setting for his first prime-time national address, a speech in which Bush would overturn the NIH guidelines and create a new policy that would confine federal funding for embryonic stem cell research to a narrow strip of frontier that had already been developed. Bush's new policy restricted federal funding of embryonic stem cell research to those cell lines that were already existent on the day he gave his speech.

REFRAMING THE FRONTIER

In the shadow of over seventy years of presidential speechmaking that celebrated scientists for tirelessly crossing the frontiers of knowledge, Bush's preemptive performance of a pioneering attitude on the Texas range would not be enough, on its own, to counterbalance the seemingly un-American act of drawing a borderline across which federally funded scientists would be forbidden to advance. All that his Marlboro Man routine did was set the stage for the speech to come, assuring Americans that his rhetorical approach would not be to directly counter the frontier myth.

This was not a foregone conclusion. In fact, an explicit critical repudiation of the frontier myth might have been a logical strategy to adopt in this situation. As Francis Collins did in the op-ed essay that I analyzed in the previous chapter, Bush might have reminded Americans that their unchecked forays onto the western frontier resulted in the massacre of countless American Indians, a result that is now recognized as an ethical outrage. The parallel would have been especially apt in this case because Bush was seeking protection for embryos, which he considers a group of people with moral and legal rights that are not being recognized, just as American Indians had moral and legal rights that were overlooked by frontier explorers.

However, what might work fairly well analogically does not necessarily work psychologically in this situation. Rhetoricians Mark West and Chris Carey have argued that the Bush White House was particularly fond of Old West tropes; in fact, compared to other American presidents, "the tactical narration of frontier rhetoric in the Bush administration's parlance far outstrips that of its predecessors."[39] Perhaps because of this fondness for the American frontier myth, the authors of Bush's stem cell policy speech chose not to explicitly counter the convention of appealing to it. Instead, this speech took a less direct approach to calling the frontier-expanding ways of American scientists into question. On August 9, 2001, Bush subtly reframed the frontier of science so it would be seen as an undesirable place to enter.

One way he did this was by using a competing metaphor. In the middle of the speech, he announced: "As the discoveries of modern science create tremendous hope, they also lay vast ethical minefields." Here the frontier that comes into view is not the wild American West, but the mined front of a foreign war between two bordering nations. "Embryonic stem cell research is at the leading edge of a series of moral hazards," he explained in the next paragraph. Coming right after the minefields metaphor, these "hazards" at the "leading edge" can be visualized as buried explosives. The front thus becomes a deadly space that we would be mad to enter.

With this minefield metaphor, Bush moved away from the Americanized meaning of "frontier," where it signifies a wilderness border, and back to its original meaning, as an international boundary between two densely populated nation-states.[40] Such a border must be respected, as his immigration policy would confirm. Bush thus subtly transformed his audience's orientation toward the frontier, encouraging them to see it as a borderline that should not be crossed. The landmine metaphor was especially apt for doing this work. The summer of 2001 saw celebrities like Paul McCartney raising awareness about the horrors of children tripping unexploded mines in former war zones.[41] In this context, Bush's claim that the discoveries of modern science are responsible for laying vast minefields connects the activity of scientists on the frontier to the gruesome deaths of innocent children. Without offering an explicit critique of the frontier myth itself, the minefield metaphor managed to achieve much of what such a critique would have offered to support Bush's policy: a recognition that the land beyond the frontier is not vacant, and a warning that decisions made by men in these dangerous spaces can result in the slaughter of innocents.

Another way that Bush reframed the frontier was by calling up a fearful image of the future. In the same paragraph where he introduced the minefield metaphor, he made reference to a dystopic science fiction novel that creates revulsion for extending the frontiers of science.

"As the genius of science extends the horizons of what we can do, we increasingly confront complex questions about what we should do. We have arrived at that brave new world that seemed so distant in 1932, when Aldous Huxley wrote about human beings created in test tubes in what he called a 'hatchery.'" In this passage, the "genius of science" is represented as an evil genius that extends a people's horizons in horrifying ways. Bush followed this reference with the "deeply troubling" revelation "that scientists have created human embryos in test tubes solely to experiment on them," a development that he would have his audience read as a "warning sign" that the dystopic future they once feared is upon them. The frontier that stem cell scientists would explore is thus transformed in this speech from the abundant wilderness of the New World to Huxley's "brave new world" of an unnatural totalitarian state. Bush then argued that human cloning is right around the corner, a procedure that he said "most Americans" oppose. "We recoil at the idea of growing human beings for spare body parts or creating life for our convenience." In this way, the president called forth science fiction scenarios from popular culture narratives of appalling possible futures to reshape his audience's thinking about scientific frontiers.[42]

Lefkowitz was most likely responsible for the *Brave New World* allusion in this speech, since he claims to have been the person who introduced passages from the book to discussions about stem cell research in the Oval Office. According to Lefkowitz, when he "read passages aloud imagining a future in which humans would be bred in hatcheries, a chill came over the room." In response, said Lefkowitz, Bush immediately made a connection between this image and the need to draw a spatial boundary across which stem cell research must not pass. "'We're tinkering with the boundaries of life here,' Bush said when I finished. 'We're on the edge of a cliff. And if we take a step off the cliff, there's no going back. Perhaps we should only take one step at a time.'"[43] By presenting the boundaries of knowledge as edging on a minefield, or a cliff that Americans could stumble off in a headlong spin toward a hellish future, Bush reframed the frontier as an undesirable space and thus justified a cautious approach toward it.

The section of Bush's August 9 speech that introduced the minefield metaphor and evoked a science fiction dystopia concluded with the only direct mention of the frontier of science metaphor in the speech: "And while we must devote enormous energy to conquering disease, it is equally important that we pay attention to the moral concerns raised by the new frontier of human embryo stem cell research." These moral concerns create an image that competes with conventional portrayals of the frontier as a place where Americans test their mettle and find their fortunes. In this competing image, the frontier is a minefield leading to a future from which Americans can only recoil in horror.

Spinning the New Policy

The minefield metaphor and the allusion to a frightening future are powerful images through which to reframe the frontier, but it is unlikely that three paragraphs in the middle of a short speech are enough to completely reverse the positive association that Americans have for the heroic crossing of scientific frontiers, an association that had been established through the better part of a century of rhetorical convention in presidential speeches. What the authors of this speech realized, to their credit, was that Bush did not need to overturn the appeal of the frontier myth; he merely needed to call the bold actions of scientists into question so that audiences would see the two competing narratives, of frontier progress and dystopian disaster, as balanced against each other, and his own policy as carefully walking a tightrope between the two (while possibly leaning just a bit toward their own side of the issue).

To appreciate this strategy, one has to realize that before Bush gave this speech, a strong majority of Americans were in favor of moving forward on the frontier of embryonic stem cell research.[44] Even staunch pro-life Republican politicians like Strom Thurmond, Orrin Hatch, and Bill Frist favored the research.[45] Frum reports having informed Bush, before the speech was written, that he was "leading an outnumbered army," since "two-thirds of the public favored stem-cell research. So did many of the party's biggest donors. So did Nancy Reagan. So did a large majority of the White House senior staff. So did Vice President Cheney and [White House Chief of Staff] Andy Card."[46]

What Bush's speech managed to do was ignore this imbalance and present the two sides of the issue as existing in equilibrium, perfectly balanced against each other, so that even listeners who were firmly on one side of the debate would think that a position of steady balance between progress and retreat was the most democratic stance for their president to take. By representing the new policy as a compromise that occupies a middle ground between two equally balanced extremes,

Bush's speech was able to gain support from a majority of Americans even though a majority did not actually agree with the policy.[47]

In conjunction with its carefully managed rhetoric of balance, the speech also managed to frame Bush's new policy ambiguously enough that it could be interpreted as either carefully pushing this important research forward or carefully shutting the door to further research, depending on which stance the auditor preferred. The result was a speech that was perfectly designed to make Bush out to be the sort of moderate triangulator that Americans in a divided nation could feel good about supporting. As Frum put it, the design of the speech allowed Bush "to win the support of his viewers for his own not at all middle-of-the-road position. . . . Bush had defended on national television the most unflinchingly pro-life position ever expressed by a president before a mass audience. . . . And he had not only protected but actually expanded his image as a moderate. It was a masterstroke—and Hughes's finest hour."[48]

This was not the only time strategists for the Bush administration took advantage of the American public's respect for two-sided argument to manufacture the appearance of a balanced controversy and thus support the interests of an outnumbered constituency. Not long after this speech was delivered, Republican language expert Frank Luntz famously recommended that Republicans recruit scientists to deny the scientific consensus on global warming, creating the appearance of a balanced debate on that issue to justify a wait-and-see attitude in the face of increasing demands for federal regulations to reduce carbon emissions.[49] In Bush's stem cell policy speech, the balanced controversy that was manufactured to justify a policy of quiescence in the face of increasing demands for forward movement was not a debate between scientists, but between scientists and ethicists, with the former imagined to be supportive of the research, and the latter opposed. Lynch has described this framing of the stem cell debate as "Manichean," the deployment of an idiom in which ethical and religious voices are assumed to speak in stark opposition to scientific voices, and vice versa.[50] In fact, at the time Bush's speech was given, ethicists had been making arguments on both sides of this issue; but after listening to Bush's speech, one might not know that since the speech framed the debate with arguments urging caution from ethicists being pit against arguments urging action from research scientists.[51] What is rhetorically significant about this framing for Bush's purpose is that in response to this imagined debate balancing scientists against ethicists, a presidential policy that is poised to stand between the two extremes can be made to seem most reasonable.

A study of the stylistic form of Bush's stem cell policy speech reveals that the dominant pattern accomplishing this sense of balance is the juxtaposition of opposites. At the beginning of the speech, Bush identified the issue of human embryonic stem cell research as "increasingly the subject of a national debate." After introducing the subject and some background information to help listeners understand it, the president modeled the rhetorical exercise of *dissoi logoi*, voicing arguments from each side of the debate. He started with the argument of "one researcher" that the five-day-old cluster of cells is not an embryo but a pre-embryo. Then the president offered a view from the other side, an "ethicist" who dismisses that argument "as a callous attempt at rationalization." In a second imagined exchange, Bush told his listeners that many on the researcher's side argue that "these embryos are byproducts," and "we should allow couples to donate them to science so they can be used for good purpose instead of wasting their potential."[52] But then Bush pointed out that others on the ethicist's side say that just because "a living being is going to die does not justify experimenting on it or exploiting it as a natural resource."[53]

After voicing these arguments from each side of the debate, Bush summarized the conflict. "At its core, this issue forces us to confront fundamental questions about the beginnings of life and the ends of science." With this pleasantly balanced phrasing (beginnings of/ends of), the president identified the two exchanges as representing two stases in the larger debate. The first exchange was about how we define the beginnings of life (pre-embryo versus embryo). The second exchange was about how we value the ends of science, particularly when considering the means used to achieve those ends. The use of the term "ends" has two meanings here. An end can be a purpose: science that sees itself as using stem cells for "good purpose" as opposed to science that is all about experimenting on or exploiting living beings. But an end can also be a spatial or temporal terminus, regarding how far Americans should go on this new frontier of knowledge. To answer that question, Bush concluded this section with the balancing claim that America was "at a difficult moral intersection" that juxtaposes "the need to protect life in all its phases with the prospect of saving and improving life in all its stages."[54]

It is only after arriving at this balanced intersection that Bush introduced the minefield metaphor and dystopian science fiction narrative.

Following the three paragraphs that reframe the frontier as an undesirable space, Bush offered a paragraph that affirms his faith in science, and then another that affirms his belief that "human life is a sacred gift from our Creator." He concluded this double affirmation with a characterization of his own policy as balanced between two extremes. "Embryonic stem cell research offers both great promise and great peril. So I have decided that we must proceed with great care."[55] This alliterative antithesis (promise and peril) is well designed to show that Bush appreciates both sides of an evenly balanced debate between scientists and ethicists.

The speech went on to announce Bush's decision to prohibit federal funding for any research on embryonic stem cells that falls outside the limit of "stem cell lines that already exist" as of August 9, 2001. This policy was characterized as a slow and careful movement forward, to "proceed" between the "great promise" and the "great peril" with "great care." But the policy was simultaneously characterized in the speech as a decision to stop at the edge of a moral minefield. He said: "This allows us to explore the promise and potential of stem cell research without crossing a fundamental moral line by providing taxpayer funding that would sanction or encourage further destruction of human embryos that have at least the potential for life."[56] The ambiguity of a policy that is described as moving us forward with great care, but also, at the same time, stopping us behind a fundamental moral line creates a speech that can be interpreted variously by different auditors.

The speech ended with yet another suggestion that science and morality are pulling Americans in opposite directions, and that Bush's decision triangulates a middle space between two extremes. "As we go forward, I hope we will always be guided by both intellect and heart, by both our capabilities and our conscience." While Bush used a both/and structure here, it turns out that the virtue that holds the spotlight, the virtue that is privileged as the one that Americans must not neglect when guided by their considerable talents, is a heartfelt sense of right and wrong. The subtle implication is that scientists, driven by their intellect and capabilities, are lacking in heart or conscience, leading us to a brave new world that is similarly deficient, unless they can be slowed down or stopped by those who are guided by religious and ethical imperatives.

Employing a rhetoric that appeared to be balanced between the appeals of scientists and ethicists, Bush thus countered the allure of the frontier myth with the prospect of a dystopian hell and offered a third way that could be interpreted either as proceeding cautiously forward or as exploring the promise and potential of science in a safe, intermediary space that would allow us to avoid crossing a perilous boundary.

I should point out that my rhetorical reading of Bush's speech here conflicts with Lynch's in significant ways. Our readings align in emphasizing the significance of Bush's recasting of the debate over stem cell research as a Manichean conflict between morality and science. However, Lynch claims that Bush's speech was an immediate failure, incoherently designed and succeeding only at "defining the middle ground of compromise he desperately seeks out of existence."[57] While this might be true logically (there being no intersection between non-overlapping magisteria), I argue that the speech was actually successful in the short term because it constructed a *rhetorical* middle ground through its policy allowing federally funded research on the limited territory of stem cell lines that already had been developed.[58] Although this was not a real or workable compromise, as scientists would soon discover, it was a rhetorical success in the short term because it could be interpreted as both pushing scientific research forward and as stopping that research on the safe side of a moral boundary. By appearing to construct a compromise position between science and morality, Bush could achieve his short-term goal of seeming moderate while also seeming to ally with scientists or, alternatively, with the religious Right, depending on which constituency was interpreting his speech. My claim about the speech's short-term success, an effect that Lynch does not acknowledge, is supported by the reception evidence offered in the next section.

Audience Reception

A review of newspaper editorials immediately after the speech was given demonstrates that at least some critics who commented on its rhetorical structure recognized its ingeniously polysemous design. *New York Times* editor Frank Bruni pointed out that "Mr. Bush did a bit of oratorical triangulation, using the language of people who advocate much broader federal support as he wended his way to his relatively narrow decision." Bruni predicted that the result would be contrary interpretations of the speech's meaning. "His speech was like a Rorschach, subject to various interpretations."[59] Bruni's newspaper published an editorial two days later that drew the same conclusion. "George W. Bush's speech about stem cell research last week was a wonder. There was a paragraph for every listener." This editorial evaluated Bush as "a skilled triangulator" who "has developed a gift for wiggling out of controversies by seizing the initiative and creating a third option." But the appearance of even-handedness in that third option was a ruse, the editors warned. "Mr. Bush's forays to the center have been mainly cosmetic."[60]

Newspaper reports that include the remarks of people responding to the speech, rather than analyzing its rhetorical structure, provide evidence that the speech worked in just this way, inviting different constituencies to interpret it positively, for very different reasons. For example, the National Right to Life Committee (NRLC) announced Bush's decision with the headline "Bush Blocks Stem Cell Funding That Would Destroy Embryos." The NRLC emphasized that with this "eloquent" speech, Bush "nullified the guidelines approved by former President Clinton that would have provided taxpayer funding for embryonic stem cell research." NRLC executive director David N. O'Steen was quoted as saying that he commends Bush's decision to "prevent the federal government from becoming involved" in this research.[61] Dr. Richard D. Land, president of the Southern Baptist Convention's Ethics and Religious Liberty Commission, used a metaphor that imagined an inferno beyond the scientific frontier of embryonic stem cell research that would be checked by the "very important firebreak" that Bush had installed with this speech.[62]

But while these pro-life auditors lauded the speech with terministic screens of blockage, nullification, and prevention, many scientists approved of the speech for the opposite reason, because they interpreted it as opening territory and promoting forward movement. For example, Dr. Robert Rich, an expert in favor of embryonic stem cell research, concluded that supporters "made a big step forward this evening."[63] Dr. John Mendelson, president of the University of Texas M.D. Anderson Cancer Center, said: "I believe President Bush made the important decision, which is to go forward."[64] "Make no mistake, this is a bold step," said Tommy Thompson, Bush's secretary of the Department of Health and Human Services. Anthony Fauci, director of the National Institute of Allergy and Infectious Diseases, agreed: "We can move forward now and do some real good for humankind."[65]

So this speech, which asserted that we must avoid "crossing a fundamental moral line," and simultaneously asserted that we must "go forward" and "proceed with great care," resulted in two very different interpretations of its orientation toward movement across the frontier of embryonic stem cell research.

This is not to suggest that the speech was positively received by everyone who heard it. Some crossed reading frames, interpreting its orientation toward the frontier of stem cell research as being against their own special interests. For example, Mary Boyert, pro-life director of the Catholic Archdiocese of Atlanta, claimed that Bush did not do enough to block the forward movement of scientists; he "leaves a little too much of a door open."[66] In contrast, a self-identified quadriplegic wrote a letter to the editor of the *New York Times* proclaiming that she was "devastated" by President Bush's decision, which "has slammed the door shut on the greatest frontier in medicine."[67]

Readings like this suggest that strategic ambiguity is not an infallible stratagem.[68] However, given that a majority of respondents approved of Bush's decision, it seems likely that the polysemous potential of the speech resulted in more people interpreting it in line with their interests than against them. Since 75 percent of Americans questioned by pollsters in the days after the speech said they favored the use of discarded embryos in stem cell research, a practice that Bush's policy would forbid in federally funded labs, the high approval rating (50–62 percent) for Bush's policy after the speech in which he announced it says a great deal about the success of that speech's ingenious rhetorical design.[69]

Subsequent Stem Cell Speeches

However cleverly designed a speech is, it can only mislead people about a policy for so long. Bush's ambiguously triangulated solution to an imagined conflict between scientists and ethicists wore thin as it became clear that the intermediary space for research that he had created was insufficiently rich to support scientists' research needs. Less than a month after Bush's stem cell policy speech, Tommy Thompson was admitting that of the "more than 60" stem cell lines that Bush's speech claimed existed, only twenty-four were close to being ready for use, with the rest "in different stages" of preparation.[70] In a matter of months, press reports informed the public that the number of cell lines available for distribution continued to be significantly smaller than the number first announced. In addition to concerns about the number of lines available, scientists also were worried about the fact that most of the cell lines were grown in culture with the help of mouse stem cells, making them potentially dangerous to humans should the research advance to the stage of producing therapies. As time passed, dissatisfaction grew over this relatively narrow and possibly polluted strip of research territory that had been left open for federally funded scientists.[71]

By the election of 2004, the campaign to further open the frontier of stem cell research was in full swing. Democratic presidential candidate John Kerry used the frontier myth freely in speeches attacking his opponent's stem cell policy. On the day after the funeral for Ronald Reagan, who had died of a disease that scientists hoped to someday cure with stem cells, Kerry blamed Bush for letting fear of the future and lack of trust in American values block scientific progress. "We must lift the barriers that stand in the way of science and push the boundaries of medical exploration so that researchers can find the cures that are there, if only they are allowed to look. . . . Above all, we must look to the future not with fear, but with the hope and the faith that advances in medicine will advance our best values. America has always been a land of discovery—of distant horizons and unconquered frontiers."[72] In a speech on the third anniversary of Bush's stem cell policy, Kerry expressed outrage that "some of the most pioneering cures and treatments are right at our fingertips, but because of the stem cell ban, they remain beyond our reach." "This is not the way we do things in America," he insisted. "We are a land of discovery—a place where innovators and optimists are free to dream and explore . . . always searching for the next breakthrough, always pushing the boundaries of our knowledge."[73] Kerry revisited the theme in a couple of speeches after Christopher Reeve, an actor with a devastating spinal cord injury who had championed stem cell research, died. Because of President Bush, Kerry said, "we stand at the edge of the next great frontier—but instead of leading the way, we're stuck on the sidelines."[74] "It's wrong to tell scientists that they can't cross the frontiers of new knowledge. It is wrong morally and it is wrong economically. When I am president, we will change this policy—and we will lead the world in stem cell research."[75] In these speeches, Kerry characterized Bush as cowardly, repressive, and un-American for halting the forward progress of American scientists across a promising new frontier.

Of course, Kerry did not become president. But his sentiments on stem cell research were shared by a bipartisan majority in Congress. In

2005 and 2006, the House and Senate respectively passed the Stem Cell Research Enhancement Act, a bill that sought to abolish the Bush restrictions and allow federal funding of human embryonic research on stem cells derived from excess embryos donated from fertility clinics. In response, Bush issued the first veto of his presidency. The speech that he gave on that occasion was less thoughtfully designed than his 2001 speech on stem cell research. Rather than enact balance through rhetorical form, Bush claimed that attribute for his stem cell policy by explicitly using the word "balance" four times to describe it. His veto speech also repeated the boundary line metaphor multiple times, saying, for example, that the bill being vetoed "crosses a moral boundary that our decent society needs to respect. . . . I made it clear to Congress that I will not allow our nation to cross this moral line. I felt like crossing this line would be a mistake, and once crossed, we would find it almost impossible to turn back."[76] Press reports on the veto speech uniformly quoted the language about not crossing a moral boundary line, but none picked up the "balance" frame that Bush also repeated so many times.[77] It was getting increasingly hard to see the president's policy as a fair and balanced middle-ground position, or to envision it as a reasonable way of moving forward with care.

Just shy of the votes needed to override the president's veto, Congress tried again with a similar bill in 2007, which President Bush also vetoed. In his second veto speech, Bush repeated the moral boundary line metaphor again, four times, drawing his own line in the sand across which he would not allow American scientists to cross.[78]

This subsequent rhetoric from Bush made it easy for Barack Obama, when he became president, to describe his own policy eliminating the previous administration's restrictions as a frontier-opening act. Early in the speech where Obama announced his Stem Cell Executive Order of 2009, he characterized scientific research as mettle-testing work, spanning "years of lonely trial and error, much of which never bears fruit," but some of which ultimately results in medical miracles. Obama identified recent successes like "pioneering cancer treatments" and "the sequencing of the human genome" as typical cases in "the story of scientific progress in America." This story, as told by Obama, triggered an American view of scientists as frontiersmen. In our current era of big science, where most laboratories are full of people and scientific papers are almost all coauthored, Obama's vision of science as a "lonely" activity bears little resemblance to the realities of scientific practice; instead, it reflects the alignment of science with the American frontier myth, where heroes cross a vast and mostly vacant wilderness. After characterizing science as a lonely, pioneering activity, Obama then argued that when the federal government fails to make investments to support science, "opportunities are missed. Promising avenues go unexplored. Some of our best scientists leave for other countries that will sponsor their work. And those countries may surge ahead of ours in the advances that transform our lives." To avoid losing this race on the frontier, he argued, we need to support stem cell research.

Obama went on to assure his American audience that the previous administration forced "a false choice between sound science and moral values. . . . I believe we have been given the capacity and will to pursue this research—and the humanity and conscience to do so responsibly," so it is the duty of Americans, even their manifest destiny, to pursue this course, "actively, responsibly, and with the urgency required to make up for lost ground." With this executive order, Obama saw himself as "opening up this new front of research today."[79] Thus was the American frontier spirit used to justify the reversal of Bush's stem cell policy. A rhetorically savvy speech in 2001 had allowed an American president to effectively justify restraining the pioneering efforts of scientists, but only temporarily. In the end, it became clear that the force of the frontier of science metaphor, a lasting convention in modern American presidential speech, could not be long subverted.

The close reading of twenty-first-century American attempts to counter the frontier of science metaphor, like the subtle reframing used by Bush or the brief but explicit rejection of the metaphor by Collins that I examined in the previous chapter, indicates that it is exceedingly difficult to check the use and influence of this pervasive commonplace in American public address. If the problem with the attempt by Collins was that his rejection was superficial, abandoning the most troubling entailments of the metaphor in words but not in thought or deed, the problem with the attempt by Bush was the reverse—he would have Americans restrain their frontier-crossing impulses without ever abandoning the frontier myth that endorses such behavior. Bush's post-September 11 renewal of a "deliberate, sustained, and unyielding frontier fantasy" extended the image that the president offered prior to his first stem cell speech of his rugged cowboy identity clearing brush on his Texas ranch.[80] These prior and subsequent endorsements of the frontier myth by Bush ultimately worked against his argument to Americans that they should curb their pioneering spirit and choose not to breach existing boundaries of knowledge in the field of stem cell research. The complicated entanglements of the frontier myth with American history, politics, and science cannot help but make a lasting withdrawal from the influence of the frontier of science metaphor a challenging proposition.

Conclusion

⌘

Patricia Nelson Limerick pointed out that "the relation between the frontier and the American mind is not a simple one."[1] This book demonstrates the truth of that statement when it comes to the "frontier of science" metaphor. The metaphor guides American thinking about science so that the prospect of halting research in a particular area becomes unimaginable. It encourages themes of competitiveness and economic exploitation even when used by rhetors sensitive to the danger of such themes; it then gets interpreted against the interests of those rhetors by diverse audiences. By studying these metaphoric entailments in the public discourse of scientists and of politicians talking about science policy, we can better understand how a frontier logic catches them in its flypaper rhetorical trap, shaping scientific research in particular ways and sometimes blocking scientists from achieving the ends they seek. A summary of how the metaphor is used and received, and also at how it is critiqued, adapted, or subverted in American public address, can help rhetors gain more control over the resources of rhetorical invention that are available to them when talking about science in the public sphere. In this conclusion, a return to the three questions that guided this book helps organize the findings of the rhetorical analyses just completed.

Question #1: Entailments of the Metaphor

The first question I asked in this book was about what is selected and what is deflected by the frontier of science metaphor. Each time we look closely at the deployment of this metaphor, we learn something more about the implications that follow it. Throughout this book, I have examined texts that offer the frontier of science as a replacement for the literal frontier that allegedly formed the character of the American people and supplied that people with an abundance of material resources. We have seen the trope used in appeals for scientists to conquer knowledge territory and extract its treasures (regardless of who else might have a legitimate claim to that territory), and we have seen it used to depict American scientists as courageous souls who have a duty to always push forward to the horizons of knowledge (regardless of who might be trampled in the process). In each case, the metaphor invites a mental picture of American science as heroic, rewarding, and uncompromising.

The earliest appearances of the metaphor established science as a national salvation at a time of anxiety about the future. When Americans found themselves lacking their former outlet for economic expansion, no longer able to tell their young men to "Go West" to seek their fortunes, science was offered as a perpetually available new territory for exploration, an infinitely extended horizon that could accommodate personal ambition and return capital gains to the nation. Frederick Jackson Turner not only introduced the idea that Americans had a unique pioneering spirit, he also introduced the idea that the discoveries of American chemists, physicists, and biologists would serve as substitutes for the vanishing material resources of the nation's frontier past.[2]

The significance of this entailment of the metaphor becomes clear when we consider an attempt to offer an alternative vision of America's future. During the Great Depression, Franklin Delano Roosevelt acknowledged the anxiety of fellow Americans when he said that the nation's "last frontier has long since been reached" so they have left "no safety valve in the form of a Western prairie"; he initially addressed this exigence by reasoning that the nation's "task now is not discovery or exploitation of natural resources" but the "more sober, less dramatic business of administering resources" that they already have, a task of "enlightened administration."[3] But such sensible analysis would hold little appeal for an anxious people, and it was not long before Roosevelt's political opponent seized the opportunity to attack him for his pessimistic failure to recognize that the frontier of science and invention remains open for development in America.[4] Chastened, Roosevelt would alter his rhetoric to accommodate this compelling new vision of science as the solution to what ails us; he admitted that while the old frontier might be closed, science and invention have opened a new frontier upon which young people will apply their considerable energies.[5]

Vannevar Bush's *Science: The Endless Frontier*, commissioned by the Roosevelt administration, would repeat this claim, arguing that while the nation's geographical frontiers might be limited, there is an inexhaustible national resource in the territory of the sciences.[6] The metaphor would continue to offer this ameliorating function throughout the twentieth century, creating for American scientists "a sense of the endless frontiers of the human mind and of human aspirations which would otherwise become increasingly confined in an ever-shrinking world."[7]

Attached to this entailment of endless opportunity for national development was a motivational appeal to those considering a career in science. The "frontiersman of science" was presented as someone who acts with "courage" and "fortitude."[8] Repeatedly, scientists were characterized as taking the roles of Lewis and Clark for the modern world.[9] Speeches given by scientists to promote their work described intellectual territory as a heroic and exciting space. With the assistance of the frontier metaphor, even tedious taxonomic work could be envisioned as the height of adventure.[10]

A consequence of these appeals was an image of the scientist that inherited both the positive and negative traits of the American frontiersman. Researchers collaborating in the modern institutions of big science could be characterized as "lonely" because they had been depicted for so long as rugged individualists who separate themselves from civilized society to venture into an unmapped wilderness.[11] Scientists, as framed through the frontiersman metaphor, have an impulse to penetrate the unknown and a temperament that is bold, aggressive, and competitive. In short, they are archetypes of hegemonic masculinity. The ability to work with vast numbers of scientific colleagues, to organize vast bodies of data, and to communicate with and across disciplinary communities remains unacknowledged in the skill set of this imagined scientist-frontiersman.

Likewise, the need to cooperate with scientists from other nations is elided when the frontier metaphor creates a mentality that sees science as a contest for territory. American scientists are expected to race competitors to claim knowledge territory and the wealth to be extracted from it, whether through bioprospecting, genome mapping, or stem cell research. The desire to see Americans win that frontier race, supported by the assumption that economic benefit will inevitably follow basic scientific research, has resulted in a duty for the federal government to fund such research, just as the government once funded frontier exploration and opened new territories for pioneer development. At the same time, the government is expected to trust the scientists who have been exploring that territory to decide which trails to take once their expeditions begin.

Texts that assume American scientists have a manifest destiny to explore, excavate, and develop territory on the frontier of science create an impression of the scientist as the "Ugly American." A negative view of the general public is also suggested by the frontier of science metaphor. Insofar as scientists see themselves as heroes who courageously break from the confines of civilization to cross the frontiers of knowledge, then by implication, those who are not scientists are regarded as a weaker class of people whose evangelical attachment to the old ways is a product of their fear of the "practical heterogeneity, rush and unsettlement" of frontier life.[12] Under the influence of this set of assumptions, any effort to block the manifest destiny of researchers who are "crossing the new horizons of science and technology" can be seen as an unreasonable act of "fear" unworthy of a true American.[13] Conflicts between scientists and their critics may be thus perpetuated by the negative characterizations of each that are implicit in the frontier of science metaphor.

An examination of these various entailments of the frontier of science metaphor exposes two paradoxes, both of which are tied to inconsistencies that exist in the broader frontier myth. The first was once hinted at by Janice Hocker Rushing, who pointed out that the idea of the frontier "is inherently paradoxical; while it implies unlimited space on the one hand, it encourages conquest on the other."[14] What is paradoxical in treatments of the literal frontier becomes more so when the frontier is reimagined as knowledge territory. Insofar as this new metaphoric frontier is made up of ideas, theories, or facts that are "discovered" by scientific frontiersmen, it has no physical properties or dimensions, and so is truly endless, a quality that the literal frontier could only claim in hyperbolic contrast with the more densely populated land that the frontiersman left behind. With a truly unlimited resource at their disposal, there should be no need for scientific frontiersmen to be driven by a largely competitive, rather than cooperative, spirit. Competition to lay claim to land in frontier territory was the consequence of a delimited space being divvied up by those who were quick enough, strong enough, and lucky enough to make the first "discoveries" there. But scientific "discoveries" on the frontiers of knowledge are ideas that, presumably, will be available as long as there are minds to think them, and such ideas can be freely shared with no loss to the total amount of knowledge being held by those doing the sharing. The belief that competition between rugged individualists is a constitutive feature of science may come more from convention than necessity. Viewing science through a frontier metaphor, the notion of intellectual property translates this convention into law; it sets out a requirement that scientific ideas be seen as equivalent to land and therefore subject to a renewed Doctrine of Discovery, with those scientists who are first to stake a "legitimate" claim to new scientific "territory" being provided legal rights to the distribution and development of it. This creates a fiercely competitive atmosphere for scientists exploring new knowledge spaces, even though those new knowledge spaces are not physically delimited in the same way that land is.

A second paradox also follows from the framing of knowledge as equivalent to land on a wilderness frontier. At the same time that the Doctrine of Discovery opened frontier territory to ownership claims by the European nations whose explorers first stepped on, mapped, and built settlements on that land, the doctrine denied the legitimacy of most ownership rights for native peoples living there. Thus frontier territory was both the common property of the nation that first staked a "legitimate" claim to it and the private property of settlers who were sold parcels or given land grants to improve it, but rarely was it acknowledged to be the property of those who had long lived there. Applying this frontier mentality to knowledge territory, it becomes easy to paradoxically claim that a biological organism or genetic sequence is both the common property of humankind and a patentable object for the scientists who "discovered" it, but not the legitimate property of those who had long lived with that organism or gene sequence.

Recognizing these paradoxes can help us understand some of the complexities of the frontier myth when applied metaphorically to the profession of science. The entailments of the metaphor are numerous, and often troubling when thoughtfully considered. But knowing some of the potentially dangerous attitudes that are selected by this metaphor and thinking about what alternatives are deflected by it are the first steps toward escaping its power.

Question #2: Power of the Metaphor

The second question I asked was whether the theoretical selections and deflections identified by answering the first question have had any real effects on rhetors and audiences. A scholar can spin out any number of hypothetical entailments, but what evidence do we have that the frontier of science metaphor actually influences the way science is perceived and developed? A closer examination of some texts produced by scientists caught in the grip of this rhetoric, and at the reception of audiences to those texts, gave us an indication of the power of this metaphor to shape our conceptions of science now and in the future.

Chapters 3 and 4 in particular showed that scientists, when ensnared by the frontier metaphor, really do tend to think in ways that this language encourages them to think, while overlooking other important perspectives that are available to them. Consider the point discussed above that language placing the scientist in the role of the frontiersman underscores the idea of ownership for those who make discoveries, while the rights of those whose lands (or traditional knowledge, or bodies) are being explored is removed from view. We saw this function of the frontier of science metaphor in chapter 3, when we looked at Edward O. Wilson's argument about ethical bioprospecting. He maintained that bioprospecting is appropriate if it is based on firm contracts between multinational corporations that provide research funding and local scientific institutions that supply the personnel to conduct basic research on commercially interesting biological specimens.[15] Egregiously missing from Wilson's field of vision were the rights of the native peoples whose knowledge was being used when scientists selected the most promising specimens for study. Reasoning from the perspective of the frontiersman, the rights of the prospector and his funders were protected through firm contracts that bound them to each other, while the rights of the people who already occupied the territory being mined were conveniently neglected. Even though a concern over indigenous rights to traditional knowledge was discussed in the texts that Wilson used to source his comments on bioprospecting, Wilson failed to mention those rights, recognizing only the rights of the scientific frontiersman and those who invest in his expedition.[16] Such thinking was enabled by language that imagines biodiversity as inert mineral wealth that a researcher is excited to discover on the frontiers of science.

A similar frontier logic blocked Francis Collins from considering the rights of native peoples who object to their genomes being explored by scientists. Although Collins acknowledged that literal frontiersmen and pioneers regrettably pushed aside American Indians in the history of this nation, when he then offered a protection against the danger of pushing aside whole groups of people as genomic exploration proceeds, he illogically endorsed legislation that would only protect the rights of individuals from having their genomic information, once collected, used against them by insurance agencies and employers.[17] Collins never mentioned the right of groups of people to block the collection of genomic information, even though this was an issue that American Indians were raising at the time. From the frontiersman of science's perspective, the right of the biologist to explore genomic territory is inviolate; no moratorium on research can be tolerated when it is the manifest destiny of scientists to press forward on the horizons of knowledge. From the frontiersman of science's perspective, genomic resources are there to be discovered by scientists, and legal wrangling is relevant only insofar as individuals and businesses dispute how those resources, once identified and extracted, should be economically valued and used. Once again, a scientist ensnared by the frontier metaphor had his attention deflected from issues that are missing from the frontiersman's mental world.

My close reading of texts to identify such deflections tells us something about how scientists use the metaphor, and also something about how the metaphor uses scientists, cultivating habits of mind that they might not even be aware of holding. It shows us that the language a rhetor selects helps shape that rhetor's thinking about the subjects being addressed, resulting in the emphasis of some things at the expense of others.

When we also look at how such language was received, often against the interests of those very scientists, we come to learn even more about the power of this metaphor. Chapters 3 and 4 introduced reception evidence that indicated that audiences resisted appeals associated with the frontier metaphor. The fact that scientists continued to use the metaphor even in the face of that resistance confirms the power of this language over their rhetorical imagination. The fact that their rhetorical choices worked against their own interests recommends reflection on how they might escape the influence of this metaphor in the future.

We saw the counterproductive effect of the frontier metaphor most obviously in the case of Wilson's appeals for public support of biodiversity research in the Amazonian rain forest. By characterizing biodiversity as riches to be discovered and mined by enterprising scientists, and by imagining the wildlands as a "global commons," Wilson rhetorically wed his cause to the frontier myth.[18] Not long after he made those arguments, Brazilians passed legislation to shut their borders to foreign scientists, severely restricting the study of biodiversity in the Amazon for fear that greedy American imperialists were out to steal their natural biological resources. A number of them recognized what was missing in Wilson's frontiersman-oriented appeal—namely, an appreciation for the "common heritage of the social group," an appreciation that should result, in the context of an intellectual-property-rights regime, in local traditional knowledge being given legal status as group-held intellectual property rights, rather than being "exploited by bioprospecting."[19] In a region with a long history of foreign interests removing its natural resources, Wilson's conflation of scientists and frontier prospectors did more to harm his cause of promoting biodiversity research than it did to help it.

Another case where audience reception included sentiments opposite to the stated interests of the rhetors who were using the frontier metaphor was the White House media event announcing the completion of the Human Genome Project. Each speaker on that day claimed that collaboration across national borders and cooperation between privately funded and publicly funded scientists was necessary and desirable; in fact, the media event was scheduled in order to make that very point. Yet the use of frontier imagery by the speakers was so compelling that media reports on the event told the story of a gold rush for genes that pits scientists from different nations in a fierce competition, and that sets researchers from public and private efforts racing against each other to plant their figurative flags on newly mapped genome territory. Unable to escape the pull of the frontier myth, the speakers at the White House evoked the frontier image of competitive individualists mapping territory to lay claim to it, even though their stated goal was to counter such an image of genomic science.

Such cases demonstrate that rhetors would do well to avoid the use of the frontier metaphor, or at least find ways in which the metaphor might be reimagined so as to serve their interests more effectively.

Question #3: Flexibility of the Metaphor

The third question I raised was how does one go about avoiding or reimagining the frontier metaphor. I sought to answer it by examining some of the specific moves that rhetors have made when trying to escape the frontier of science metaphor. A metaphor with enough power to dominate the rhetorical imaginations of American scientists, even when it works against their interests, is troubling. But the metaphor is not all-powerful. When the frontier of science metaphor was first introduced in American public address, its connotations were presented as uniformly positive; but more recently there is evidence of a shift in public consciousness, as some contemporary scientists step back, if only temporarily, from some aspects of the frontier myth.

When Robert B. Gagosian admitted in 2004 that Columbus was an agent of European economic imperialism, and even briefly considered disavowing the analogy between Columbus and modern scientists because of the dark acts committed by Columbus and his ilk, he voiced a postmodern ambivalence about frontier heroism.[20] When Wilson complained in 2002 that the European conquest of the United States treated wilderness as nothing more than a frontier region to be rolled back, he hinted at a dawning critical perspective toward the American frontier myth.[21] When Collins reminded us in 2005 of the American Indians who were unjustly pushed aside when the white settlers came to the Pacific Northwest, he offered a revisionist history lesson that cast a shadow on the frontier myth.[22] In the end, all of these rhetors continued to promote a positive vision of the scientist as frontiersman, indicating that their orientation toward the frontier myth had not really shifted. But the fact that each of them felt a need to pay lip service to a critique of the myth, critiques that were missing in earlier texts that employed the frontier metaphor, suggests that something is changing in public attitudes toward the frontier.[23] A fractured sense of the frontier explorer is available to rhetors today, in a way that was not evident when the metaphor first began appearing in American public discourse about science.

American scientists might not be doing much yet with the negative connotations carried by the frontier of science metaphor, beyond conceding that they exist, but critics of science have exploited this contemporary fractured sense of the frontier myth to make arguments for stopping some controversial research projects. Bioprospecting projects in South America were successfully curtailed when they were reframed as biopiracy, thus focusing attention on the avarice and injustice of explorers on the scientific frontier of biodiversity research. The Human Genome Diversity Project was halted after American Indian activists relabeled it as biocolonialism and framed it as yet another way of subjugating indigenous bodies. These cases, mentioned in chapters 3 and 4, respectively, show us that political activists who focus on the negative entailments of the frontier metaphor can successfully block research that scientists have been promoting with that metaphor. Whether these activists would have had as much success without such an easy target in the public rhetoric of scientists advocating "frontier" research projects is unclear, but scientists would do well to consider the possibility that their rhetorical choices are setting them up for failure.

One of the cases I selected for examination also shows us that a critical reading of the frontier myth might not be equally available to everyone who wants to oppose a line of scientific research. George W. Bush did not explicitly critique the frontier myth in his efforts to shut down embryonic stem cell research, but chose instead to subtly undermine the power of frontier-expanding rhetoric by using negative images from other narratives—recalling landmines on the front of a foreign war and a dystopic science fiction landscape.[24] Why did he choose these images rather than directly assailing the frontier myth as critics of bioprospecting and the Human Genome Diversity Project had done so successfully? It is likely that the victims of colonialism are able to point to the dark side of a frontier story in public arguments about science more readily than an American president, especially one with the ethos of a conservative Texan.

Willingness to publicly acknowledge the unfavorable aspects of an American frontier story probably varies according to ideological commitment, with conservative speakers less eager to cast aspersions on this traditional way of defining national identity. However, the strength of conservative attachment to the frontier myth does not mean that progressive speakers are more weakly attached to it; progressives are not quick to eschew a frontier of science metaphor that valorizes escape from constraining traditions and unending movement toward a better future. Both conservative and progressive voices have long seen their values embodied in the figure of the frontiersman of science, whether he is imaged as Hoover's rugged individualist reviving American prosperity through scientific entrepreneurism or Dewey's progressive biologist standing up against the fearful containment efforts of religious fundamentalists. Republican and Democratic presidents have all used the frontier of science metaphor over the last eighty years, and there is little reason to expect that this performative tradition will be abandoned in American public address anytime soon. As we have seen, contemporary American scientists of various political leanings have thus far shown only shallow or temporary recognition of the metaphor's negative entailments, while clinging to the image it creates of an exciting and nationally revitalizing scientific vocation.

Recommendations for Scientists (and Those Who Teach Rhetoric to Them)

If the frontier of science metaphor is dangerous for scientists to use, directing their attention through the narrow mind-set of the frontiersman and leaving scientific projects open to critique from postcolonial, transnational, or feminist audiences, what should they do to avoid these problems? The most obvious answer would be to stop using the frontier of science metaphor. As Limerick has put it, one might seek to retire "the f-word" from our vocabulary.[25] But given the lengthy history and powerful influence of this trope on American public discourse, that is not likely to be a viable solution. Even if individual scientists were able to avoid the trope, its alignment with the ethos of modern American science has been so well established that its influence over our impression of scientists would likely continue for quite some time.

It also seems shortsighted to suppress a metaphor in order to avoid criticism based on the negative aspects of the history it evokes. Critical reflection on that history would do more to broaden the perspectives of rhetors than attempts to police language use in an effort to eliminate potentially troubling metaphors.[26] Scientists making an analogy between their activities and frontier exploration would be better off if they examined the metaphor from multiple angles, seeing the frontier of science from the perspective of the colonized as well as the colonizer. Such self-reflexive language use might, for example, result in more scientists coming to endorse contracts and laws that go beyond protecting scientific frontiersmen, their investors, and markets, to protecting the group rights of native peoples to ownership of their knowledge and genomes.

In addition to critically examining their own use of the frontier metaphor, another way for scientific rhetors to improve thinking about the future of American science might be to introduce other related metaphors that, when mixed with this one, bring neglected aspects of an issue to our attention. When activists introduced the figure of the biopirate to stand alongside the figure of the bioprospector, readers were encouraged to consider the complexity of ownership claims over the biological "wealth" discovered by scientific researchers. When Bush introduced a landmine metaphor to discussions of stem cell research, the scientific front that might have been envisioned as filled only with promise was seen as one that contains dangers too. Neither of these alternative metaphors dismissed the historical resonance and spatial logic of the frontier of science. Instead, when presented in discursive exchanges that also included the frontier metaphor, these metaphors gave us other, more complicated perspectives toward actions being taken on the boundaries of knowledge—a frontier containing pirates as well as heroes, a frontier filled not only with the potential for treasure but also with the potential for destruction.

A scientist contemplating rhetorical invention might try to throw a few different metaphors into the mix, directing the attention of audiences not only to the exploitative and competitive themes attached to scientific frontiersmen but also toward the puzzle-solving skills of scientific detectives who search for clues to unravel the mysteries of the natural world, or toward the miraculous feats of scientific magicians who reveal the astonishing complexities that surround us in this vast cosmos. These figures are not going to cancel out the frontier metaphor, and each has its own limitations that make it less than ideal as a replacement for the frontier metaphor. But by drawing on characters from a multiplicity of genres when configuring the identity of American scientists, a variety of virtues can be evoked and encouraged to guide future thought and action.

Yet another alternative for scientists concerned about the implications of their language choice when using the frontier of science metaphor is to adjust the specific application of that metaphor in their discourse, so that the focus is shifted to some of the less frequently evoked aspects of the frontier myth. We saw Franklin Delano Roosevelt do that when he emphasized the wagon train cooperativeness of American pioneers as a quality to be emulated by modern young people, rather than the rugged individualism that Hoover had promoted.[27] Rhetors seeking to transform our understanding of American science could do something similar, focusing on the organization and collaboration required for (scientific) pioneers to make it past the edge of their known world, thus emphasizing the cooperative aspects of science over its competitive aspects. Feminist scientists might find it easier to encourage young women to consider a career in science if they held out Sacagawea as a praiseworthy model for the scientist on the frontier of knowledge, rather than just Lewis and Clark. Such reframing could emphasize how Sacagawea's communication skills allowed the group to negotiate its way out of danger, and how she balanced work with family life, quite literally, on her capable back.[28] These adjustments to what the important bits are in the analogy between scientists and frontier heroes would take advantage of our contemporary postmodern understanding of American history to create a more inclusive and less objectionable vision of the ideal American scientist.

Each of these recommendations would take for granted that the relationship between the frontier myth and the American mind is not a simple one, drawing on the very complexity of that relationship to create a more sophisticated public understanding of American science. Without seeking to eradicate a metaphor that has long guided our thinking, scientists could disrupt that thinking, trouble it, and expand it by critically examining the metaphor, mixing it with other metaphors, and drawing our attention to associated commonplaces that are not normally brought to mind upon hearing it used.

A Final Recommendation for Scholars of Rhetoric

Rhetoricians are not immune to the influence of the frontier of science metaphor, so as a final note, I turn to a critique of its appearance in the language used by a prominent rhetorician of science. In an important essay that I mentioned in the introduction, John Lyne identified "bio-rhetoric" as a concept to guide scholarship on the relationship between the biological sciences and the public sphere. At a time when some scholars were arguing that science was rhetorical "without remainder," and others were arguing that critics would do well to adopt "some cautionary strictures against the too easy assumption that scientific texts are as susceptible to rhetorical analysis as are texts in other disciplines," Lyne argued that his position toward the relationship between ideology and epistemology was a moderate one:[29]

> It would be misleading to assimilate science fully to social discourse, since science is focused on phenomena that are presocial, and not yet squared with what is known and understood. The scientist is not acting just as a voice of society in advancing knowledge claims. Before making a claim, one might say, the scientist is first *staking* a claim, which if redeemed becomes society's. In that sense, science is a discourse of the frontier and a "socializing" of the unknown. It succeeds only if it is accountable to what is on both sides of that frontier—and there are various ways of accountability. The error of scientism is to think that science can meet society strictly on its own terms and rewrite society's rules; the error on the other side is to treat science as though it were not a frontier and thus already fully socialized.[30]

Lyne's use of the frontier metaphor here is telling because it is like the many other uses I have examined in this book, drawing on an American myth by treating the frontier not as a line that divides one sovereign country from another, but as the border between civilization and an unknown wilderness. Like the scientists who use this metaphor, Lyne was characterizing scientists as heroic individuals who are unafraid to separate themselves from the provincial morality of the settled towns-folk as they blaze new trails and stake out new intellectual territory.

But as I have argued elsewhere in this book, one of the problems with the frontier of science metaphor is the dependent and somewhat antagonistic relationship it calls forth between the heroic scientist-frontiersman and the more common nonscientific townsfolk. There is a hierarchy implied by the metaphor, with scientists taking the superior position because they boldly strike out into the unknown, and in so doing, tame the wilderness for the benefit of the townsfolk, who can then profit from the new discoveries that were made out there. The nonscientists in this narrative are timid, afraid of what lies beyond their borders, but dependent on scientists who have the true grit to open up the new territories. The morality of the townsfolk is fine and good for civilized living, but worse than useless once you move out past the frontier, where what you are likely to encounter is not yet "fully socialized."

Another problem with thinking about science in this way is that it inscribes a border between the social and presocial, civilization and wilderness, science and the territory that scientists would explore. But just as the American frontiersman did not really enter an unpeopled wilderness (the land already being occupied by Indians), so too do a great many scientists venture into intellectual territory that is already occupied by others—the tribes of social scientists, scholars of the humanities, and theologians, just to name a few. Some of the most interesting uses toward which Lyne's term "bio-rhetoric" has been employed in the rhetoric of science literature are cases where the biologist has ventured into territory already occupied by researchers from other fields. Consider, for example, Lyne's own critique of Richard Dawkins's "selfish gene" metaphor, a terministic screen that sociobiologists use when they trespass into territory already occupied by social scientists and scholars of the humanities; or consider Robert Brookey's critique of scientists who, seeking a "gay gene," design experiments that anyone with even the slightest awareness of queer theory would recognize as hopelessly riddled with prejudicial stereotypes; or consider John Lynch's study of public discourse about stem cell research, in which the bio-rhetoric of proponents intensifies into a scientism that subjugates ethics and religion by claiming that the "primitive streak" of the protospinal cord that appears on the fifteenth day after conception is a clear scientific dividing line between human life and human cells.[31]

If we carry the terms of the scientific frontier-as-wilderness analogy through to its logical conclusion, then characterizing the subject matter that science takes on in these cases as not "already fully socialized" is little better than characterizing Indians as savage, part of a hostile environment that needs to be tamed through the heroic actions of frontiersmen. But if, as Lyne says at the end of his 1990 essay on bio-rhetorics, the job of the rhetorical analyst is "to raise [our] consciousness" of rhetorical elements in science, "so that intellectual investigation, irreducibly social and communicative, can be held more socially accountable and be more carefully moralized," then I think we would be better off *not* thinking of scientists as frontiersmen entering an unpopulated, not-fully-socialized space.[32] If we imagine them as American frontiersmen, the rhetorical analyst's ethos becomes that of the townsfolk, timid and sometimes downright dangerous in our irrelevant moralizing at those brave men who act as they do only because they regularly face the uncivilized unknown; or the rhetorical analyst's ethos becomes that of the American Indian as constructed in the Euro-American imaginary, savage and undeserving of the intellectual territory we occupy.

Instead, what if rhetoricians were to think about the frontier of science through that older meaning of the word "frontier," as a border between sovereign countries? Then a bio-rhetoric would continue to be a strategy for mediating discourses, but the territories crossed could be conceived as sovereign domains of intellectual investigation—biology and the social sciences, psychology and queer theory, embryology and theology. The success of a bio-rhetoric would then depend on the ability of the scientist-rhetors to negotiate the languages, customs, and values of these independent domains.[33]

This perspective does not assimilate science fully to the social discourse of any of these other independent domains; the biological scientist would continue to cling to his or her own specialized vocabulary, research practices, and aims. But this version of the metaphor would recognize biological science as just one mode of knowledge-production, one mode of explanation, that needs to negotiate with other modes of intellectual investigation when venturing into the shared territory where humans are defined and studied. The border is not between an expert technical sphere and a nonexpert public sphere, but between different types of expertise, each accomplished at doing different work. A bio-rhetoric negotiates that border from the perspective of the biologist, and in so doing comes into contact with other rhetorics (a sociologist rhetoric, a queer rhetoric, a religious rhetoric), each of which negotiates the border from its own domain of expertise.

Thinking about the frontier of science through the Americanized meaning of the term "frontier," as a border between the civilized known and the savage unknown, privileges science in a way that paradoxically encourages the very scientism that Lyne has so effectively worked to counter in his critiques of sociobiologists like Richard Dawkins and Edward O. Wilson.[34] Thinking about bio-rhetoric as the discursive strategy of one mode of intellectual inquiry that communicates with other valued and sovereign modes might do more to hold these modes accountable to each other and to the common subjects of their investigation. By rethinking our use of the frontier of science metaphor, rhetoricians of science can help to create a less antagonistic relationship between the culture of science and the various other cultures that surround it.

Notes

⌘

Introduction

1. Ronald Reagan, "Remarks at the Annual Convention of the Texas State Bar Association in San Antonio," July 6, 1984, in *The American Presidency Project,* ed. Gerhard Peters and John T. Woolley, http://www.presidency.ucsb.edu/.

2. Mario Cuomo, "1984 Democratic National Convention Keynote," July 16, 1984, in *American Rhetoric*, ed. Michael E. Eidenmuller , http://www.americanrhetoric.com/.

3. Reagan won the election, but Republicans acknowledged that this speech by Cuomo was especially well designed to appeal to Americans and forced the Reagan campaign to do some rhetorical repair work that they otherwise would not have been forced to do. See David Henry, "The Rhetorical Dynamics of Mario Cuomo's 1984 Keynote Address," in *Contemporary American Public Discourse*, 3rd ed., ed. Halford Ross Ryan (Prospect Heights, Ill.: Waveland Press, 1992), 303–4, 314.

4. E. G. Adelberger et al. "Torsion Balance Experiments: A Low-Energy Frontier of Particle Physics," August 19, 2008, http://www.npl.washington.edu/eotwash/publications/pdf/lowfrontier2.pdf; Edward D. Lazowska and David A. Patterson, "An Endless Frontier Postponed," *Science* 308, no. 5723 (2005): 757,

http://lazowska.cs.washington.edu/Science.pdf; Cary Alan Johnson, "The Final Frontier: Why LGBT Rights Are a Game Changer and Will Liberate Us All," University of Washington Department of Global Health, October 25, 2011, http://globalhealth.washington.edu/media/gallery/5274.

5. Patricia Nelson Limerick, "The Adventures of the Frontier in the Twentieth Century," in *The Frontier in American Culture*, ed. James R. Grossman (Berkeley: University of California Press, 1994), 67, 94.

6. Kenneth Burke, *Language as Symbolic Action: Essays on Life, Literature and Method* (Berkeley: University of California Press, 1966), 50.

7. Richard Slotkin, *Gunfighter Nation: The Myth of the Frontier in Twentieth-Century America* (New York: Maxwell Macmillan International, 1992), 2.

8. Tarla Rai Peterson, "Jefferson's Yeoman Farmer as Frontier Hero: A Self Defeating Mythic Structure," *Agriculture and Human Values* 7, no. 1 (1990): 9.

9. Limerick, "Adventures," 68.

10. Mary E. Stuckey, "The Donner Party and the Rhetoric of Westward Expansion," *Rhetoric & Public Affairs* 14, no. 2 (2011): 232; Hillary A. Jones, "'Them as Feel the Need to Be Free': Reworking the Frontier Myth," *Southern Communication Journal* 76, no. 3 (2011): 231.

11. Janice Hocker Rushing, "Mythic Evolution of 'The New Frontier' in Mass Mediated Rhetoric," *Critical Studies in Mass Communication* 3, no. 3 (1986): 265.

12. Richard Slotkin, *Regeneration through Violence: The Mythology of the American Frontier, 1600–1860* (Middletown, Conn.: Wesleyan University Press, 1973), 5. See also Richard Slotkin, *The Fatal Environment: The Myth of the Frontier in the Age of Industrialization, 1800–1890* (New York: Atheneum, 1985); and Slotkin, *Gunfighter Nation*.

13. Slotkin, *Regeneration through Violence*, 4.

14. Leroy G. Dorsey, "The Myth of War and Peace in Presidential Discourse: John Kennedy's 'New Frontier' Myth and the Peace Corps," *Southern Communication Journal* 62, no. 1 (1996): 42–55.

15. Ronald H. Carpenter, "America's Tragic Metaphor: Our Twentieth-Century Combatants as Frontiersmen," *Quarterly Journal of Speech* 76, no. 1 (1990): 1–22.

16. Mark West and Chris Carey, "(Re)Enacting Frontier Justice: The Bush Administration's Tactical Narration of the Old West Fantasy after September 11," *Quarterly Journal of Speech* 92, no. 4 (2006): 379–412.

17. Rushing, "Mythic Evolution," 266, 294. See also Janice Hocker Rushing, "Ronald Reagan's 'Star Wars' Address: Mythic Containment of Technical Reasoning," *Quarterly Journal of Speech* 72, no. 4 (1986): 415–33; Janice Hocker Rushing, "Evolution of 'The New Frontier' in *Alien* and *Aliens*: Patriarchal Co-optation of the Feminine Archetype," *Quarterly Journal of Speech* 75, no. 1 (1989): 1–25.

18. Ray A. Williamson, "Outer Space as Frontier: Lessons for Today," *Western Folklore* 46, no. 4 (1987): 260. See also Linda T. Krug, *Presidential Perspectives on*

Space Exploration: Guiding Metaphors from Eisenhower to Bush (New York: Praeger, 1991): 68–74, 82–86, 94; James L. Kauffman, *Selling Outer Space: Kennedy,
the Media, and Funding for Project Apollo, 1961–1963* (Tuscaloosa: University of
Alabama Press, 1994): 132–34; John W. Jordan, "Kennedy's Romantic Moon and
Its Rhetorical Legacy for Space Exploration," *Rhetoric & Public Affairs* 6, no. 2
(2003): 209–32; Catherine Gouge, "The Great Storefront of American Nationalism: Narratives of Mars and the Outerspatial Frontier," *Americana: The Journal of
American Popular Culture (1900–present)* 1, no. 2 (2002).

19. James P. McDaniel, "Figures for New Frontiers, From Davy Crockett to Cyberspace Gurus," *Quarterly Journal of Speech* 88, no. 1 (2002): 94.

20. David J. Gunkel and Ann Hetzel Gunkel, "Terra Nova 2.0: The New World of
MMORPGs," *Critical Studies in Media Communication* 26, no. 2 (2009): 110.

21. Beverly J. Stoeltje, "Making the Frontier Myth: Folklore Process in a Modern
Nation," *Western Folklore* 46, no. 4 (1987): 250, 252.

22. Gunkel and Gunkel, "Terra Nova 2.0," 108, 110.

23. Kenneth Burke, *The Philosophy of Literary Form* (Berkeley: University of California Press, 1973), 110–11.

24. I imagine some of the participants in that conversation to be the scholars who
contributed to Kendall Phillips, ed., *Framing Public Memory* (Tuscaloosa: University of Alabama Press, 2004).

25. Texts dominating this discussion would include Mary E. Stuckey, *Defining Americans: The Presidency and National Identity* (Lawrence: University Press of Kansas,
2004); Vanessa B. Beasley, *You the People: American National Identity in Presidential Rhetoric* (College Station: Texas A&M University Press, 2004); and Leroy G.
Dorsey, *We Are All Americans, Pure and Simple: Theodore Roosevelt and the Myth
of Americanism* (Tuscaloosa: University of Alabama Press, 2007).

26. Most of these tensions arise from the influential late-twentieth-century conflict
between rhetorical critics Michael Leff and Michael McGee. That tension is
most famously represented by Michael Leff and Andrew Sachs, "Words Most
Like Things: Iconicity and the Rhetorical Text," *Western Journal of Communication* 54, no. 3 (1990): 252–73; and Michael McGee, "Text, Context, and the
Fragmentation of Contemporary Culture," *Western Journal of Communication* 54,
no. 3 (1990): 274–89. My insistence that one need not choose between such
binaries, but can manage tensions on a case-by-case basis, borrows from several
scholars, but most recently from David Zarefsky, "Public Address Scholarship in
the New Century: Achievements and Challenges," in *The Handbook of Rhetoric
and Public Address*, ed. Shawn J. Parry-Giles and J. Michael Hogan (Malden,
Mass.: Wiley-Blackwell, 2010), 80.

27. See James Jasinski, "The Status of Theory and Method in Rhetorical Criticism,"
Western Journal of Communication 65, no. 3 (2001): 249–70; Karlyn Kohrs Camp-
bell, "Rhetorical Criticism 2009: A Study in Method," in Parry-Giles and Hogan,
Handbook of Rhetoric and Public Address, 86–107.

28. Jeanne Fahnestock, "The Rhetoric of the Natural Sciences," in *The Sage Handbook of Rhetorical Studies*, ed. Andrea A. Lunsford, Kirt H. Wilson, and Rosa A. Eberly (Thousand Oaks, Calif.: Sage, 2009): 184.

29. Thomas M. Lessl, "The Priestly Voice," *Quarterly Journal of Speech* 75, no. 2 (1989): 190–93.

30. I should make it clear that I do not dispute Lessl's argument that scientists employ the priestly voice; I am merely calling attention to the fact that another voice is present in these texts that also deserves critical scrutiny from rhetoricians.

31. Celeste M. Condit, John Lynch, and Emily Winderman, "Recent Rhetorical Studies in Public Understanding of Science: Multiple Purposes and Strengths," *Public Understanding of Science* 21, no. 4 (2012): 390, 391.

32. Dorothy Nelkin, "Promotional Metaphors and Their Popular Appeal," *Public Understanding of Science* 3, no. 1 (1994): 30.

33. Joanna Ploeger, "Techno-Scientific Spectacle: The Rhetoric of IMAX in the Contemporary Science Museum," *Poroi* 3, no. 2 (2004): 82, 86.

34. Maureen Burns and Joan Leach, "Science as an Extra Dividend: *Frontiers of Science*," *International Journal of Cultural Studies* 14, no. 5 (2011): 537. This comic was produced in Australia, but Burns and Leach maintain that the trope of the frontier it conveyed drew on a cultural history and meaning very similar to the frontier described in American contexts.

35. For example, Mary Rosner and T. R. Johnson, "Telling Stories: Metaphors of the Human Genome Project," *Hypatia* 10, no. 4 (1995): 115–22; Donna J. Haraway, *Modest_Witness@Second_Millennium.FemaleMan©_Meets_OncoMouseTM* (New York: Routledge, 1997), 162–67; José van Dijck, *Imagenation: Popular Images of Genetics* (Washington Square: New York University Press, 1998), 111–14, 126–28, 139, 182; Davi Johnson Thornton, *Brain Culture: Neuroscience and Popular Media* (New Brunswick, N.J.: Rutgers University Press, 2011), 150–61.

36. Rosner and Johnson identified one Lewis and Clark analogy introduced by a scientist, with the rest of their examples of frontier rhetoric authored by journalists or public relations experts; Haraway critiqued explorer rhetoric from images and a news article in a special issue of *Science* and from an advertisement for a biotech company, all of which were the product of science writers rather than scientists; Van Dijck focused mostly on texts written by journalists, including just one quote including frontier language from an essay written by a scientist and one mention of the frontier myth in a popular book written by a scientist; and Johnson Thornton included only one frontier quote uttered by a scientist.

37. Adrienne Kolb and Lillian Hoddeson, "A New Frontier in the Chicago Suburbs: Settling Fermilab, 1963–1972," *Illinois Historical Journal* 88, no. 1 (1995): 4, 7; Lillian Hoddeson and Adrienne W. Kolb, "The Superconducting Super Collider's Frontier Outpost, 1983–1988," *Minerva* 38, no. 1 (2000): 271–310. See also Lillian Hoddeson, Adrienne W. Kolb, and Catherine Westfall, *Fermilab: Physics, the Frontier, and Megascience* (Chicago: University of Chicago Press, 2008); Joanna

S. Ploeger, *The Boundaries of the New Frontier: Rhetoric and Communication at Fermi National Accelerator Laboratory* (Columbia: University of South Carolina Press, 2009); John M. Findlay and Bruce Hevly, *Atomic Frontier Days: Hanford and the American West* (Seattle: University of Washington Press, 2011).

38. Alice Domurat Dreger, "Metaphors of Morality in the Human Genome Project," in *Controlling Our Destinies: Historical, Philosophical, Ethical, and Theological Perspectives on the Human Genome Project*, ed. Phillip R. Sloan (Notre Dame, Ind.: University of Notre Dame Press, 2000), 159–67.

39. Dreger, "Metaphors of Morality," 160.

40. An exception is chapter 5, where I look at how an American political leader orients toward the frontier of science metaphor.

41. Janice Hocker Rushing and Thomas S. Frentz, "The Rhetoric of 'Rocky': A Social Value Model of Criticism," *Western Journal of Communication* 42, no. 2 (1978): 67.

42. Rushing identified the myth of the Old West as an American adaptation of the "hero archetype" in Rushing, "Mythic Evolution," 271.

43. Michael Osborn, "Memories of Miz Myth," *Southern Communication Journal* 71, no. 2 (2006): 149–50.

44. Robert C. Rowland, "On a Limited Approach to Mythic Criticism: Rowland's Rejoinder," *Communication Studies* 41, no. 2 (1990): 155.

45. Dorsey, *We Are All Americans,* 5.

46. Leroy Dorsey, "The Rhetorical Presidency and the Myth of the American Dream," in *The Prospect of Presidential Rhetoric*, ed. James Arnt Aune and Martin J. Medhurst (College Station: Texas A&M University Press, 2008), 136. Barthes argues that myth "abolishes the complexity of human acts, it gives them the simplicity of essences, it does away with all dialectics." Roland Barthes, *Mythologies*, trans. Annette Lavers (New York: Hill and Wang, 1972), 143.

47. Robert C. Rowland, "On Mythic Criticism," *Communication Studies* 41, no. 2 (1990): 107–12.

48. Rowland, "On Mythic Criticism," 105–6.

49. Rowland, "On Mythic Criticism," 112.

50. Michael Osborn, "In Defense of Broad Mythic Criticism," *Communication Studies* 41, no. 2 (1990): 126.

51. Janice Hocker Rushing, "On Saving Mythic Criticism: A Reply to Rowland," *Communication Studies* 41, no. 2 (1990): 146. The early study that she referenced was Waldo W. Braden, "Myths in a Rhetorical Context," *Southern Speech Communication Journal* 40, no. 2 (1975): 113–26.

52. One exception is George W. Bush's stem cell rhetoric, which avoids elaboration of the frontier myth because it was trying to counter the appeal of that myth as applied to that particular subject. See chapter 5.

53. Rowland suggests that in addition to textual interpretation, audience reception is a way of developing a persuasive argument for the presence of a mythic appeal

in a text, and Osborn agrees. Rowland, "Limited Approach," 157–58; Osborn, "Broad Mythic Criticism," 127.

54. Kenneth Burke, *A Grammar of Motives* (Berkeley: University of California Press, 1969), 503–4.

55. I. A. Richards, *The Philosophy of Rhetoric* (New York: Oxford University Press, 1936), 96–97. If this distinction seems imprecise, that is because it is. See David Douglass, "Issues in the Use of I. A. Richards' Tenor-Vehicle Model of Metaphor," *Western Journal of Communication* 64, no. 4 (2000): 405–24.

56. Max Black, "Metaphor," *Proceedings of the Aristotelian Society* 55 (1954): 286–91.

57. Michael Osborn, "The Trajectory of My Work with Metaphor," *Southern Communication Journal* 74, no. 1 (2009): 83.

58. A search in the database *Communication and Mass Media Complete* using the terms "rhetoric" and "metaphor" turns up almost 450 results, far more than searches that combine rhetoric with other tropes like metonymy, synecdoche, or irony, and even more than searches that combine rhetoric with other traditional concepts like ethos, kairos, or genre.

59. See, for example, David Zarefsky, *President Johnson's War on Poverty: Rhetoric and History* (Tuscaloosa: University of Alabama Press, 1986); Francis A. Beer and Christ'l De Landtsheer, eds., *Metaphorical World Politics* (East Lansing: Michigan State University Press, 2004); Karrin Vasby Anderson and Kristina Horn Sheeler, *Governing Codes: Gender, Metaphor, and Political Identity* (Lanham, Md.: Lexington Books, 2005); Robert Asen, *Invoking the Invisible Hand: Social Security and the Privatization Debates* (East Lansing: Michigan State University Press, 2009).

60. Michael Osborn, "Archetypal Metaphor in Rhetoric: The Light-Dark Family," *Quarterly Journal of Speech* 53, no. 2 (1967): 115–26.

61. Michael Osborn, *Orientations to Rhetorical Style* (Chicago: Science Research Associates, 1976), 16.

62. Osborn identifies "the image of the frontiersman in our tradition" as a "culture-type" in "Trajectory of My Work," 84.

63. George Lakoff and Mark Johnson, *Metaphors We Live By* (Chicago: University of Chicago Press, 1980). A well-known example of criticism in this vein is Robert L. Ivie, "Metaphor and the Rhetorical Invention of Cold War 'Idealists,'" *Communication Monographs* 54, no. 2 (1987): 165–82. An essay that precedes Lakoff and Johnson but that anticipates this approach to criticism is Edwin Black, "The Second Persona," *Quarterly Journal of Speech* 56, no. 2 (1970): 109–19. More recent examples include Marita Gronnvoll and Jamie Landau, "From Viruses to Russian Roulette to Dance: A Rhetorical Critique and Creation of Genetic Metaphors," *Rhetoric Society Quarterly* 40, no. 1 (2010): 46–70; Theresa Ann Donofrio, "Ground Zero and Place-Making Authority: The Conservative Metaphors in 9/11 Families' Take Back the Memorial' Rhetoric," *Western Journal of Communication* 74, no. 2 (2010): 150–69.

64. Osborn, "Broad Mythic Criticism," 122; Jeanne Fahnestock, *Rhetorical Style: The Uses of Language in Persuasion* (New York: Oxford University Press, 2011), 105; Randy Harris, review of *Tropical Truth(s)*, ed. Armin Burkhardt and Brigitte Nerlich, *Quarterly Journal of Speech* 97, no. 4 (2011): 474.

65. Douglass, "Issues," 419.

66. See, for example, Celeste M. Condit, "How the Public Understands Genetics: Non-deterministic and Non-discriminatory Interpretations of the 'Blueprint' Metaphor," *Public Understanding of Science* 8, no. 3 (1999): 169–80; Celeste M. Condit et al., "Recipes or Blueprints for Our Genes? How Contexts Selectively Activate the Multiple Meanings of Metaphors," *Quarterly Journal of Speech* 88, no. 3 (2002): 303–25; Celeste M. Condit, "Pathos in Criticism: Edwin Black's Communism-As-Cancer Metaphor," *Quarterly Journal of Speech* 99, no. 1 (2013): 1–26.

67. Cornelia Müller, *Metaphors Dead and Alive, Sleeping and Waking: A Dynamic View* (Chicago: University of Chicago Press, 2008).

68. John Lyne, "Learning the Lessons of Lysenko: Biology, Politics, and Rhetoric in Historical Controversy," in *Argument and Critical Practices: Proceedings of the Fifth SCA/AFA Conference on Argumentation*, ed. Joseph W. Wenzel (Annandale, Va.: Speech Communication Association, 1987), 508.

69. John Lyne, "Bio-Rhetorics: Moralizing the Life Sciences," in *The Rhetorical Turn: Invention and Persuasion in the Conduct of Inquiry*, ed. Herbert W. Simons (Chicago: University of Chicago Press, 1990), 38.

70. I use the term "postcolonial" here and elsewhere in this book to refer to the period after colonialism, an era in which imperialist assumptions are destabilized, but not abandoned, in public rhetoric. I am not claiming to develop a postcolonial analysis in this book, although I draw on postcolonial critical perspectives in a limited manner to draw attention to some of the unacknowledged assumptions of the frontier myth.

Chapter One. History of the Frontier of Science Metaphor

1. James Jasinski, "Instrumentalism, Contextualism, and Interpretation in Rhetorical Criticism," in *Rhetorical Hermeneutics: Invention and Interpretation in the Age of Science*, ed. William Keith and Alan G. Gross (Albany, N.Y.: SUNY Press, 1997), 214–15.

2. Frederick Jackson Turner, *The Frontier in American History* (New York: Henry Holt, 1920).

3. Vannevar Bush, *Science—The Endless Frontier* (Washington, D.C.: Government Printing Office, 1945).

4. Francis Bacon, *The Advancement of Learning* [1605], Project Gutenberg.

5. *Oxford English Dictionary*, s.v. "pioneer."

6. Victoria Neufeldt, ed., *Webster's New World College Dictionary*, 3rd ed. (New York: Macmillan, 1997), s.v. "frontier," 542.

7. Sidney I. Landau, ed., *Cambridge Dictionary of American English* (New York: Cambridge University Press 2001), s.v. "frontier," 349.

8. *Webster's Collegiate Dictionary*, 5th ed. (Springfield, Mass.: G. & C. Merriam, 1941), s.v. "frontier," 403.

9. *Webster's Collegiate Dictionary*, 4th ed. (Springfield, Mass.: G. & C. Merriam, 1934), s.v. "frontier," 404.

10. Charles Earle Funk, ed., *Funk and Wagnalls New Practical Standard Dictionary of the English Language*, Britannica World Language Edition, vol. 1 (New York: Funk and Wagnalls, 1955), s.v. "frontier," 533.

11. *Funk and Wagnalls New Standard Dictionary of the English Language* (New York: Funk and Wagnalls, 1946), s.v. "frontier," 986.

12. John A. Simpson and Edmund S. C. Weiner, eds., *Oxford English Dictionary*, 2nd ed., vol. 6 (New York: Oxford University Press, 1989), s.v. "frontier," 218; John A. Simpson and Edmund S. C. Weiner, eds., *Oxford English Dictionary Additions Series* (New York: Oxford University Press, 1993); John A. Simpson and Edmund S. C. Weiner, eds., *Oxford English Dictionary Additions Series* (New York: Oxford University Press, 1997); *Oxford English Dictionary*, s.v. "frontier."

13. For example, see A. S. Hornby, A. P. Cowie, and J. Windsor Lewis, eds., *Oxford Advanced Learner's Dictionary of Current English* (London: Oxford University Press, 1974), s.v. "frontier," 352; R. E. Allen, ed., *The Concise Oxford Dictionary of Current English*, 8th ed. (New York: Oxford University Press, 1990), s.v. "frontier," 473.

14. For example, see Clarence L. Barnhart, ed., *The American College Dictionary* (New York: Harper & Brothers, 1951), s.v. "frontier," 489; Elizabeth J. Jewell and Frank Abate, eds., *The New Oxford American Dictionary* (New York: Oxford University Press, 2001), s.v. "frontier," 681; Landau, *Cambridge Dictionary of American English*, s.v. "frontier," 349.

15. As I mentioned in the introduction, almost all the texts I examine in this book activate the metaphor by extended, rather than passing, reference that foregrounds and elaborates the source domain (frontier as wilderness region). For discussion of the distinction between active and inactive (or waking and sleeping) metaphors and the problems with defining metaphors as dead or alive, see Cornelia Müller, *Metaphors Dead and Alive, Sleeping and Waking: A Dynamic View* (Chicago: University of Chicago Press, 2008).

16. The paper was first published in *Proceedings of the State Historical Society of Wisconsin at Its Forty-First Annual Meeting, December 14, 1893* (Madison, Wis.: Democrat Printing, 1894): 79–112, and *The Annual Report of the American Historical Association for the Year 1893* (Washington, D.C.: Government Printing Office, 1894), 199–227. It was subsequently anthologized in several places, including the first chapter of his 1920 book, *The Frontier in American History*. All citations to Turner in this chapter appear in the text and refer to that book.

17. Catherine Gouge, "The American Frontier: History, Rhetoric, Concept," *Americana: The Journal of American Popular Culture (1900–present)* 6, no. 1 (Spring 2007).

18. Jack D. Forbes, "The Indian in the West: A Challenge for Historians," *Arizona and the West* 1, no. 3 (Autumn 1959): 206–15.

19. Mary E. Stuckey and John M. Murphy, "By Any Other Name: Rhetorical Colonialism in North America," *American Indian Culture and Research Journal* 24, no. 4 (2001): 87. See also Mary E. Stuckey, "The Donner Party and the Rhetoric of Westward Expansion," *Rhetoric & Public Affairs* 14, no. 2 (2011): 232.

20. Greg Dickinson, Brian L. Ott, and Eric Aoki, "Memory and Myth at the Buffalo Bill Museum," *Western Journal of Communication* 69, no. 2 (2005): 97.

21. Timothy Maurice O'Donnell, "Vannevar Bush, the Endless Frontier, and the Rhetoric of American Science Policy" (Ph.D. diss., University of Pittsburgh, 2000), 83.

22. Ronald H. Carpenter, "America's Opinion Leader Historians on Behalf of Success," *Quarterly Journal of Speech* 69, no. 2 (1983): 115.

23. Ronald H. Carpenter, "Frederick Jackson Turner and the Rhetorical Impact of the Frontier Thesis," *Quarterly Journal of Speech* 63, no. 2 (1977): 128. See also Ronald H. Carpenter, *The Eloquence of Frederick Jackson Turner* (San Marino, Calif.: Huntington Library, 1983).

24. Carpenter, "Frederick Jackson Turner," 120.

25. Carpenter, "Frederick Jackson Turner," 123. See also Carpenter, "America's Opinion," 115; Ronald H. Carpenter, *History as Rhetoric: Style, Narrative, and Persuasion* (Columbia: University of South Carolina Press, 1995): 47–48, 52–54.

26. Chaim Perelman and Lucie Olbrechts-Tyteca, *The New Rhetoric: A Treatise on Argumentation*, trans. John Wilkinson and Purcell Weaver (Notre Dame, Ind.: University of Notre Dame Press, 1969), 287.

27. Carpenter, "America's Opinion," 117.

28. Carpenter, "Frederick Jackson Turner," 123, 125.

29. Herbert Hoover, *American Individualism* (Garden City, N.Y.: Doubleday, Page & Company, 1922). For evidence that Hoover and Turner exchanged books and mutually admiring letters, see Ray Allen Billington, *Frederick Jackson Turner: Historian, Scholar, Teacher* (New York: Oxford University Press, 1973), 442.

30. David M. Wrobel, *The End of American Exceptionalism: Frontier Anxiety from the Old West to the New Deal* (Lawrence: University Press of Kansas, 1993), 101.

31. Hoover, *American Individualism*, 64.

32. John Dewey, "The American Intellectual Frontier," *New Republic* 30, no. 388 (May 10, 1922): 303–5.

33. J. Arthur Harris, "Frontiers," *Scientific Monthly* 30, no. 1 (1930): 19–32. Further references to this article appear in the text. The journal in which it was published, put out by the American Association for the Advancement of Science, was incorporated into the journal *Science* in 1957. Harris died four months after this article was published; he was eulogized as "a pioneer of indomitable spirit in scientific work until the day of his untimely passing." A. E. Treloar, "James Arthur Harris," *Journal of the American Statistical Association* 25, no. 171 (September 1930): 356.

34. For more on the genre of "inspirational" texts that seek to recruit readers to pursue careers in science, see Leah Ceccarelli, *Shaping Science with Rhetoric: The Cases of Dobzhansky, Schrödinger, and Wilson* (Chicago: University of Chicago Press, 2001).

35. For the interaction theory of metaphor, see I. A. Richards, *The Philosophy of Rhetoric* (New York: Oxford University Press, 1936); Max Black, "Metaphor," *Proceedings of the Aristotelian Society* 55 (1954): 286–91.

36. O'Donnell, "Vannevar Bush," 39, 166, 177–78.

37. O'Donnell, "Vannevar Bush," 81.

38. Franklin D. Roosevelt to Vannevar Bush, November 17, 1944, reprinted in Bush, *Science*, viii.

39. Daniel J. Kevles, "The National Science Foundation and the Debate over Postwar Research Policy, 1942–1945: A Political Interpretation of *Science—The Endless Frontier*," *Isis* 68, no. 1 (1977): 23; Daniel J. Kevles, "FDR's Science Policy," *Science* 183, no. 4127 (1974): 798, 800.

40. Vannevar Bush, "The Engineer and His Relation to Government," *Science* 86, no. 2222 (1937): 91. This essay is identified in a footnote as the concluding part of an address delivered to the American Institute of Electrical Engineers on June 22, 1937.

41. O'Donnell, "Vannevar Bush," 70–71.

42. Bush, *Science*. Further references to this publication appear in the text.

43. The committee reports were appendixes to the overall report, focusing on medicine (40–64), science and public welfare (65–127), the discovery and development of scientific talent (128–77), and the publication of scientific information (178–84).

44. Daniel Lee Kleinman, *Politics on the Endless Frontier: Postwar Research Policy in the United States* (Durham, N.C.: Duke University Press, 1995), 45; O'Donnell, "Vannevar Bush," 46.

45. O'Donnell, "Vannevar Bush," 103.

46. John F. Kennedy, "Address of Senator John F. Kennedy Accepting the Democratic Party Nomination for the Presidency of the United States—Memorial Coliseum, Los Angeles," July 15, 1960, in *The American Presidency Project*, ed. Gerhard Peters and John T. Woolley.

Chapter Two. The Frontier Metaphor in Public Speeches by American Scientists

1. Because the live performance of a speech is ephemeral, this chapter examines speech manuscripts. Each manuscript in the sample was attributed to a scientist speaking in an authoritative role as a leader of some academic, government, or

industry organization that distributed a text version of the speech in an effort to extend its influence beyond the moment of its original presentation.

2. Two recent exceptions are Christian F. Casper, "In Praise of Carbon, In Praise of Science: The Epideictic Rhetoric of the 1996 Nobel Lectures in Chemistry," *Journal of Business and Technical Communication* 21, no. 3 (2007): 303–23; and Lisa Keränen, Jason Lesko, Alison Vogelaar, and Lisa Irvin, "'Myth, Mask, Shield, and Sword': Dr. John H. Marburger III's Rhetoric of Neutral Science for the Nation," *Cultural Studies <=> Critical Methodologies* 8, no. 2 (2008): 159–86. Casper, however, considers the primary audience for the Nobel "lectures" he examines to be scientists, not a larger public, so he does not consider his artifacts to be *public* speech texts. I discuss the findings of the other study in more detail later in this chapter.

3. Consider, for example, the scholarship collected in Randy Allen Harris, ed., *Landmark Essays on Rhetoric of Science: Case Studies* (Mahwah, N.J.: Lawrence Erlbaum, 1997). A recent move in the field toward the study of material artifacts expands the range of objects considered, but continues the general neglect of public speech texts by scientists. See Jordynn Jack, "Object Lessons: Recent Work in the Rhetoric of Science," *Quarterly Journal of Speech* 96, no. 2 (2010): 209–16.

4. The transcript of the speech was not published, but the address was revised into an article that was published in the AAAS journal *Science*. Leon M. Lederman, "The Advancement of Science," *Science* 256, no. 5060 (1992): 1119–24. References to the speech appear in the text and cite this revised printed version.

5. Leon M. Lederman, "Science: The End of the Frontier?" *Science* 251, no. 4990 (1991): S1–S20.

6. Leon Lederman, "Scientific Retreat Demise of the SSC Is a National Loss," *Chicago Tribune*, November 18, 1993.

7. Arden L. Bement Jr., "From Commitment to Engagement: How Industry Can Cultivate Competitiveness," http://www.nsf.gov/news/speeches/bement/06/alb060628_digital.jsp. This speech was presented to the Digital Dialogue Forum in Washington, D.C., on June 28, 2006.

8. For more on this history of the mission, see Robert J. Miller, *Native America, Discovered and Conquered: Thomas Jefferson, Lewis & Clark, and Manifest Destiny* (Westport, Conn.: Praeger, 2006).

9. Evelyn Fox Keller, *Reflections on Gender and Science* (New Haven, Conn.: Yale University Press, 1985), 90, 78.

10. Shirley M. Tilghman, "Science: The Last Frontier," http://www.princeton.edu/president/speeches/20060228/index.xml. This speech was presented on February 28, 2006, at Sidwell Friends School in Washington, D.C.

11. Jeanne Fahnestock, "Accommodating Science: The Rhetorical Life of Scientific Facts," *Written Communication* 3, no. 3 (July 1986): 279.

12. Casper, "In Praise of Carbon," 320.

13. Keränen et al., "'Myth, Mask, Shield, and Sword,'" 162.

14. Keränen et al., "'Myth, Mask, Shield, and Sword,'" 167, 169–70, 177–79.

15. Bement, "From Commitment to Engagement."

16. See chapter 1 for discussion of Bacon's metaphor of the pioneers and smiths of science.

17. Arden L. Bement Jr., "Testimony before the Senate Commerce, Science and Transportation Subcommittee on Technology, Innovation and Competitiveness," March 29, 2006, http://commerce.senate.gov/pdf/bement-032906.pdf.

18. Arden L. Bement Jr., "Speech at the 30th Annual AAAS Forum on Science and Technology Policy," Washington, D.C., April 21, 2005, http://www.aaas.org/news/releases/2005/0422bementText.shtml.

19. Frederick Jackson Turner, *The Frontier in American History* (New York: Henry Holt, 1920), 153, 269–89.

20. For a detailed study of this doctrine, see Miller, *Native America*.

21. Tilghman, "Science."

22. Bement, "Testimony before the Senate."

23. Bement, "Speech at the 30th Annual AAAS Forum."

24. Davida Charney makes a similar point about the "horse-race" framing found in popular treatments of science, which focuses on heroic individuals competing with each other and "devalues the collective sharing" that makes science a communal venture. Davida Charney, "Lone Geniuses in Popular Science: The Devaluation of Scientific Consensus," *Written Communication* 20, no. 3 (2003): 215, 217.

25. August M. Watanabe, "Leveraging Scientific Research for the Next American Century: The Future of Science and Technology in the Heartland," *Vital Speeches of the Day* 60, no. 1 (1996): 12–14. This speech was delivered to the Future of Science and Technology in the Heartland Conference on August 21, 1996.

26. Robert B. Gagosian, "An Old Idea for New Science: Discovery Means Taking Risks," *Vital Speeches of the Day* 71, no. 4 (2004): 122–25. This speech was delivered on June 7, 2004, to IdeasBoston 2004.

27. Gagosian, "Old Idea," 125, 124.

28. Gagosian, "Old Idea," 123.

29. Gagosian, "Old Idea," 123–24.

30. Sheila Jasanoff, *Designs on Nature: Science and Democracy in Europe and the United States* (Princeton, N.J.: Princeton University Press, 2005), 250.

31. Choon Fong Shih, "Speech Presented at the Brown University Commencement Forum," May 24, 2008, http://www.kaust.edu.sa/about/presidents-speech-brown.aspx.

Chapter Three. The Dangers of Bioprospecting on the Frontier: The Rhetoric of Edward O. Wilson's Biodiversity Appeals

1. D. Graham Burnett, "A View from the Bridge: The Two Cultures Debate, Its Legacy, and the History of Science," *Daedalus* 128, no. 2 (1999): 214. The book to which Burnett refers is Edward O. Wilson, *Consilience: The Unity of Knowledge* (New York: Alfred A. Knopf, 1998).

2. Leah Ceccarelli, *Shaping Science with Rhetoric: The Cases of Dobzhansky, Schrödinger, and Wilson* (Chicago: University of Chicago Press, 2001), 129–37.

3. Ceccarelli, *Shaping Science with Rhetoric*, 137–39.

4. Edward O. Wilson, *The Diversity of Life* (1992; repr., New York: W. W. Norton, 1999), 351. Further references to this publication are cited in the text as "*D*" followed by the page number.

5. Edwin Black, "The Second Persona," *Quarterly Journal of Speech* 56, no. 2 (1970): 119.

6. Edward O. Wilson, *The Future of Life* (New York: Vintage Books, 2002). Further references to this publication are cited in the text as "*F*" followed by the page number.

7. Gregg Sapp, review of *The Future of Life*, by Edward O. Wilson, *Library Journal* 127, no. 1 (2002): 147; John Terborgh, "A Matter of Life and Death," review of *The Diversity of Life*, by Edward O. Wilson, *New York Review of Books* 39, no. 18 (1992): 3, 6; Wayne H. Davis, review of *The Diversity of Life*, by Edward O. Wilson, *Growth and Change* 24, no. 2 (1993): 278; Kevin Shapiro, "Biophiliac," review of *The Future of Life*, by Edward O. Wilson, *Commentary* 113, no. 4 (2002): 67, 68.

8. Alice L. Clarke, review of *The Diversity of Life*, by Edward O. Wilson, *Politics and Life Sciences* 13, no. 1 (1994): 129.

9. This Kipling poem, titled "The Explorer," seems to hold a special appeal for Americans attracted to the frontier myth. Frederick Jackson Turner mentions it in a footnote to the reprinting of his University of Indiana commencement address. The botanist and mathematician J. Arthur Harris quotes from this poem in his 1930 argument that scientists should think of themselves as new frontiersmen. Frederick Jackson Turner, *The Frontier in American History* (New York: Henry Holt, 1920), 270; J. Arthur Harris, "Frontiers," *Scientific Monthly* 30, no. 1 (1930): 20–21. See chapter 1 for more on Turner and Harris.

10. Robert L. Ivie, "Metaphor and the Rhetorical Invention of Cold War 'Idealists,'" *Communication Monographs* 54, no. 2 (1987): 167.

11. Walter V. Reid et al., *Biodiversity Prospecting: Using Genetic Resources for Sustainable Development* (Washington, D.C.: World Resources Institute, 1993).

12. Leslie Roberts, "Chemical Prospecting: Hope for Vanishing Ecosystems?" *Science* 256, no. 5060 (1992): 1143; Ricardo Bonalume Neto and David Dickson, "$3m Deal Launches Major Hunt for Drug Leads in Brazil," *Nature* 400, no. 6742 (1999): 302.

13. Ana Isla, "An Ecofeminist Perspective on Biopiracy in Latin America," *Signs: Journal of Women in Culture and Society* 32, no. 2 (2007): 323–31.

14. Beth Burrows, "Patents, Ethics and Spin," in *Redesigning Life? The Worldwide Challenge to Genetic Engineering*, ed. Brian Tokar (Montreal and Kingston: McGill-Queen's University Press, 2001), 239.

15. Victoria Tauli-Corpuz, "Biotechnology and Indigenous Peoples," in Tokar, *Redesigning Life?* 255.

16. Vandana Shiva, "Bioprospecting as Sophisticated Biopiracy," *Signs: Journal of Women in Culture and Society* 32, no. 2 (2007): 309–10.

17. Shiva, "Bioprospecting," 313.

18. Edward O. Wilson, *A Diversidade Da Vida*, trans. Carlos Afonso Malferrari (São Paulo: Companhia das Letras, 1994); Edward O. Wilson, *O Futuro Da Vida: Um Estudo Da Bioesfera Para A Proteção De Todas As Espécies, Inclusive A Humana*, trans. Ronaldo Sérgio de Biasi (Rio de Janeiro: Editora Campus, 2002).

19. Larry Rohter, "As Brazil Defends Its Bounty, Rules Ensnare Scientists," *New York Times*, August 28, 2007. The term "biopiracy" is an interesting countermetaphor to the term "bioprospecting." Activist organizations like the ETC Group use this language to evoke another frontier-era character whose theft, because it was against the powerful, can be more easily recognized as transgressive. See ETC Group, "Biopiracy + 10. Captain Hook Awards—2002," *Communiqué* 75 (March/April 2002).

20. Marina Silva, "Recursos Biológicos: A Riqueza Brasileira," interview by Maria Fernanda Diniz Avidose and Lucas Tadeu Ferreira, *Revista Biotecnologia Ciência & Desenvolvimento* 1, no. 2 (1997): 44–45. All Brazilian texts cited in this chapter were translated from Portuguese into English by Patricia Narvaes.

21. Antonio Silveira R. dos Santos, "Biodiversidade, Bioprospecção, Conhecimento Tradicional e o Futuro da Vida," *Revista de Informação e Tecnologia* (March 2001).

22. Lorenzo Carrasco quoted in Larry Rohter, "In the Amazon: Conservation or Colonialism," *New York Times*, July 26, 2007.

23. Rohter, "In the Amazon." A widely reproduced map of the Amazon as an "international reserve," said to be extracted from an American middle-school geography textbook, is most certainly a hoax, as Rohter suggests. It has also been widely reported that Brazilians bristled when Senator Al Gore purportedly said in 1989 that "contrary to what Brazilians think, the Amazon is not their property, it belongs to all of us." See Alexei Barrionuevo, "Whose Rain Forest Is This, Anyway?" *New York Times*, May 18, 2008; Sonia Gallego, "Alarm Bells Sound for the Amazon," *ABC News*, May 29, 2008. Irrespective of the accuracy of claims that Americans

want to internationalize the Amazon, the angry reaction of Brazilians to such comments indicates how sensitive this issue is.

24. Barrionuevo, "Whose Rain Forest?"

25. Brazilian military intelligence report, quoted in Rohter, "In the Amazon."

26. Darlene Menconi and Leonel Rocha, "Riqueza Ameaçada," *Isto É* 1773 (September 24, 2003).

27. "Amazônia a soberania está em xeque," *Isto É*, 2012 (May 28, 2008).

28. Rohter, "In the Amazon."

29. Esa Väliverronen and Iina Hellsten, "From 'Burning Library' to 'Green Medicine': The Role of Metaphors in Communicating Biodiversity," *Science Communication* 24, no. 2 (2002): 229–45.

30. Väliverronen and Hellsten, "From 'Burning Library' to 'Green Medicine,'" 234, 240. They label this image "positive" because their study, which focuses on British and American texts, finds little uptake on potential controversies such as strained North-South relations, property rights, and the rights of indigenous peoples. Had they examined other texts from indigenous groups or from nations that see themselves as being targeted for exploitation by foreign powers, I suspect they would have found the image of untapped biological riches to be more contested.

31. Väliverronen and Hellsten, "From 'Burning Library' to 'Green Medicine,'" 234.

32. James Lovelock, review of *The Diversity of Life*, by Edward O. Wilson, *TLS—The Times Literary Supplement* 4731 (December 3, 1993): 9.

33. James E. Lovelock, *Gaia: A New Look at Life on Earth* (Oxford: Oxford University Press, 1979), 28, 129, 111.

34. Lovelock, review, 9.

35. Eric Reis, "Rainbow Warrior," review of *The Diversity of Life*, by Edward O. Wilson, *Public Interest* 110 (Winter 1993): 106; Gunther Stent, "Save Biodiversity," review of *The Diversity of Life*, by Edward O. Wilson, *Partisan Review* 61, no. 4 (1994): 694.

36. Stent, "Save Biodiversity," 689, 694–95.

37. An example of his critique of Wilson's sociobiology is found in Stephen Jay Gould, review of *On Human Nature*, by Edward O. Wilson, *Human Nature* 1, no. 10 (1978): 20–28. Wilson's gratuitous savaging of Gould's theory of punctuated equilibrium appears on pages 88–89 of *The Diversity of Life*. One reviewer takes exception to this "loftily dismissive" treatment of Gould; see Marek Kohn, "The Soft Machine," review of *The Diversity of Life*, by Edward O. Wilson, *New Statesman and Society* 6, no. 240 (1993): 37.

38. Stephen Jay Gould, "Prophet for the Earth," review of *The Diversity of Life*, by Edward O. Wilson, *Nature* 361, no. 6410 (1993): 311–12.

39. Gould, "Prophet," 311–12.

40. "About Us," *Commentary Magazine*, www.commentarymagazine.com/about.

41. Shapiro, "Biophiliac," 66–68.

42. Kenan Malik, "The End Is Not Nigh: This Ecological Jeremiad by a Scientist Who Believes in Both Man and in Nature Is Too Gloomy by Half," review of *The Future of Life*, by Edward O. Wilson, *Sunday Telegraph*, April 21, 2002.

43. Patricia Nelson Limerick, "The Persistence of the Frontier," *Harper's* 289, no. 1733 (1994): 21–23.

Chapter Four. Biocolonialism and Human Genomics Research: The Frontier Mapping Expedition of Francis Collins

1. "Remarks Made by the President, Prime Minister Tony Blair of England (via satellite), Dr. Francis Collins, Director of the National Human Genome Research Institute, and Dr. Craig Venter, President and Chief Scientific Officer, Celera Genomics Corporation, on the Completion of the First Survey of the Entire Human Genome Project," June 26, 2000, the White House, http://www.genome.gov/10001356.

2. Bita Amani and Rosemary J. Coombe, "The Human Genome Diversity Project: The Politics of Patents at the Intersection of Race, Religion, and Research Ethics," *Law & Policy* 27, no. 1 (2005): 164–65.

3. Francis S. Collins, *The Language of Life: DNA and the Revolution in Personalized Medicine* (New York: HarperCollins, 2010), 303. Venter's personal history of how the event came about is, in some ways, strikingly different from the one that Collins tells, but he too describes it as a "truce" between groups who were engaged in a competitive race to sequence the genome. See J. Craig Venter, *A Life Decoded: My Genome: My Life* (New York: Viking Penguin, 2007).

4. "Remarks Made by the President."

5. "Remarks Made by the President."

6. "Remarks Made by the President."

7. Francis S. Collins, *The Language of God: A Scientist Presents Evidence for Belief* (New York: Free Press, 2006), 2.

8. "Remarks Made by the President."

9. Collins, *Language of Life*, 304.

10. Matt Ridley quoted in Collins, *Language of Life*, 304. The quote is from Matt Ridley, *Genome: The Autobiography of a Species in 23 Chapters* (New York: HarperCollins, 2000), 6.

11. Collins, *Language of Life*, 2.

12. Francis Collins interview, May 23, 1998, Jackson Hole, Wyo., *Academy of Achievement*.

13. Collins, *Language of Life*, 2. See also his somewhat different use of a mountain-climbing metaphor in his comments during the "Millennium Evening at the White House: Informatics Meets Genomics," October 12, 1999, http://www.genome.gov/10001397. In that discussion with Hillary Clinton, Collins claimed that "the top of the mountain is curing diabetes, curing hypertension, curing cancer, curing schizophrenia," with the Human Genome Project serving merely as the "base camp" that scientists build before taking a pathway toward the top of the mountain. When using another mountain-climbing metaphor eleven years later, Collins shifted from the mountaineer's context, where reaching the top is the achievement, to the frontiersman's context, in which the mountain is something to climb *over* to get to the other side. In 1999, the top of the mountain was the cure; in 2010, the top of the mountain was redefined as the Human Genome Project, with cures to be found in some distant valley on the other side.

14. Francis Collins, "Statement on Frontiers of Science before Committee on Appropriations, Subcommittee on Labor, Health and Human Services, Education and Related Agencies, U.S. Senate," April 30, 2007, http://www.hhs.gov/asl/testify/2007/04/t20070430e.html; Francis Collins, "Remarks of NIH Director Francis Collins," September 30, 2009, http://www.nih.gov/about/director/09302009remarks_POTUS.htm.

15. Brigitte Nerlich and Iina Hellsten, "Genomics: Shifts in Metaphorical Landscape between 2000 and 2003," *New Genetics and* Society 23, no. 3 (2004): 256–57. See also Hub Zwart, "The Adoration of a Map: Reflections on a Genome Metaphor," *Genomics, Society and Policy* 5, no. 3 (2009): 39. The essay mentioned is Francis Collins, Eric D. Green, Alan E. Guttmacher, and Mark S. Guyer, "A Vision for the Future of Genomics Research: A Blueprint for the Genomic Era," *Nature* 422, no. 6934 (2003): 835–47.

16. Nerlich and Hellsten, "Genomics," 266.

17. José van Dijck, *Imagenation: Popular Images of Genetics* (Washington Square: New York University Press, 1998), 127.

18. Alice Domurat Dreger, "Metaphors of Morality in the Human Genome Project," in *Controlling Our Destinies: Historical, Philosophical, Ethical, and Theological Perspectives on the Human Genome Project*, ed. Phillip R. Sloan (Notre Dame, Ind.: University of Notre Dame Press, 2000), 159–60, 163, 167, 175.

19. Mary Rosner and T. R. Johnson, "Telling Stories: Metaphors of the Human Genome Project," *Hypatia* 10, no. 4 (1995): 104, 117.

20. Zwart, "Adoration of a Map," 30, 33.

21. "Remarks Made by the President."

22. Brigitte Nerlich, Robert Dingwall, and David D. Clarke, "The Book of Life: How the Completion of the Human Genome Project Was Revealed to the Public,"

health: An Interdisciplinary Journal for the Social Study of Health, Illness and Medicine 6, no. 4 (2002): 446.

23. Nerlich, Dingwall, and Clarke, "Book of Life," 450.

24. One reception study of the White House announcement that focuses on the "genome is a text" metaphor cluster and mentions the instruction book vehicle as part of this cluster is Helena Calsamiglia and Teun A. van Dijk, "Popularization Discourse and Knowledge About the Genome," *Discourse & Society* 15, no. 4 (2004): 369–89.

25. "Remarks Made by the President."

26. This interpretation of the "book of life" metaphor in the speech by Collins is mentioned in Nerlich, Dingwall, and Clarke, "Book of Life," 451.

27. Collins, "Remarks."

28. Collins, *Language of God*, 86, 88.

29. For a look at how another interaction of two seemingly conflicting metaphors in this media event ends up resolving into a single image that favors the entailments of one metaphor over the other, see Leah Ceccarelli, "Neither Confusing Cacophony Nor Culinary Complements: A Case Study of Mixed Metaphors for Genomic Science," *Written Communication* 21, no. 1 (2004): 92–105.

30. Cor van der Weele, "Roads towards a *Lingua Democratica* on Genomics: How Can Metaphors Guide Us?" *Genomics, Society and Policy* 5, no. 3 (2009): v.

31. Martin Döring, "A Sequence of 'Factishes': The Media-Metaphorical Knowledge Dynamics Structuring the German Press Coverage of the Human Genome," *New Genetics and Society* 24, no. 3 (2005): 331.

32. Zwart, "Adoration of a Map," 37.

33. Collins, "Remarks."

34. Eleni Gogorosi, "Untying the Gordian Knot of Creation: Metaphors for the Human Genome Project in Greek Newspapers," *New Genetics and Society* 24, no. 3 (2005): 306.

35. Andrew Smart, "Reporting the Dawn of the Post-Genomic Era: Who Wants to Live Forever?" *Sociology of Health & Illness* 25, no. 1 (2003): 35–36.

36. Döring, "Sequence of 'Factishes,'" 328, 329.

37. Nerlich, Dingwall, and Clarke, "Book of Life," 448.

38. Zwart, "Adoration of a Map," 36.

39. Collins, "Remarks."

40. "Remarks Made by the President."

41. "Remarks Made by the President."

42. Marouf Hasian Jr. and Emily Plec, "The Cultural, Legal, and Scientific Arguments in the Human Genome Diversity Debate," *Howard Journal of Communications* 13, no. 4 (2002): 314. For a history of the HGDP, see Jenny Reardon, *Race to the Finish: Identity and Governance in an Age of Genomics* (Princeton, N.J.: Princeton

University Press, 2005). Another excellent study of the issues involved, this one written before the White House media event and thus presumably available to those participating in it, is Hilary Cunningham, "Colonial Encounters in Postcolonial Contexts: Patenting Indigenous DNA and the Human Genome Diversity Project," *Critique of Anthropology* 18, no. 2 (1998): 205–33.

43. "Declaration of Indigenous Peoples of the Western Hemisphere Regarding the Human Genome Diversity Project," Phoenix, Ariz., February 19, 1995, http://www.indians.org/welker/genome.htm.

44. Leona Lone Dog, "Whose Genes Are They? The Human Genome Diversity Project," *Journal of Health and Social Policy* 10, no. 4 (1999): 58.

45. Debra Harry, "The Human Genome Diversity Project: Implications for Indigenous Peoples," *Abya Yala News* 8, no. 4 (1994).

46. Susan Hawthorne, "Land, Bodies, and Knowledge: Biocolonialism of Plants, Indigenous Peoples, Women, and People with Disabilities," *Signs: Journal of Women in Culture and Society* 32, no. 2 (2007): 318.

47. Victoria Tauli-Corpuz, "Biotechnology and Indigenous Peoples," in *Redesigning Life? The Worldwide Challenge to Genetic Engineering*, ed. Brian Tokar (Montreal and Kingston: McGill-Queen's University Press, 2001), 255.

48. See Government Accountability Office, "Native American Graves Protection and Repatriation Act: After Almost 20 Years, Key Federal Agencies Still Have Not Fully Complied with the Act," July 2010, GAO-10–768, http://www.gao.gov/assets/310/307856.pdf; Government Accountability Office, "Smithsonian Institution: Much Work Still Needed to Identify and Repatriate Indian Human Remains and Objects," May 2011, GAO-11–515, http://www.gao.gov/assets/320/318818.pdf.

49. Paul Smaglik, "Genetic Diversity Project Fights for Its Life . . ." *Nature* 912, no. 6781 (2000): 912.

50. See Marouf Hasian Jr., "The Internet and the Human Genome," *Peace Review* 13, no. 3 (2001): 375–80; Reardon, *Race to the Finish*, 145–46, 157; Jenny Reardon, "Democratic Mis-haps: The Problem of Democratization in a Time of Biopolitics," *BioSocieties* 2, no. 2 (2007): 243; Joanne Barker, "The Human Genome Diversity Project: 'Peoples,' 'Populations,' and the Cultural Politics of Identification," *Cultural Studies* 18, no. 4 (2004): 588, 598. Both Reardon and Barker note, however, that while the HGDP was defeated by this criticism, its advocates have found ways to see their goals met in other research proposals, like the HapMap project and the Genographic project.

51. Reardon, "Democratic Mis-haps," 243.

52. Francis S. Collins, "Exploring the Frontiers of Life: Northwest at Forefront of Pioneering Effort to Mine the Secrets of the Human Genome," *Seattle Times*, August 7, 2005.

53. Collins, "Exploring the Frontiers of Life."

54. Collins, "Exploring the Frontiers of Life."

55. The rhetorician Celeste Condit argues that people respond to genomic meta-phors with their emotions as much as through a rational comparison of tenor and vehicle. This might explain why Collins would develop a solution to the problem of the frontier of science metaphor that is not rationally sound. Familiar with both the triumphalism of the frontier myth and with revisionist histories of the current era, it is likely that Collins feels ambivalent about the frontier of science metaphor, which allows him to embrace it and reject it simultaneously, but does not force him to respond with a rational conclusion that takes into account the most troubling analogical inferences of the metaphor. See Celeste M. Condit, "Dynamic Feelings about Metaphors for Genes: Implications for Research and Genetic Policy," *Genomics, Society and Policy* 5, no. 3 (2009): 44–58.

56. Laurie Anne Whitt, "Value-Bifurcation in Bioscience: The Rhetoric of Research Justification," *Perspectives on Science* 7, no. 4 (1999): 420.

57. Hasian and Plec, "Cultural, Legal, and Scientific Arguments," 309, 313.

58. Reardon, "Democratic Mis-haps," 254.

59. Collins, "Exploring the Frontiers of Life."

Chapter Five. Reframing the Frontier of Science: George W. Bush's Stem Cell Rhetoric

1. Polls suggest that 32–45 percent of Americans watched Bush's speech on televi-sion. Matthew C. Nisbet, "The Polls—Trends: Public Opinion about Stem Cell Research and Human Cloning," *Public Opinion Quarterly* 68, no. 1 (2004): 141.

2. George W. Bush, "Address to the Nation on Stem Cell Research," August 9, 2001, in *The American Presidency Project*, ed. Gerhard Peters and John T. Woolley.

3. In addition to the studies that I cite in the remainder of this chapter, some examples of this research include Leroy G. Dorsey, *We Are All Americans, Pure and Simple: Theodore Roosevelt and the Myth of Americanism* (Tuscaloosa, Uni-versity of Alabama Press, 2007); J. Justin Gustainis, "John F. Kennedy and the Green Berets: The Rhetorical Use of the Hero Myth," *Communication Studies* 40, no. 1 (1989): 41–53; Janice Hocker Rushing, "Ronald Reagan's 'Star Wars' Address: Mythic Containment of Technical Reasoning," *Quarterly Journal of Speech* 72 (1986): 415–33; Linda T. Krug, *Presidential Perspectives on Space Exploration: Guiding Metaphors from Eisenhower to Bush* (New York: Praeger, 1991).

4. For more on Turner's frontier thesis and how it was received by Americans, see chapter 1.

5. Calvin Coolidge, "Address Accepting the Statue of President Andrew Jack-son at Washington, D.C.," April 15, 1928, in Peters and Woolley, *American Presidency Project*.

6. Coolidge, "Address Accepting the Statue."

7. Recall that he used the frontier of science metaphor ten years earlier as well, in a 1922 book; see chapter 1 for more on this.

8. Herbert Hoover, "Address at Madison Square Garden in New York City," October 31, 1932, in Peters and Woolley, *American Presidency Project*.

9. Davis W. Houck, "FDR's Commonwealth Club Address: Redefining Individualism, Adjudicating Greatness," *Rhetoric & Public Affairs* 7, no. 3 (2004): 268, 272–73, 276.

10. Franklin Delano Roosevelt, "Radio Address to the Young Democratic Clubs of America," August 24, 1935, in Peters and Woolley, *American Presidency Project*.

11. Roosevelt, "Radio Address." For more on the contours of Roosevelt's prudential reasoning in the earlier Commonwealth Club speech, see Michael Leff, "Prudential Argument and the Use of History in Franklin Delano Roosevelt's 'Commonwealth Club' Address," in *Proceedings of the Second International Conference on Argumentation*, ed. F. H. van Eemeren, R. Grootendorshet, J. A. Blair, and C. A. Willard (Amsterdam: SICSAT, 1991), 931–36.

12. Roosevelt, "Radio Address."

13. Recall from chapter 1 that it was also the FDR administration that used such stirring frontier language to commission Vannevar Bush's *Science—The Endless Frontier*.

14. See Leroy G. Dorsey, "The Frontier Myth in Presidential Rhetoric: Theodore Roosevelt's Campaign for Conservation," *Western Journal of Communication* 59, no. 1 (1995): 1–19; Leroy G. Dorsey, "The Myth of War and Peace in Presidential Discourse: John Kennedy's 'New Frontier' Myth and the Peace Corps," *Southern Communication Journal* 62, no. 1 (1996): 42–55.

15. John F. Kennedy, "Address of Senator John F. Kennedy Accepting the Democratic Party Nomination for the Presidency of the United States—Memorial Coliseum, Los Angeles," July 15, 1960, in Peters and Woolley, *American Presidency Project*.

16. Kennedy, "Accepting the Democratic Party Nomination."

17. James L. Kauffman, *Selling Outer Space: Kennedy, the Media, and Funding for Project Apollo, 1961–1963* (Tuscaloosa: University of Alabama Press, 1994), 10; see also 132–33.

18. John W. Jordan, "Kennedy's Romantic Moon and Its Rhetorical Legacy for Space Exploration," *Rhetoric & Public Affairs* 6, no. 2 (2003): 221.

19. John F. Kennedy, "Address at Rice University in Houston on the Nation's Space Effort," September 12, 1962, in Peters and Woolley, *American Presidency Project*.

20. Gerald R. Ford, "Remarks at Dedication Ceremonies for the National Air and Space Museum," July 1, 1976, in Peters and Woolley, *American Presidency Project*.

21. George H. W. Bush, "Remarks at the Superconducting Super Collider Laboratory in Waxahachie, Texas," July 30, 1992, in Peters and Woolley, *American Presidency Project*.

22. Mary E. Stuckey, *Slipping the Surly Bonds: Reagan's* Challenger *Address* (College Station: Texas A&M University Press, 2006).

23. Ronald Reagan, "Address to the Nation on the Explosion of the Space Shuttle *Challenger*," January 28, 1986, in Peters and Woolley, *American Presidency Project*.

24. Ronald Reagan, "Remarks at the Memorial Service for the Crew of the Space Shuttle *Challenger* in Houston, Texas," January 31, 1986, in Peters and Woolley, *American Presidency Project*.

25. Dwight D. Eisenhower, "Address in Convention Hall, Philadelphia, Pennsylvania," November 1, 1956, in Peters and Woolley, *American Presidency Project*.

26. Ford, "Remarks at Dedication Ceremonies."

27. William J. Clinton, "Remarks on Presenting the National Medals of Science and Technology," April 27, 1999, in Peters and Woolley, *American Presidency Project*. As I demonstrated in the previous chapter, Clinton also invoked the metaphor in celebrating the Human Genome Project.

28. George W. Bush, "Remarks on Presenting the National Medals of Science and Technology," March 14, 2005, in Peters and Woolley, *American Presidency Project*.

29. George W. Bush, "The President's News Conference," August 9, 2007, in Peters and Woolley, *American Presidency Project*.

30. George W. Bush, "The President's Radio Address," September 22, 2001, in Peters and Woolley, *American Presidency Project*.

31. Bush, "Address to the Nation."

32. There are several sources that relate this history. See, for example, "Stem Cell 101: Legislators Toolkit: Federal Public Policy," Kansas University Medical Center, http://www.kumc.edu/stem-cell-101/federal-public-policy.html; "AAAS Policy Brief: Stem Cell Research," http://www.aaas.org/spp/cstc/briefs/stemcells/#ban.

33. William J. Clinton, "Remarks on the Electricity Shortage in California and an Exchange with Reporters," August 23, 2000, in Peters and Woolley, *American Presidency Project*.

34. "National Institutes of Health Guidelines for Research Using Human Pluripotent Stem Cells and Notification of Request for Emergency Clearance," *Federal Register* 65, no. 166 (2000), 51975–81.

35. "Nobel Laureates' Letter to President Bush," *Washington Post*, February 21, 2001.

36. John Lynch, *What Are Stem Cells? Definitions at the Intersection of Science and Politics* (Tuscaloosa: University of Alabama Press, 2011), 119.

37. Hughes acknowledged authorship of the speech, claiming to have received help from "policy expert" Lefkowitz and from Bush himself, in Karen Hughes, *Ten Minutes from Normal* (New York: Viking Penguin, 2004), 229. Lefkowitz confirmed that he and Bush worked on the speech with Hughes in Jay P. Lefkowitz, "Stem Cells and the President: An Inside Account," *Commentary* 125, no. 1 (January 2008): 23.

38. David Frum, *The Right Man: The Surprise Presidency of George W. Bush* (New York: Random House, 2003), 105.

39. Mark West and Chris Carey, "(Re)Enacting Frontier Justice: The Bush Administration's Tactical Narration of the Old West Fantasy after September 11," *Quarterly Journal of Speech* 92, no. 4 (2006): 380.

40. For more on these different meanings, recall the etymological analysis in chapter 1.

41. "McCartney Launches Landmine Campaign," *CNN.com*, June 4, 2001.

42. Scholars who have examined the public discourse over embryonic research in the United Kingdom have found that allusions to negative science fiction scenarios such as *Brave New World* are used there almost exclusively by proponents of the research, who (inaccurately) attribute such references to opponents and use such references in a rhetorically dismissive way to argue that opponents are being unreasonable in attacking hysterical fictions rather than realities. Michael Mulkay, "Frankenstein and the Debate over Embryo Research," *Science, Technology, & Human Values* 21, no. 2 (Spring 1996): 164, 167–69; Jenny Kitzinger and Clare Williams, "Forecasting Science Futures: Legitimising Hope and Calming Fears in the Embryo Stem Cell Debate," *Social Science and Medicine* 61, no. 3 (2005): 736–37. However, a study of public discourse over cloning in the United Kingdom found a strategy similar to the one used by Bush to be prevalent there, with critics of the research evoking an apocalyptic future through science fiction references in an effort to counter the arguments of supporters that scientists are on a journey that must not be blocked. Iina Hellsten, "Dolly: Scientific Breakthrough or Frankenstein's Monster? Journalistic and Scientific Metaphors of Cloning," *Metaphor and Symbol* 15, no. 4 (2000): 213–21. These divergent findings indicate that further study of how science fiction dystopias are used in public discourse about science is warranted, especially regarding how different scientific controversies are treated in different national contexts.

43. Lefkowitz, "Stem Cells," 22.

44. Nisbet, "Polls," 135–36.

45. Sheryl Gay Stolberg, "Stem Cell Research Advocates in Limbo," *New York Times*, January 20, 2001; Lynch, *What Are Stem Cells?* 49, 51.

46. Frum, *Right Man*, 107.

47. Polls taken after the speech indicate that 75 percent of Americans favored the use of "discarded embryos" in stem cell research. The president's policy would prohibit federal funding of such research. Yet polls taken at the same time report that from 50 to 62 percent of Americans approved of Bush's decision. Nisbet, "Polls," 146, 149.

48. Frum, *Right Man*, 110.

49. Frank Luntz, "The Environment: A Cleaner, Safer, Healthier America," Luntz Research Companies—Straight Talk, n.d., http://www.ewg.org/files/LuntzResearch _environment.pdf. I document elsewhere that this memo was produced sometime

between November 2001 and November 2002. See Leah Ceccarelli, "Manufactured Scientific Controversy: Science, Rhetoric, and Public Debate," *Rhetoric & Public Affairs* 14, no. 2 (2011): 224.

50. Lynch, *What Are Stem Cells?* 12–13, 124.

51. For some arguments by ethicists in favor of embryonic stem cell research that would have been available to the Bush administration prior to this speech, see George J. Annas, Arthur Caplan, and Sherman Ellias, "The Politics of Human-Embryo Research: Avoiding Ethical Gridlock," *New England Journal of Medicine* 334, no. 20 (1996): 1329–32; Geron Ethics Advisory Board, "Research with Human Embryonic Stem Cells: Ethical Considerations," *Hastings Center Report* 29, no. 2 (1999): 31–36; National Bioethics Advisory Commission, *Ethical Issues in Human Stem Cell Research: Executive Summary*, September 1999, http://bioethics .georgetown.edu/nbac/execsumm.pdf.

52. In using the term "embryo" rather than "pre-embryo" in framing this second exchange, Bush signaled that he was swayed by the argument of the ethicist who opposed embryonic stem cell research in the first exchange. But this is a subtle signal, and probably lost on those not reading the speech closely.

53. Bush, "Address to the Nation." The idea of treating the human body as a "natural resource" subject to exploitation is an abhorrent one, but as we saw in the previous chapter on Francis Collins and the map of the human genome, it is an idea that can arise when terms from the American frontier myth are applied to biomedical issues. Although Bush's speech did not make a direct critique of the application of the frontier myth to biomedical science, it did subtly hint here that the exploitation of natural resources is inappropriate when the territory being explored is human bodies.

54. Bush, "Address to the Nation."

55. Bush, "Address to the Nation."

56. Bush, "Address to the Nation."

57. Lynch, *What Are Stem Cells?* 120.

58. "Nonoverlapping magisteria" is the idea that science and religion exist in separate domains encompassing the empirical and the moral respectively, and that those spheres do not intersect. Stephen Jay Gould, "Nonoverlapping Magisteria," *Natural History* 106, no. 2 (1997): 16–22.

59. Frank Bruni, "Of Principles and Politics: Decision Helps Define the President's Image," *New York Times*, August 10, 2001.

60. "William Jefferson Bush," *New York Times*, August 12, 2001.

61. "Bush Blocks Stem Cell Funding That Would Destroy Embryos," *NRLC News* 28, no. 8 (2001).

62. Robin Toner, "The Reaction: Each Side Finds Something to Like, and Not," *New York Times*, August 10, 2001.

63. Quoted in Patricia Guthrie, "In Atlanta, Decision Elicits Support, Dismay, Concern," *Atlanta Journal Constitution*, August 10, 2001.

64. Quoted in Sheryl Gay Stolberg, "A Question of Research: Disappointed by Limits, Scientists Doubt Estimate of Available Cell Lines," *New York Times*, August 10, 2001.

65. Quoted in Sheryl Gay Stolberg, "U.S. Acts Quickly to Put Stem Cell Policy in Effect," *New York Times*, August 11, 2001.

66. Quoted in Guthrie, "In Atlanta."

67. Peggy Thomas, letter to the editor, *New York Times*, August 11, 2001.

68. In fact, the fallibility of the stratagem might have ironically worked in Bush's favor. Frum pointed out that when the nation's Catholic bishops "rather ungenerously" caviled at the speech the next day, "they did him a favor," reassuring supporters of the research that Bush had aligned with them rather than with the religious Right. Frum, *Right Man*, 110. At the same time, a pro-life organization gleefully quoted the presidents of two pro-choice leaders who were railing against this "setback" for scientists interpreting their anger as proof that Bush created an effective barrier to the research. "Bush Blocks Stem Cell Funding."

69. Nisbet, "Polls," 146, 149.

70. Senate Committee on Health, Education, Labor and Pensions, *Hearing Examining the Scientific and Ethical Implications of Stem Cell Research and Its Potential to Improve Human Health*, 107th Cong., 1st Sess., September 5, 2001.

71. "AAAS Policy Brief."

72. John Kerry, "Democratic Radio Address," June 12, 2004, in Peters and Woolley, *American Presidency Project*.

73. John Kerry, "Radio Address to the Nation," August 7, 2004, in Peters and Woolley, *American Presidency Project*.

74. John Kerry, "Radio Address to the Nation," October 16, 2004, in Peters and Woolley, *American Presidency Project*.

75. John Kerry, "Remarks in Columbus, Ohio," October 21, 2004, in Peters and Woolley, *American Presidency Project*.

76. George W. Bush, "Remarks on Signing the Fetus Farming Prohibition Act and Returning without Approval to the House of Representatives the 'Stem Cell Research Enhancement Act of 2005,'" July 19, 2006, in Peters and Woolley, *American Presidency Project*.

77. See, for example, Sheryl Gay Stolberg, "First Bush Veto Maintains Limits on Stem Cell Use," *New York Times*, July 20, 2006; Sarah Lueck, "Bush Vetoes Stem-Cell Bill; House Override Fails," *Wall Street Journal*, July 20, 2006; Bob Deans, "Veto Halts Stem Cell Bill for Now," *Atlanta Journal Constitution*, July 20, 2006.

78. George W. Bush, "Remarks on Returning without Approval to the Senate the 'Stem Cell Research Enhancement Act of 2007,'" June 20, 2007, in Peters and Woolley, *American Presidency Project*.

79. Barack Obama, "Remarks on Signing an Executive Order Removing Barriers to Responsible Scientific Research Involving Human Stem Cells and a Memorandum on Scientific Integrity," March 9, 2009, in Peters and Woolley, *American Presidency Project*.

80. West and Carey, "(Re)Enacting Frontier Justice," 380.

Conclusion

1. Patricia Nelson Limerick, "The Adventures of the Frontier in the Twentieth Century," in *The Frontier in American Culture*, ed. James R. Grossman (Berkeley: University of California Press, 1994), 68.

2. Frederick Jackson Turner, *The Frontier in American History* (New York: Henry Holt, 1920), 284, 287.

3. Franklin Delano Roosevelt, "Campaign Address on Progressive Government at the Commonwealth Club in San Francisco, California," September 23, 1932, in *The American Presidency Project*, ed. Gerhard Peters and John T. Woolley.

4. Herbert Hoover, "Address at Madison Square Garden in New York City," October 31, 1932, in Peters and Woolley, *American Presidency Project*.

5. Franklin Delano Roosevelt, "Radio Address to the Young Democratic Clubs of America," August 24, 1935, in Peters and Woolley, *American Presidency Project*.

6. Vannevar Bush, *Science—The Endless Frontier* (Washington, D.C.: Government Printing Office, 1945), 68.

7. Leon M. Lederman, "Science: The End of the Frontier?" *Science* 251, no. 4990 (1991): S17.

8. J. Arthur Harris, "Frontiers," *Scientific Monthly* 30, no. 1 (1930): 26.

9. Arden L. Bement, Jr., "From Commitment to Engagement: How Industry Can Cultivate Competitiveness," Address to the Digital Dialogue Forum in Washington, D.C., June 28, 2006, http://www.nsf.gov/news/speeches/bement/06/alb060628_digital.jsp; "Remarks Made by the President, Prime Minister Tony Blair of England (via satellite), Dr. Francis Collins, Director of the National Human Genome Research Institute, and Dr. Craig Venter, President and Chief Scientific Officer, Celera Genomics Corporation, on the Completion of the First Survey of the Entire Human Genome Project," June 26, 2000, the White House, http://www.genome.gov/10001356; Francis S. Collins, *The Language of Life: DNA and the Revolution in Personalized Medicine* (New York: HarperCollins, 2010), 2; Francis S. Collins, interview, May 23, 1998, Jackson Hole, Wyo., *Academy of Achievement*; Francis S. Collins, "Exploring the Frontiers of Life: Northwest at Forefront of Pioneering Effort to Mine the Secrets of the Human Genome," *Seattle Times*, August 7, 2005; George W. Bush, "Remarks on Presenting the National

Medals of Science and Technology," March 14, 2005, in Peters and Woolley, *American Presidency Project*.

10. Edward O. Wilson, *The Future of Life* (New York: Vintage Books, 2002), 15.

11. Barack Obama, "Remarks on Signing an Executive Order Removing Barriers to Responsible Scientific Research Involving Human Stem Cells and a Memorandum on Scientific Integrity," March 9, 2009, in Peters and Woolley, *American Presidency Project*.

12. John Dewey, "The American Intellectual Frontier," *New Republic* 30, no. 388 (May 10, 1922): 304.

13. John Kerry, "Remarks in Denver, Colorado," June 21, 2004, in Peters and Woolley, *American Presidency Project*.

14. Janice Hocker Rushing, "Mythic Evolution of 'The New Frontier' in Mass Mediated Rhetoric," *Critical Studies in Mass Communication* 3, no. 3 (1986): 266.

15. Wilson, *Future of Life*, 127–28.

16. Leslie Roberts, "Chemical Prospecting: Hope for Vanishing Ecosystems?" *Science* 256, no. 5060 (1992): 1143; Ricardo Bonalume Neto and David Dickson, "$3m Deal Launches Major Hunt for Drug Leads in Brazil," *Nature* 400, no. 6742 (1999): 302.

17. Collins, "Exploring the Frontiers of Life."

18. Edward O. Wilson, *The Diversity of Life* (1992; repr., New York: W. W. Norton, 1999), 326, 329.

19. Antonio Silveira R. dos Santos, "Biodiversidade, Bioprospecção, Conhecimento Tradicional e o Futuro da Vida," *Revista de Informação e Tecnologia* (March 2001).

20. Robert B. Gagosian, "An Old Idea for New Science: Discovery Means Taking Risks," *Vital Speeches of the Day* 71, no. 4 (2004): 123.

21. Wilson, *Future of Life*, 144.

22. Collins, "Exploring the Frontiers of Life."

23. An analysis of American public opinion and textbook treatments of Columbus corroborates this suggestion that public consciousness is shifting, if ever so slightly, at least among the better educated. Howard Schuman, Barry Schwartz, and Hannah D'Arcy, "Elite Revisionists and Popular Beliefs: Christopher Columbus, Hero or Villain?" *Public Opinion Quarterly* 69, no. 1 (2005): 2–29.

24. George W. Bush, "Address to the Nation on Stem Cell Research," August 9, 2001, in Peters and Woolley, *American Presidency Project*.

25. Patricia Nelson Limerick, "The Persistence of the Frontier," *Harper's* 289, no. 1733 (1994): 22.

26. Tarla Rai Peterson makes a similar argument, that the perseverance of frontier imagery "suggests that critical analysis of the myth would accomplish more than attempts to discredit it." Tarla Rai Peterson, "Jefferson's Yeoman Farmer as Frontier Hero: A Self Defeating Mythic Structure," *Agriculture and Human Values* 7, no. 1 (1990): 16–17.

27. This was also the vision of the frontier that Cuomo emphasized in the speech discussed in the introduction.

28. I am not suggesting that this model be used to entice American Indians to consider a career in science; Sacagawea is a contested figure in Native history, seen by some as a collaborator whose actions served the interests of Euro-American imperialists. Rather, I am drawing attention to the gender of this historic character to suggest that women and qualities typically associated with women, like the ability to communicate, to negotiate, and to integrate the interests of private and public spheres, can also be emphasized as vital to the advancement of science. For an account of Native treatments of Sacagawea, see Mary Lawlor, *Public Native America: Tribal Self-Representations in Museums, Powwows, and Casinos* (Piscataway, N.J.: Rutgers University Press, 2006). For an account of how American feminists of the early twentieth century first began using the figure of Sacagawea as a model of female leadership in order to alter public norms, see Cindy Koenig Richards, "Inventing Sacagawea: Public Women and the Transformative Potential of Epideictic Rhetoric," *Western Journal of Communication* 73, no. 1 (2009): 1–22.

29. See Alan G. Gross, *The Rhetoric of Science* (Cambridge, Mass.: Harvard University Press, 1990), 33; J. E. McGuire and Trevor Melia, "Some Cautionary Strictures on the Writing of the Rhetoric of Science," *Rhetorica* 7, no. 1 (1989): 87.

30. John Lyne, "Bio-Rhetorics: Moralizing the Life Sciences," in *The Rhetorical Turn: Invention and Persuasion in the Conduct of Inquiry*, ed. Herbert W. Simons (Chicago: University of Chicago Press, 1990), 54.

31. Lyne, "Bio-Rhetorics"; Robert Alan Brookey, "Bio-Rhetoric, Background Beliefs and the Biology of Homosexuality," *Argumentation and Advocacy* 37, no. 4 (2001): 171–83; John Lynch, "Stem Cells and the Embryo: Biorhetoric and Scientism in Congressional Debate," *Public Understanding of Science* 18, no. 3 (2009): 309–24.

32. Lyne, "Bio-Rhetorics," 55.

33. The metaphoric structures typically used to describe disciplines are already drawn from geopolitics. See Julie Thompson Klein, *Interdisciplinarity: History, Theory and Practice* (Detroit: Wayne State University Press, 1990), 77–78. This tendency to view disciplines as sovereign domains makes the European frontier a natural alternative to the American frontier myth as a metaphorical vehicle to characterize a scientific discipline like genomics or biodiversity studies.

34. John Lyne and Henry F. Howe, "The Rhetoric of Expertise: E. O. Wilson and Sociobiology," *Quarterly Journal of Speech* 76, no. 2 (1990): 134–51; Henry Howe and John Lyne, "Gene Talk in Sociobiology," *Social Epistemology* 6, no. 2 (1992): 109–63.

Bibliography

⌘

"AAAS Policy Brief: Stem Cell Research." http://www.aaas.org/spp/cstc/briefs/stemcells/#ban.

"About Us." *Commentary Magazine*.

Adelberger, E. G., J. H. Gundlach, B. R. Heckel, S. Hoedl, and S. Schlamminger. "Torsion Balance Experiments: A Low-Energy Frontier of Particle Physics." August 19, 2008. http://www.npl.washington.edu/eotwash/publications/pdf/lowfrontier2.pdf.

Allen, R. E., ed. *The Concise Oxford Dictionary of Current English*. 8th ed. New York: Oxford University Press, 1990.

Amani, Bita, and Rosemary J. Coombe. "The Human Genome Diversity Project: The Politics of Patents at the Intersection of Race, Religion, and Research Ethics." *Law & Policy* 27, no. 1 (2005): 152–88.

"Amazônia a soberania está em xeque." *Isto É* 2012 (May 28, 2008).

Anderson, Karrin Vasby, and Kristina Horn Sheeler. *Governing Codes: Gender, Metaphor, and Political Identity*. Lanham, Md.: Lexington Books, 2005.

Annas, George J., Arthur Caplan, and Sherman Ellias. "The Politics of Human-Embryo Research: Avoiding Ethical Gridlock." *New England Journal of Medicine* 334, no. 20 (1996): 1329–32.

Asen, Robert. *Invoking the Invisible Hand: Social Security and the Privatization Debates.* East Lansing: Michigan State University Press, 2009.

Bacon, Francis. *The Advancement of Learning* [1605]. Project Gutenberg.

Barker, Joanne. "The Human Genome Diversity Project: 'Peoples,' 'Populations,' and the Cultural Politics of Identification." *Cultural Studies* 18, no. 4 (2004): 571–606.

Barnhart, Clarence L., ed. *The American College Dictionary.* New York: Harper & Brothers, 1951.

Barrionuevo, Alexei. "Whose Rain Forest Is This, Anyway?" *New York Times,* May 18, 2008.

Barthes, Roland. *Mythologies.* Trans. Annette Lavers. New York: Hill and Wang, 1972.

Beasley, Vanessa B. *You the People: American National Identity in Presidential Rhetoric.* College Station: Texas A&M University Press, 2004.

Beer, Francis A., and Christ'l De Landtsheer, eds. *Metaphorical World Politics.* East Lansing: Michigan State University Press, 2004.

Bement, Arden L., Jr. "From Commitment to Engagement: How Industry Can Cultivate Competitiveness." Address to the Digital Dialogue Forum in Washington, D.C., June 28, 2006. http://www.nsf.gov/news/speeches/bement/06/alb060628_digital.jsp.

———. "Speech at the 30th Annual AAAS Forum on Science and Technology Policy." Washington, D.C., April 21, 2005. http://www.aaas.org/news/releases/2005/0422bementText.shtml.

———. "Testimony before the Senate Commerce, Science and Transportation Subcommittee on Technology, Innovation and Competitiveness." March 29, 2006. http://commerce.senate.gov/pdf/bement-032906.pdf.

Billington, Ray Allen. *Frederick Jackson Turner: Historian, Scholar, Teacher.* New York: Oxford University Press, 1973.

Black, Edwin. "The Second Persona." *Quarterly Journal of Speech* 56, no. 2 (1970): 109–19.

Black, Max. "Metaphor." *Proceedings of the Aristotelian Society* 55 (1954): 286–91.

Braden, Waldo W. "Myths in a Rhetorical Context." *Southern Speech Communication Journal* 40, no. 2 (1975): 113–26.

Brookey, Robert Alan. "Bio-Rhetoric, Background Beliefs and the Biology of Homosexuality." *Argumentation and Advocacy* 37, no. 4 (2001): 171–83.

Bruni, Frank. "Of Principles and Politics: Decision Helps Define the President's Image." *New York Times*, August 10, 2001.

Burke, Kenneth. *A Grammar of Motives*. Berkeley: University of California Press, 1969.

———. *Language as Symbolic Action: Essays on Life, Literature and Method*. Berkeley: University of California Press, 1966.

———. *The Philosophy of Literary Form*. Berkeley: University of California Press, 1973.

Burnett, D. Graham. "A View from the Bridge: The Two Cultures Debate, Its Legacy, and the History of Science." *Daedalus* 128, no. 2 (1999): 193–218.

Burns, Maureen, and Joan Leach. "Science as an Extra Dividend: *Frontiers of Science*." *International Journal of Cultural Studies* 14, no. 5 (2011): 531–46.

Burrows, Beth. "Patents, Ethics and Spin." In *Redesigning Life? The Worldwide Challenge to Genetic Engineering*, ed. Brian Tokar, 238–51. Montreal and Kingston: McGill-Queen's University Press, 2001.

Bush, George H. W. "Remarks at the Superconducting Super Collider Laboratory in Waxahachie, Texas." July 30, 1992. In *The American Presidency Project*, ed. Gerhard Peters and John T. Woolley.

Bush, George W. "Address to the Nation on Stem Cell Research." August 9, 2001. In *The American Presidency Project*, ed. Gerhard Peters and John T. Woolley.

———. "The President's News Conference." August 9, 2007. In *The American Presidency Project*, ed. Gerhard Peters and John T. Woolley.

———. "The President's Radio Address." September 22, 2001. In *The American Presidency Project*, ed. Gerhard Peters and John T. Woolley.

———. "Remarks on Presenting the National Medals of Science and Technology." March 14, 2005. In *The American Presidency Project*, ed. Gerhard Peters and John T. Woolley.

———. "Remarks on Returning without Approval to the Senate the 'Stem Cell Research Enhancement Act of 2007.'" June 20, 2007. In *The American Presidency Project*, ed. Gerhard Peters and John T. Woolley.

———. "Remarks on Signing the Fetus Farming Prohibition Act and Returning without Approval to the House of Representatives the 'Stem Cell Research Enhancement Act of 2005.'" July 19, 2006. In *The American Presidency Project*, ed. Gerhard Peters and John T. Woolley.

Bush, Vannevar. "The Engineer and His Relation to Government." *Science* 86, no. 2222 (1937): 87–91.

———. *Science—The Endless Frontier*. Washington, D.C.: Government Printing Office, 1945. "Bush Blocks Stem Cell Funding That Would Destroy Embryos." *NRLC News* 28, no. 8 (2001).

Calsamiglia, Helena, and Teun A. van Dijk. "Popularization Discourse and Knowledge About the Genome." *Discourse & Society* 15, no. 4 (2004): 369–89.

Campbell, Karlyn Kohrs. "Rhetorical Criticism 2009: A Study in Method." In *The Handbook of Rhetoric and Public Address*, ed. Shawn J. Parry-Giles and J. Michael Hogan, 86–107. Malden, Mass.: Wiley-Blackwell, 2010.

Carpenter, Ronald H. "America's Opinion Leader Historians on Behalf of Success." *Quarterly Journal of Speech* 69, no. 2 (1983): 111–26.

———. "America's Tragic Metaphor: Our Twentieth-Century Combatants as Frontiersmen." *Quarterly Journal of Speech* 76, no. 1 (1990): 1–22.

———. *The Eloquence of Frederick Jackson Turner*. San Marino, Calif.: Huntington Library, 1983.

———. "Frederick Jackson Turner and the Rhetorical Impact of the Frontier Thesis." *Quarterly Journal of Speech* 63, no. 2 (1977): 117–29.

———. *History as Rhetoric: Style, Narrative, and Persuasion*. Columbia: University of South Carolina Press, 1995.

Casper, Christian F. "In Praise of Carbon, In Praise of Science: The Epideictic Rhetoric of the 1996 Nobel Lectures in Chemistry." *Journal of Business and Technical Communication* 21, no. 3 (2007): 303–23.

Ceccarelli, Leah. "Manufactured Scientific Controversy: Science, Rhetoric, and Public Debate." *Rhetoric & Public Affairs* 14, no. 2 (2011): 195–228.

———. "Neither Confusing Cacophony Nor Culinary Complements: A Case Study of Mixed Metaphors for Genomic Science." *Written Communication* 21, no. 1 (2004): 92–105.

———. *Shaping Science with Rhetoric: The Cases of Dobzhansky, Schrödinger, and Wilson*. Chicago: University of Chicago Press, 2001.

Charney, Davida. "Lone Geniuses in Popular Science: The Devaluation of Scientific Consensus." *Written Communication* 20, no. 3 (2003): 215–41.

Choon Fong Shih. "Speech Presented at the Brown University Commencement Forum." May 24, 2008. http://www.kaust.edu.sa/about/presidents-speech -brown.aspx.

Clarke, Alice L. Review of *The Diversity of Life*, by Edward O. Wilson. *Politics and Life Sciences* 13, no. 1 (1994): 129–30.

Clinton, William J. "Remarks on Presenting the National Medals of Science and Technology." April 27, 1999. In *The American Presidency Project*, ed. Gerhard Peters and John T. Woolley.

———. "Remarks on the Electricity Shortage in California and an Exchange with Reporters." August 23, 2000. In *The American Presidency Project*, ed. Gerhard Peters and John T. Woolley.

Collins, Francis S. "Exploring the Frontiers of Life: Northwest at Forefront of Pioneering Effort to Mine the Secrets of the Human Genome." *Seattle Times,* August 7, 2005.

———. Interview. May 23, 1998. Jackson Hole, Wyo. *Academy of Achievement.*

———. *The Language of God: A Scientist Presents Evidence for Belief.* New York: Free Press, 2006.

———. *The Language of Life: DNA and the Revolution in Personalized Medicine.* New York: HarperCollins, 2010.

———. "Remarks of NIH Director Francis Collins." September 30, 2009. http://www.nih.gov/about/director/09302009remarks_POTUS.htm.

———. "Statement on Frontiers of Science before Committee on Appropriations, Subcommittee on Labor, Health and Human Services, Education and Related Agencies, U.S. Senate." April 30, 2007. http://www.hhs.gov/asl/testify/2007/04/t20070430e.html.

Collins, Francis, Eric D. Green, Alan E. Guttmacher, and Mark S. Guyer. "A Vision for the Future of Genomics Research: A Blueprint for the Genomic Era." *Nature* 422, no. 6934 (2003): 835–47.

Condit, Celeste M. "Dynamic Feelings about Metaphors for Genes: Implications for Research and Genetic Policy." *Genomics, Society and Policy* 5, no. 3 (2009): 44–58.

———. "How the Public Understands Genetics: Non-deterministic and Non-discriminatory Interpretations of the 'Blueprint' Metaphor." *Public Understanding of Science* 8, no. 3 (1999): 169–80.

———. "Pathos in Criticism: Edwin Black's Communism-As-Cancer Metaphor." *Quarterly Journal of Speech* 99, no. 1 (2013): 1–26.

Condit, Celeste M., Benjamin R. Bates, Ryan Galloway, Sonja Brown Givens, Caroline K. Haynie, John W. Jordan, Gordon Stables, and Hollis Marshall West. "Recipes or Blueprints for Our Genes? How Contexts Selectively Activate the Multiple Meanings of Metaphors." *Quarterly Journal of Speech* 88, no. 3 (2002): 303–25.

Condit, Celeste M., John Lynch, and Emily Winderman. "Recent Rhetorical Studies in Public Understanding of Science: Multiple Purposes and Strengths." *Public Understanding of Science* 21, no. 4 (2012): 386–400.

Coolidge, Calvin. "Address Accepting the Statue of President Andrew Jackson at Washington, D.C." April 15, 1928. In *The American Presidency Project,* ed. Gerhard Peters and John T. Woolley.

Cunningham, Hilary. "Colonial Encounters in Postcolonial Contexts: Patenting Indigenous DNA and the Human Genome Diversity Project." *Critique of Anthropology* 18, no. 2 (1998): 205–33.

Cuomo, Mario. "1984 Democratic National Convention Keynote." July 16, 1984. In *American Rhetoric*, ed. Michael E. Eidenmuller.

Davis, Wayne H. Review of *The Diversity of Life*, by Edward O. Wilson. *Growth and Change* 24, no. 2 (1993): 277–79.

Deans, Bob. "Veto Halts Stem Cell Bill for Now." *Atlanta Journal Constitution*, July 20, 2006.

"Declaration of Indigenous Peoples of the Western Hemisphere Regarding the Human Genome Diversity Project." Phoenix, Ariz. February 19, 1995. http://www.indians.org/welker/genome.htm.

Dewey, John. "The American Intellectual Frontier." *New Republic* 30, no. 388 (May 10, 1922): 303–5.

Dickinson, Greg, Brian L. Ott, and Eric Aoki. "Memory and Myth at the Buffalo Bill Museum." *Western Journal of Communication* 69, no. 2 (2005): 85–108.

Donofrio, Theresa Ann. "Ground Zero and Place-Making Authority: The Conservative Metaphors in 9/11 Families' 'Take Back the Memorial' Rhetoric." *Western Journal of Communication* 74, no. 2 (2010): 150–69.

Döring, Martin. "A Sequence of 'Factishes': The Media-Metaphorical Knowledge Dynamics Structuring the German Press Coverage of the Human Genome." *New Genetics and Society* 24, no. 3 (2005): 317–36.

Dorsey, Leroy G. "The Frontier Myth in Presidential Rhetoric: Theodore Roosevelt's Campaign for Conservation." *Western Journal of Communication* 59, no. 1 (1995): 1–19.

———. "The Myth of War and Peace in Presidential Discourse: John Kennedy's 'New Frontier' Myth and the Peace Corps." *Southern Communication Journal* 62, no. 1 (1996): 42–55.

———. "The Rhetorical Presidency and the Myth of the American Dream." In *The Prospect of Presidential Rhetoric*, ed. James Arnt Aune and Martin J. Medhurst, 130–59. College Station: Texas A&M University Press, 2008.

———. *We Are All Americans, Pure and Simple: Theodore Roosevelt and the Myth of Americanism*. Tuscaloosa: University of Alabama Press, 2007.

Douglass, David. "Issues in the Use of I. A. Richards' Tenor-Vehicle Model of Metaphor." *Western Journal of Communication* 64, no. 4 (2000): 405–24.

Dreger, Alice Domurat. "Metaphors of Morality in the Human Genome Project." In *Controlling Our Destinies: Historical, Philosophical, Ethical, and Theological Perspectives on the Human Genome Project*, ed. Phillip R. Sloan, 159–67. Notre Dame, Ind.: University of Notre Dame Press, 2000.

Eisenhower, Dwight D. "Address in Convention Hall, Philadelphia, Pennsylvania." November 1, 1956. In *The American Presidency Project*, ed. Gerhard Peters and John T. Woolley.

ETC Group. "Biopiracy + 10. Captain Hook Awards—2002." *Communiqué* 75 (March/April 2002).

Fahnestock, Jeanne. "Accommodating Science: The Rhetorical Life of Scientific Facts." *Written Communication* 3, no. 3 (July 1986): 275–96.

———. *Rhetorical Style: The Uses of Language in Persuasion.* New York: Oxford University Press, 2011.

———. "The Rhetoric of the Natural Sciences." In *The Sage Handbook of Rhetorical Studies*, ed. Andrea A. Lunsford, Kirt H. Wilson, and Rosa A. Eberly, 175–95. Thousand Oaks, Calif.: Sage, 2009.

Findlay, John M., and Bruce Hevly. *Atomic Frontier Days: Hanford and the American West.* Seattle: University of Washington Press, 2011.

Forbes, Jack D. "The Indian in the West: A Challenge for Historians." *Arizona and the West* 1, no. 3 (Autumn 1959): 206–15.

Ford, Gerald R. "Remarks at Dedication Ceremonies for the National Air and Space Museum." July 1, 1976. In *The American Presidency Project*, ed. Gerhard Peters and John T. Woolley.

Frum, David. *The Right Man: The Surprise Presidency of George W. Bush.* New York: Random House, 2003.

Funk, Charles Earle, ed. *Funk and Wagnalls New Practical Standard Dictionary of the English Language.* Britannica World Language Edition. Vol. 1. New York: Funk and Wagnalls, 1955.

Funk and Wagnalls New Standard Dictionary of the English Language. New York: Funk and Wagnalls, 1946.

Gagosian, Robert B. "An Old Idea for New Science: Discovery Means Taking Risks." *Vital Speeches of the Day* 71, no. 4 (2004): 122–25.

Gallego, Sonia. "Alarm Bells Sound for the Amazon." *ABC News*, May 29, 2008.

Geron Ethics Advisory Board. "Research with Human Embryonic Stem Cells: Ethical Considerations." *Hastings Center Report* 29, no. 2 (1999): 31–36.

Gogorosi, Eleni. "Untying the Gordian Knot of Creation: Metaphors for the Human Genome Project in Greek Newspapers." *New Genetics and Society* 24, no. 3 (2005): 299–315.

Gouge, Catherine. "The American Frontier: History, Rhetoric, Concept." *Americana: The Journal of American Popular Culture (1900–present)* 6, no. 1 (Spring 2007).

———. "The Great Storefront of American Nationalism: Narratives of Mars and the Outerspatial Frontier." *Americana: The Journal of American Popular Culture (1900–present)* 1, no. 2 (2002).

Gould, Stephen Jay. Review of *On Human Nature*, by Edward O. Wilson. *Human Nature* 1, no. 10 (1978): 20–28.

————. "Prophet for the Earth." Review of *The Diversity of Life*, by Edward O. Wilson. *Nature* 361, no. 6410 (1993): 311–12.

————. "Nonoverlapping Magisteria." *Natural History* 106, no. 2 (1997): 16–22.

Government Accountability Office. "Native American Graves Protection and Repatriation Act: After Almost 20 Years, Key Federal Agencies Still Have Not Fully Complied with the Act." July 2010, GAO-10–768. http://www .gao.gov/assets/310/307856.pdf.

————. "Smithsonian Institution: Much Work Still Needed to Identify and Repatriate Indian Human Remains and Objects." May 2011, GAO-11–515. http://www.gao.gov/assets/320/318818.pdf.

Gronnvoll, Marita, and Jamie Landau. "From Viruses to Russian Roulette to Dance: A Rhetorical Critique and Creation of Genetic Metaphors." *Rhetoric Society Quarterly* 40, no. 1 (2010): 46–70.

Gross, Alan G. *The Rhetoric of Science.* Cambridge, Mass.: Harvard University Press, 1990.

Gunkel, David J., and Ann Hetzel Gunkel. "Terra Nova 2.0: The New World of MMORPGs." *Critical Studies in Media Communication* 26, no. 2 (2009): 104–27.

Gustainis, J. Justin. "John F. Kennedy and the Green Berets: The Rhetorical Use of the Hero Myth." *Communication Studies* 40, no. 1 (1989): 41–53.

Guthrie, Patricia. "In Atlanta, Decision Elicits Support, Dismay, Concern." *Atlanta Journal Constitution*, August 10, 2001.

Haraway, Donna J. *Modest_Witness@Second_Millennium.FemaleMan©_Meets _OncoMouseTM*. New York: Routledge, 1997.

Harris, J. Arthur. "Frontiers." *Scientific Monthly* 30, no. 1 (1930): 19–32.

Harris, Randy Allen, ed. *Landmark Essays on Rhetoric of Science: Case Studies.* Mahwah, N.J.: Lawrence Erlbaum, 1997.

————. Review of *Tropical Truth(s)*, ed. Armin Burkhardt and Brigitte Nerlich. *Quarterly Journal of Speech* 97, no. 4 (2011): 473–77.

Harry, Debra. "The Human Genome Diversity Project: Implications for Indigenous Peoples." *Abya Yala News* 8, no. 4 (1994).

Hasian, Marouf, Jr. "The Internet and the Human Genome." *Peace Review* 13, no. 3 (2001): 375–80.

Hasian, Marouf, Jr., and Emily Plec. "The Cultural, Legal, and Scientific Arguments in the Human Genome Diversity Debate." *Howard Journal of Communications* 13, no. 4 (2002): 301–19.

Hawthorne, Susan. "Land, Bodies, and Knowledge: Biocolonialism of Plants, Indigenous Peoples, Women, and People with Disabilities." *Signs: Journal of Women in Culture and Society* 32, no. 2 (2007): 314–22.

Hellsten, Iina. "Dolly: Scientific Breakthrough or Frankenstein's Monster? Journalistic and Scientific Metaphors of Cloning." *Metaphor and Symbol* 15, no. 4 (2000): 213–21.

Henry, David. "The Rhetorical Dynamics of Mario Cuomo's 1984 Keynote Address." In *Contemporary American Public Discourse*. 3rd ed., ed. Halford Ross Ryan, 303–15. Prospect Heights, Ill.: Waveland Press, 1992.

Hoddeson, Lillian, and Adrienne W. Kolb. "The Superconducting Super Collider's Frontier Outpost, 1983–1988." *Minerva* 38, no. 3 (2000): 271–310.

Hoddeson, Lillian, Adrienne W. Kolb, and Catherine Westfall. *Fermilab: Physics, the Frontier, and Megascience*. Chicago: University of Chicago Press, 2008.

Hoover, Herbert. "Address at Madison Square Garden in New York City." October 31, 1932. In *The American Presidency Project*, ed. Gerhard Peters and John T. Woolley.

———. *American Individualism*. Garden City, N.Y.: Doubleday, Page & Company, 1922.

Hornby, A. S., A. P. Cowie, and J. Windsor Lewis, eds. *Oxford Advanced Learner's Dictionary of Current English*. London: Oxford University Press, 1974.

Houck, Davis W. "FDR's Commonwealth Club Address: Redefining Individualism, Adjudicating Greatness." *Rhetoric & Public Affairs* 7, no. 3 (2004): 259–82.

Howe, Henry, and John Lyne. "Gene Talk in Sociobiology." *Social Epistemology* 6, no. 2 (1992): 109–63.

Hughes, Karen. *Ten Minutes from Normal*. New York: Viking Penguin, 2004.

Isla, Ana. "An Ecofeminist Perspective on Biopiracy in Latin America." *Signs: Journal of Women in Culture and Society* 32, no. 2 (2007): 323–31.

Ivie, Robert L. "Metaphor and the Rhetorical Invention of Cold War 'Idealists.'" *Communication Monographs* 54, no. 2 (1987): 165–82.

Jack, Jordynn. "Object Lessons: Recent Work in the Rhetoric of Science." *Quarterly Journal of Speech* 96, no. 2 (2010): 209–16.

Jasanoff, Sheila. *Designs on Nature: Science and Democracy in Europe and the United States*. Princeton, N.J.: Princeton University Press, 2005.

Jasinski, James. "Instrumentalism, Contextualism, and Interpretation in Rhetorical Criticism." In *Rhetorical Hermeneutics: Invention and Interpretation in the Age of Science*, ed. William Keith and Alan G. Gross, 195–224. Albany, N.Y.: SUNY Press, 1997.

———. "The Status of Theory and Method in Rhetorical Criticism." *Western Journal of Communication* 65, no. 3 (2001): 249–70.

Jewell, Elizabeth J., and Frank Abate. *The New Oxford American Dictionary*. New York: Oxford University Press, 2001.

Johnson, Cary Alan. "The Final Frontier: Why LGBT Rights Are a Game Changer and Will Liberate Us All." University of Washington Department of Global Health. October 25, 2011. http://globalhealth.washington.edu/media/gallery/5274.

Johnson Thornton, Davi. *Brain Culture: Neuroscience and Popular Media*. New Brunswick, N.J.: Rutgers University Press, 2011.

Jones, Hillary A. "'Them as Feel the Need to Be Free': Reworking the Frontier Myth." *Southern Communication Journal* 76, no. 3 (2011): 230–47.

Jordan, John W. "Kennedy's Romantic Moon and Its Rhetorical Legacy for Space Exploration." *Rhetoric & Public Affairs* 6, no. 2 (2003): 209–32.

Kauffman, James L. *Selling Outer Space: Kennedy, the Media, and Funding for Project Apollo, 1961–1963*. Tuscaloosa: University of Alabama Press, 1994.

Keller, Evelyn Fox. *Reflections on Gender and Science*. New Haven, Conn.: Yale University Press, 1985.

Kennedy, John F. "Address at Rice University in Houston on the Nation's Space Effort." September 12, 1962. In *The American Presidency Project*, ed. Gerhard Peters and John T. Woolley.

———. "Address of Senator John F. Kennedy Accepting the Democratic Party Nomination for the Presidency of the United States—Memorial Coliseum, Los Angeles." July 15, 1960. In *The American Presidency Project*, ed. Gerhard Peters and John T. Woolley.

Keränen, Lisa, Jason Lesko, Alison Vogelaar, and Lisa Irvin. "'Myth, Mask, Shield, and Sword': Dr. John H. Marburger III's Rhetoric of Neutral Science for the Nation." *Cultural Studies <=> Critical Methodologies* 8, no. 2 (2008): 159–86.

Kerry, John. "Democratic Radio Address." June 12, 2004. In *The American Presidency Project*, ed. Gerhard Peters and John T. Woolley.

———. "Radio Address to the Nation." August 7, 2004. In *The American Presidency Project*, ed. Gerhard Peters and John T. Woolley.

———. "Radio Address to the Nation." October 16, 2004. In *The American Presidency Project*, ed. Gerhard Peters and John T. Woolley.

———. "Remarks in Columbus, Ohio." October 21, 2004. In *The American Presidency Project*, ed. Gerhard Peters and John T. Woolley.

———. "Remarks in Denver, Colorado." June 21, 2004. In *The American Presidency Project*, ed. Gerhard Peters and John T. Woolley.

Kevles, Daniel J. "FDR's Science Policy." *Science* 183, no. 4127 (1974): 798, 800.

———. "The National Science Foundation and the Debate over Postwar Research Policy, 1942–1945: A Political Interpretation of *Science—The Endless Frontier*." *Isis* 68, no. 1 (1977): 4–26.

Kitzinger, Jenny, and Clare Williams. "Forecasting Science Futures: Legitimising Hope and Calming Fears in the Embryo Stem Cell Debate." *Social Science and Medicine* 61, no. 3 (2005): 731–40.

Klein, Julie Thompson. *Interdisciplinarity: History, Theory and Practice.* Detroit: Wayne State University Press, 1990.

Kleinman, Daniel Lee. *Politics on the Endless Frontier: Postwar Research Policy in the United States.* Durham, N.C.: Duke University Press, 1995.

Kohn, Marek. "The Soft Machine." Review of *The Diversity of Life*, by Edward O. Wilson. *New Statesman and Society* 6, no. 240 (1993): 37–38.

Kolb, Adrienne, and Lillian Hoddeson. "A New Frontier in the Chicago Suburbs: Settling Fermilab, 1963–1972." *Illinois Historical Journal* 88, no. 1 (1995): 2–18.

Krug, Linda T. *Presidential Perspectives on Space Exploration: Guiding Metaphors from Eisenhower to Bush.* New York: Praeger, 1991.

Lakoff, George, and Mark Johnson. *Metaphors We Live By.* Chicago: University of Chicago Press, 1980.

Landau, Sidney I., ed. *Cambridge Dictionary of American English.* New York: Cambridge University Press, 2001.

Lawlor, Mary. *Public Native America: Tribal Self-Representations in Museums, Powwows, and Casinos.* Piscataway, N.J.: Rutgers University Press, 2006.

Lazowska Edward D., and David A. Patterson. "An Endless Frontier Postponed." *Science* 308, no. 5723 (2005): 757.

Lederman, Leon M. "The Advancement of Science." *Science* 256, no. 5060 (1992): 1119–24.

———. "Science: The End of the Frontier?" *Science* 251, no. 4990 (1991): S1–S20.

———. "Scientific Retreat Demise of the SSC Is a National Loss." *Chicago Tribune*, November 18, 1993.

Leff, Michael. "Prudential Argument and the Use of History in Franklin Delano Roosevelt's 'Commonwealth Club' Address." In *Proceedings of the Second International Conference on Argumentation*, ed. F. H. van Eemeren, R. Grootendorshet, J. A. Blair, and C. A. Willard, 931–36. Amsterdam: SICSAT, 1991.

Leff, Michael, and Andrew Sachs. "Words Most Like Things: Iconicity and the Rhetorical Text." *Western Journal of Communication* 54, no. 3 (1990): 252–73.

Lefkowitz, Jay P. "Stem Cells and the President: An Inside Account." *Commentary* 125, no. 1 (2008): 19–24.

Lessl, Thomas M. "The Priestly Voice." *Quarterly Journal of Speech* 75, no. 2 (1989): 183–97.

Limerick, Patricia Nelson. "The Adventures of the Frontier in the Twentieth Century." In *The Frontier in American Culture*, ed. James R. Grossman, 66–102. Berkeley: University of California Press, 1994.

———. "The Persistence of the Frontier." *Harper's* 289, no. 1733 (1994): 21–24.

Lone Dog, Leona. "Whose Genes Are They? The Human Genome Diversity Project." *Journal of Health and Social Policy* 10, no. 4 (1999): 51–66.

Lovelock, James E. *Gaia: A New Look at Life on Earth*. Oxford: Oxford University Press, 1979.

———. Review of *The Diversity of Life*, by Edward O. Wilson. *TLS—The Times Literary Supplement* 4731 (December 3, 1993): 9.

Lueck, Sarah. "Bush Vetoes Stem-Cell Bill; House Override Fails." *Wall Street Journal*, July 20, 2006.

Luntz, Frank. "The Environment: A Cleaner, Safer, Healthier America." Luntz Research Companies—Straight Talk, n.d. http://www.ewg.org/files/Luntz Research_environment.pdf.

Lynch, John. "Stem Cells and the Embryo: Biorhetoric and Scientism in Congressional Debate." *Public Understanding of Science* 18, no. 3 (2009): 309–24.

———. *What Are Stem Cells? Definitions at the Intersection of Science and Politics*. Tuscaloosa: University of Alabama Press, 2011.

Lyne, John. "Bio-Rhetorics: Moralizing the Life Sciences." In *The Rhetorical Turn: Invention and Persuasion in the Conduct of Inquiry*, ed. Herbert W. Simons, 35–57. Chicago: University of Chicago Press, 1990.

———. "Learning the Lessons of Lysenko: Biology, Politics, and Rhetoric in Historical Controversy." In *Argument and Critical Practices: Proceedings of the Fifth SCA/AFA Conference on Argumentation*, ed. Joseph W. Wenzel, 507–12. Annandale, Va.: Speech Communication Association, 1987.

Lyne, John, and Henry F. Howe. "The Rhetoric of Expertise: E. O. Wilson and Sociobiology." *Quarterly Journal of Speech* 76, no. 2 (1990): 134–51.

Malik, Kenan. "The End Is Not Nigh: This Ecological Jeremiad by a Scientist Who Believes in Both Man and in Nature Is Too Gloomy by Half." Review of *The Future of Life*, by Edward O. Wilson. *Sunday Telegraph*, April 21, 2002.

"McCartney Launches Landmine Campaign." *CNN.com*, June 4, 2001.

McDaniel, James P. "Figures for New Frontiers, From Davy Crockett to Cyberspace Gurus." *Quarterly Journal of Speech* 88, no. 1 (2002): 91–111.

McGee, Michael. "Text, Context, and the Fragmentation of Contemporary Culture." *Western Journal of Communication* 54, no. 3 (1990): 274–89.

McGuire, J. E., and Trevor Melia. "Some Cautionary Strictures on the Writing of the Rhetoric of Science." *Rhetorica* 7, no. 1 (1989): 87–99.

Menconi, Darlene, and Leonel Rocha. "Riqueza Ameaçada." *Isto É* 1773 (September 24, 2003).

"Millennium Evening at the White House: Informatics Meets Genomics." October 12, 1999. http://www.genome.gov/10001397.

Miller, Robert J. *Native America, Discovered and Conquered: Thomas Jefferson, Lewis & Clark, and Manifest Destiny*. Westport, Conn.: Praeger, 2006.

Mulkay, Michael. "Frankenstein and the Debate over Embryo Research." *Science, Technology, & Human Values* 21, no. 2 (Spring 1996): 157–76.

Müller, Cornelia. *Metaphors Dead and Alive, Sleeping and Waking: A Dynamic View*. Chicago: University of Chicago Press, 2008.

National Bioethics Advisory Commission. *Ethical Issues in Human Stem Cell Research: Executive Summary*. September 1999. http://bioethics.georgetown.edu/nbac/execsumm.pdf.

"National Institutes of Health Guidelines for Research Using Human Pluripotent Stem Cells and Notification of Request for Emergency Clearance." *Federal Register* 65, no. 166 (2000): 51975–81.

Nelkin, Dorothy. "Promotional Metaphors and Their Popular Appeal." *Public Understanding of Science* 3, no. 1 (1994): 23–31.

Nerlich, Brigitte, and Iina Hellsten. "Genomics: Shifts in Metaphorical Landscape between 2000 and 2003." *New Genetics and* Society 23, no. 3 (2004): 255–68.

Nerlich, Brigitte, Robert Dingwall, and David D. Clarke. "The Book of Life: How the Completion of the Human Genome Project Was Revealed to the Public." *health: An Interdisciplinary Journal for the Social Study of Health, Illness and Medicine* 6, no. 4 (2002): 445–69.

Neto, Ricardo Bonalume, and David Dickson. "$3m Deal Launches Major Hunt for Drug Leads in Brazil." *Nature* 400, no. 6742 (1999): 302.

Neufeldt, Victoria, ed. *Webster's New World College Dictionary*. 3rd ed. New York: Macmillan, 1997.

Nisbet, Matthew C. "The Polls—Trends: Public Opinion about Stem Cell Research and Human Cloning." *Public Opinion Quarterly* 68, no. 1 (2004): 131–54.

"Nobel Laureates' Letter to President Bush." *Washington Post*, February 21, 2001.

Obama, Barack. "Remarks on Signing an Executive Order Removing Barriers to Responsible Scientific Research Involving Human Stem Cells and a Memorandum on Scientific Integrity." March 9, 2009. In *The American Presidency Project*, ed. Gerhard Peters and John T. Woolley.

O'Donnell, Timothy Maurice. "Vannevar Bush, the Endless Frontier, and the Rhetoric of American Science Policy." Ph.D. diss., University of Pittsburgh, 2000.

Osborn, Michael. "Archetypal Metaphor in Rhetoric: The Light-Dark Family." *Quarterly Journal of Speech* 53, no. 2 (1967): 115–26.

———. "In Defense of Broad Mythic Criticism." *Communication Studies* 41, no. 2 (1990): 121–27.

———. "Memories of Miz Myth." *Southern Communication Journal* 71, no. 2 (2006): 149–51.

———. *Orientations to Rhetorical Style.* Chicago: Science Research Associates, 1976.

———. "The Trajectory of My Work with Metaphor." *Southern Communication Journal* 74, no. 1 (2009): 79–87.

Oxford English Dictionary.

Perelman, Chaim, and Lucie Olbrechts-Tyteca. *The New Rhetoric: A Treatise on Argumentation.* Trans. John Wilkinson and Purcell Weaver. Notre Dame, Ind.: University of Notre Dame Press, 1969.

Peters, Gerhard, and John T. Woolley, eds. *The American Presidency Project.*

Peterson, Tarla Rai. "Jefferson's Yeoman Farmer as Frontier Hero: A Self Defeating Mythic Structure." *Agriculture and Human Values* 7, no. 1 (1990): 9–19.

Phillips, Kendall, ed. *Framing Public Memory.* Tuscaloosa: University of Alabama Press, 2004.

Ploeger, Joanna S. *The Boundaries of the New Frontier: Rhetoric and Communication at Fermi National Accelerator Laboratory.* Columbia: University of South Carolina Press, 2009.

———. "Techno-Scientific Spectacle: The Rhetoric of IMAX in the Contemporary Science Museum." *Poroi* 3, no. 2 (2004): 73–93.

Reagan, Ronald. "Address to the Nation on the Explosion of the Space Shuttle *Challenger.*" January 28, 1986. In *The American Presidency Project,* ed. Gerhard Peters and John T. Woolley.

———. "Remarks at the Annual Convention of the Texas State Bar Association in San Antonio." July 6, 1984. In *The American Presidency Project,* ed. Gerhard Peters and John T. Woolley.

———. "Remarks at the Memorial Service for the Crew of the Space Shuttle *Challenger* in Houston, Texas." January 31, 1986. In *The American Presidency Project,* ed. Gerhard Peters and John T. Woolley.

Reardon, Jenny. "Democratic Mis-haps: The Problem of Democratization in a Time of Biopolitics." *BioSocieties* 2, no. 2 (2007): 239–56.

———. *Race to the Finish: Identity and Governance in an Age of Genomics.* Princeton, N.J.: Princeton University Press, 2005.

Reid, Walter V., Sarah A. Laird, Carrie A. Meyer, Rodrigo Gámez, Ana Sittenfeld, Daniel H. Janzen, Michael A. Gollin, and Calestous Juma. *Biodiversity Prospecting: Using Genetic Resources for Sustainable Development*. Washington, D.C.: World Resources Institute, 1993.

Reis, Eric. "Rainbow Warrior." Review of *The Diversity of Life*, by Edward O. Wilson. *Public Interest* 110 (Winter 1993): 102–8.

"Remarks Made by the President, Prime Minister Tony Blair of England (via satellite), Dr. Francis Collins, Director of the National Human Genome Research Institute, and Dr. Craig Venter, President and Chief Scientific Officer, Celera Genomics Corporation, on the Completion of the First Survey of the Entire Human Genome Project." The White House. June 26, 2000. http://www.genome.gov/10001356.

Richards, Cindy Koenig. "Inventing Sacagawea: Public Women and the Transformative Potential of Epideictic Rhetoric." *Western Journal of Communication* 73, no. 1 (2009): 1–22.

Richards, I. A. *The Philosophy of Rhetoric*. New York: Oxford University Press, 1936.

Ridley, Matt. *Genome: The Autobiography of a Species in 23 Chapters*. New York: HarperCollins, 2000.

Roberts, Leslie. "Chemical Prospecting: Hope for Vanishing Ecosystems?" *Science* 256, no. 5060 (1992): 1142–43.

Rohter, Larry. "As Brazil Defends Its Bounty, Rules Ensnare Scientists." *New York Times*, August 28, 2007.

———. "In the Amazon: Conservation or Colonialism." *New York Times*, July 26, 2007.

Roosevelt, Franklin Delano. "Campaign Address on Progressive Government at the Commonwealth Club in San Francisco, California." September 23, 1932. In *The American Presidency Project*, ed. Gerhard Peters and John T. Woolley.

———. "Radio Address to the Young Democratic Clubs of America." August 24, 1935. In *The American Presidency Project*, ed. Gerhard Peters and John T. Woolley.

Rosner, Mary, and T. R. Johnson. "Telling Stories: Metaphors of the Human Genome Project." *Hypatia* 10, no. 4 (1995): 104–29.

Rowland, Robert C. "On a Limited Approach to Mythic Criticism: Rowland's Rejoinder." *Communication Studies* 41, no. 2 (1990): 150–60.

———. "On Mythic Criticism." *Communication Studies* 41, no. 2 (1990): 101–16.

Rushing, Janice Hocker. "Evolution of 'The New Frontier' in *Alien* and *Aliens*: Patriarchal Co-optation of the Feminine Archetype." *Quarterly Journal of Speech* 75, no. 1 (1989): 1–25.

———. "Mythic Evolution of 'The New Frontier' in Mass Mediated Rhetoric." *Critical Studies in Mass Communication* 3, no. 3 (1986): 265–96.

———. "On Saving Mythic Criticism: A Reply to Rowland." *Communication Studies* 41, no. 2 (1990): 136–49.

———. "Ronald Reagan's 'Star Wars' Address: Mythic Containment of Technical Reasoning." *Quarterly Journal of Speech* 72, no. 4 (1986): 415–33.

Rushing, Janice Hocker, and Thomas S. Frentz. "The Rhetoric of 'Rocky': A Social Value Model of Criticism." *Western Journal of Communication* 42, no. 2 (1978): 63–72.

Santos, Antonio Silveira R. dos. "Biodiversidade, Bioprospecção, Conhecimento Tradicional e o Futuro da Vida." *Revista de Informação e Tecnologia* (March 2001).

Sapp, Gregg. Review of *The Future of Life*, by Edward O. Wilson. *Library Journal* 127, no. 1 (2002): 147.

Schuman, Howard, Barry Schwartz, and Hannah D'Arcy. "Elite Revisionists and Popular Beliefs: Christopher Columbus, Hero or Villain?" *Public Opinion Quarterly* 69, no. 1 (2005): 2–29.

Senate Committee on Health, Education, Labor and Pensions. *Hearing Examining the Scientific and Ethical Implications of Stem Cell Research and Its Potential to Improve Human Health*. 107th Cong., 1st Sess., September 5, 2001.

Shapiro, Kevin. "Biophiliac." Review of *The Future of Life*, by Edward O. Wilson. *Commentary* 113, no. 4 (2002): 65–68.

Shiva, Vandana. "Bioprospecting as Sophisticated Biopiracy." *Signs: Journal of Women in Culture and Society* 32, no. 2 (2007): 307–13.

Silva, Marina. "Recursos Biológicos: A Riqueza Brasileira." Interview by Maria Fernanda Diniz Avidose and Lucas Tadeu Ferreira. *Revista Biotecnologia Ciência & Desenvolvimento* 1, no. 2 (1997): 44–45.

Simpson, John A., and Edmund S. C. Weiner, eds. *Oxford English Dictionary*. 2nd ed. Vol. 6. New York: Oxford University Press, 1989.

———. *Oxford English Dictionary Additions Series*. New York: Oxford University Press, 1993.

———. *Oxford English Dictionary Additions Series*. New York: Oxford University Press, 1997.

Slotkin, Richard. *The Fatal Environment: The Myth of the Frontier in the Age of Industrialization, 1800–1890*. New York: Atheneum, 1985.

————. *Gunfighter Nation: The Myth of the Frontier in Twentieth-Century America.* New York: Maxwell Macmillan International, 1992.

————. *Regeneration through Violence: The Mythology of the American Frontier, 1600–1860.* Middletown, Conn.: Wesleyan University Press, 1973.

Smaglik, Paul. "Genetic Diversity Project Fights for Its Life . . ." *Nature* 912, no. 6781 (2000): 912.

Smart, Andrew. "Reporting the Dawn of the Post-Genomic Era: Who Wants to Live Forever?" *Sociology of Health & Illness* 25, no. 1 (2003): 24–49.

"Stem Cell 101: Legislators Toolkit: Federal Public Policy." Kansas University Medical Center. http://www.kumc.edu/stem-cell-101/federal-public-policy .html.

Stent, Gunther. "Save Biodiversity." Review of *The Diversity of Life*, by Edward O. Wilson. *Partisan Review* 61, no. 4 (1994): 689–95.

Stoeltje, Beverly J. "Making the Frontier Myth: Folklore Process in a Modern Nation." *Western Folklore* 46, no. 4 (1987): 235–53.

Stolberg, Sheryl Gay. "First Bush Veto Maintains Limits on Stem Cell Use." *New York Times*, July 20, 2006.

————. "A Question of Research: Disappointed by Limits, Scientists Doubt Estimate of Available Cell Lines." *New York Times*, August 10, 2001.

————. "Stem Cell Research Advocates in Limbo." *New York Times*, January 20, 2001.

————. "U.S. Acts Quickly to Put Stem Cell Policy in Effect." *New York Times*, August 11, 2001.

Stuckey, Mary E. *Defining Americans: The Presidency and National Identity.* Lawrence: University Press of Kansas, 2004.

————. "The Donner Party and the Rhetoric of Westward Expansion." *Rhetoric & Public Affairs* 14, no. 2 (2011): 229–60.

————. *Slipping the Surly Bonds: Reagan's Challenger Address.* College Station: Texas A&M University Press, 2006.

Stuckey, Mary E., and John M. Murphy. "By Any Other Name: Rhetorical Colonialism in North America." *American Indian Culture and Research Journal* 24, no. 4 (2001): 73–98.

Tauli-Corpuz, Victoria. "Biotechnology and Indigenous Peoples." In *Redesigning Life? The Worldwide Challenge to Genetic Engineering*, ed. Brian Tokar, 252–70. Montreal and Kingston: McGill-Queen's University Press, 2001.

Terborgh, John. "A Matter of Life and Death." Review of *The Diversity of Life*, by Edward O. Wilson. *New York Review of Books* 39, no. 18 (1992): 3, 5–6.

Thomas, Peggy. Letter to the editor. *New York Times*, August 11, 2001.

Tilghman, Shirley M. "Science: The Last Frontier." Address to the Sidwell Friends School in Washington, D.C. February 28, 2006. http://www.princeton.edu/president/speeches/20060228/index.xml.

Tokar, Brian, ed. *Redesigning Life? The Worldwide Challenge to Genetic Engineering.* Montreal and Kingston: McGill-Queen's University Press, 2001.

Toner, Robin. "The Reaction: Each Side Finds Something to Like, and Not." *New York Times,* August 10, 2001.

Treloar, A. E. "James Arthur Harris." *Journal of the American Statistical Association* 25, no. 171 (September 1930): 356–58.

Turner, Frederick Jackson. *The Frontier in American History.* New York: Henry Holt, 1920.

————. "The Significance of the Frontier in American History." In *Proceedings of the State Historical Society of Wisconsin at Its Forty-First Annual Meeting, December 14, 1893,* 79–112. Madison, Wis.: Democrat Printing, 1894.

————. "The Significance of the Frontier in American History." In *The Annual Report of the American Historical Association for the Year 1893,* 199–227. Washington, D.C.: Government Printing Office, 1894.

Väliverronen, Esa, and Iina Hellsten. "From 'Burning Library' to 'Green Medicine': The Role of Metaphors in Communicating Biodiversity." *Science Communication* 24, no. 2 (2002): 229–45.

Van der Weele, Cor. "Roads towards a *Lingua Democratica* on Genomics: How Can Metaphors Guide Us?" *Genomics, Society and Policy* 5, no. 3 (2009): ii–vii.

Van Dijck, José. *Imagenation: Popular Images of Genetics.* Washington Square: New York University Press, 1998.

Venter, J. Craig. *A Life Decoded: My Genome: My Life.* New York: Viking Penguin, 2007.

Watanabe, August M. "Leveraging Scientific Research for the Next American Century: The Future of Science and Technology in the Heartland." *Vital Speeches of the Day* 60, no. 1 (1996): 12–14.

Webster's Collegiate Dictionary. 4th ed. Springfield, Mass.: G. & C. Merriam, 1934.

Webster's Collegiate Dictionary. 5th ed. Springfield, Mass.: G. & C. Merriam, 1941.

West, Mark, and Chris Carey. "(Re)Enacting Frontier Justice: The Bush Administration's Tactical Narration of the Old West Fantasy after September 11." *Quarterly Journal of Speech* 92, no. 4 (2006): 379–412.

Whitt, Laurie Anne. "Value-Bifurcation in Bioscience: The Rhetoric of Research Justification." *Perspectives on Science* 7, no. 4 (1999): 413–46.

"William Jefferson Bush." *New York Times,* August 12, 2001.

Williamson, Ray A. "Outer Space as Frontier: Lessons for Today." *Western Folklore* 46, no. 4 (1987): 255–67.

Wilson, Edward O. *Consilience: The Unity of Knowledge.* New York: Alfred A. Knopf, 1998.

———. *A Diversidade Da Vida.* Trans. Carlos Afonso Malferrari. São Paulo: Companhia das Letras, 1994.

———. *The Diversity of Life.* 1992. Reprint, New York: W. W. Norton, 1999.

———. *The Future of Life.* New York: Vintage Books, 2002.

———. *O Futuro Da Vida: Um Estudo Da Bioesfera Para A Proteção De Todas As Espécies, Inclusive A Humana.* Trans. Ronaldo Sérgio de Biasi. Rio de Janeiro: Editora Campus, 2002.

Wrobel, David M. *The End of American Exceptionalism: Frontier Anxiety from the Old West to the New Deal.* Lawrence: University Press of Kansas, 1993.

Zarefsky, David. *President Johnson's War on Poverty: Rhetoric and History.* Tuscaloosa: University of Alabama Press, 1986.

———. "Public Address Scholarship in the New Century: Achievements and Challenges." In *The Handbook of Rhetoric and Public Address,* ed. Shawn J. Parry-Giles and J. Michael Hogan, 67–85. Malden, Mass.: Wiley-Blackwell, 2010.

Zwart, Hub. "The Adoration of a Map: Reflections on a Genome Metaphor." *Genomics, Society and Policy* 5, no. 3 (2009): 29–43.

Index

⌘

A

American Indians. *See* Native Americans

American Individualism (Hoover), 39–40

"American Intellectual Frontier, The" (Dewey), 40

applied science, 31, 69; denigrated by Bacon, 31–32; denigrated in speeches by scientists, 55, 59–62; and Vannevar Bush's report, 47–49

argument from unlimited development, 37, 53, 140, 142–43; American presidents' use of, 114–16, 118–19, 140–43; Lederman's use of, 55–56; Tilghman's use of, 58; Turner's use of, 37–38; Vannevar Bush's use of, 46–47, 141; Wilson's use of, 87, 89–90

B

Bacon, Francis, 31–32, 47, 62

Barthes, Roland, 17

basic science, 24, 31, 67, 69, 142, 144; Bacon introduces pioneer metaphor for, 31–32; promoted by George W. Bush, 121; promoted in speeches by scientists, 53–55, 57, 59–62; promoted in Vannevar Bush's report, 45–49; promoted by Wilson, 80

Bement, Arden, Jr., 56–58, 60–62, 63–64

biocolonialism, criticism of, 82, 97, 104–6, 108, 148. *See also* biopiracy, criticism of

biodiversity studies, 25–26, 72–90, 146

biopiracy, criticism of, 81, 105, 148, 150, 170 (n. 19)